Praise for The L

Cantor Moshe Kraus. across Europe, the An Jewish children tragically murdered and the late Elie Weisel. His singing save his life as a prisoner in Bergen-Belsen concentration camp, although he weighed only 35 kilos [75 pounds] when the camp was finally liberated. His memoirs, written for general readers, contain virtually not a dull line and countless insightful and often highly amusing anecdotes. In short, a fascinating book.

Hon. David Kilgour JD
Nobel Peace Prize nominee

Although Cantor Moshe Kraus was not the cantor of our synagogue, I met him quite often. He was everywhere, inspiring with his melodies, emotionally moving with his prayers. And if he wanted, he could recite the prayers with a rarely matched combination of speed and accuracy.

But forget about speed when you read this book. Take your time and digest it. And if you want inspiration, grab this book.

Every time I met Cantor Kraus, he had a story. A different story, always either funny or uplifting. As the years went by, I was wishing more and more that he would find a way to preserve all these stories. I suspect that there are many more stories in his arsenal, but the time being, we should all be grateful to Cantor Kraus for his extraordinary memory, for his enormous life achievements in often impossible circumstances, and for committing to writing the legacy he breathed all his life.

Rabbi Dr. Reuven P. Bulka CM
Rabbi Emeritus, Congregation Machzikei Hadas

When I was Canadian ambassador to Hungary, Cantor Moshe Kraus came to Budapest during Hanukka in December 2005 to light the candles in the menorah in front of the magnificent Parliament buildings. I still remember the sight of this man in his eighties being lifted up by a cherry picker, torch in hand, on eight cold and wintry evenings. I later accompanied him on a tour of Budapest's Great Synagogue and heard him sing before the Torah ark. He told me that it was from the ghetto around the synagogue that he and other Jews were led away to the concentration camps.

In the years since returning to Ottawa, I have learned much from Moshe about the love of God, humanity, and the power of forgiveness. As Moshe says in his book, he is a storyteller – a wonderful storyteller where tales are offered with a dose of wisdom. This book is Moshe's gift to our town and future generation who will be able to share his joy and sorrows and benefit from his wisdom and compassion.

Robert Hage
Former Canadian Ambassador to Hungary and Slovenia

The Life of Moshele Der Zinger
How Singing Saved My Life

Moshe Kraus

THE LIFE OF
Moshele Der Zinger

How Singing Saved My Life

The Toby Press

The Life of Moshele Der Zinger:
How Singing Saved My Life

First edition, 2023

The Toby Press
PO Box 8531, New Milford, CT 06776-8531, USA
& PO Box 4044, Jerusalem 9104001, Israel
www.tobypress.com

Copyright © Moshe Kraus 2023

The publication of this book was made possible through the generous support of The Jewish Book Trust.

All rights reserved. No part of this book may be used or reproduced or transmitted in any form or by any means, electronic or mechanical, including photocopying, recording, or by any information storage and retrieval system, without written permission from the publisher.

Hardcover ISBN: 978-1-59264-630-2

Printed and bound in Turkey

Contents

Foreword ix
Acknowledgements xiii
Introduction xv

Chapter One: Uzhhorod   *1*
Chapter Two: Childhood   *21*
Chapter Three: Bergen-Belsen   *75*
Chapter Four: Israel   *121*
Chapter Five: Antwerp   *141*
Chapter Six: Johannesburg   *157*
Chapter Seven: Mexico City   *195*
Chapter Eight: Ottawa   *209*

Conclusion   *231*
Tales My Father Told Me   *237*
Mementos   *253*

Foreword

I first met Cantor Moshe Kraus over twenty years ago, when we were both members of the Holocaust Remembrance Committee in Ottawa. I was charmed and fascinated by the diminutive man with snowy white hair, old-school manners, and regal bearing.

Little did I know that Cantor Kraus and his lovely wife Rivka would become such an important part of my life. To this day, he is the only person in the world who calls me Brachele, the Yiddish version of my Hebrew name, Bracha.

I knew that Cantor Kraus was highly respected in Ottawa. But it was not until I had the privilege of traveling to Germany with him in 2005 that I truly realized how many lives he has touched around the world.

We were there to commemorate the sixtieth anniversary of the liberation of the Bergen-Belsen concentration camp. At every event – even walking to synagogue in Hanover – people came up to Cantor Kraus to introduce themselves, shake his hand, and remind him of something he had taught them or done for them.

The Life of Moshele Der Zinger

Many Bergen-Belsen survivors remembered him as "Moshele der Zinger," whose beautiful tenor voice and trove of Yiddish and sacred music had kept their hopes alive – and in many cases restored their faith – during the living nightmare of the Holocaust.

But the true highlight of this trip with "Moshe Kraus, Superstar," as I teasingly called him, was the memorial ceremony among the mass graves at Bergen-Belsen. When Cantor Kraus sang the *El Maalei Rahamim*, the Jewish prayer for the souls of the departed, I felt as if his voice had captured the collective anguish of those who had been murdered by the Nazis.

He was remembering them, yes, but he was also speaking to the Eternal on behalf of those who had no one to speak for them.

I have been fortunate enough to hear some of the stories in this book firsthand, told in his inimitable style – sometimes with tears in his eyes, sometimes with his trademark twinkle. But to read so many of these stories and anecdotes in one book, along with details of his life and the rich tales his father told him, is a real gift.

And I love the fact that the reader doesn't need to know anything about Judaism or the traditions of hasidic Jews to appreciate the book. Cantor Kraus, a lifelong teacher, has made sure that we have the background and context to understand his stories and his principles.

This book includes a photo of Cantor Kraus with the late Elie Wiesel. When the renowned writer, Holocaust survivor, and human rights activist came to speak in Ottawa in 2005, he made time in his whirlwind schedule to have tea with the Krauses.

As we sat on the Krauses' balcony on a balmy September afternoon, it was clear that Prof. Wiesel still looked up to his *rebbe*, the man who had been his cantor, teacher, and mentor in the Transylvanian city of Sighet (now part of Romania).

Foreword

They sang snippets of the old songs, and the years melted away as they reveled in each other's company and anecdotes. It was a gift to bear witness to this touching reunion.

This book beautifully captures the life of the ḥazan, teacher, sage, and storyteller the world knows as Cantor Moshe Kraus. And as I read it, I hear the voice and feel the laughter and tears of my dear friend, Moshele.

Barbara Crook
Ottawa
January 2023

Acknowledgements

I wish to thank my wife Rivka for her support, not only during the writing of this book, but also throughout all the adventures we have shared during our life together.

Many other people deserve special recognition:

Rabbi Moshe Berger of Cleveland, who started it all by planting the idea in my mind to write my autobiography, and then interviewed me at length as a prelude to the actual writing of my story;

Mr. Mitchell Rose, who put my spoken words into written form;

Mrs. Lynne Cohen, whose assistance was invaluable as I was attempting to bring my story to life in a straightforward and engaging manner;

My dear friends Larry Mervine and Rabbi Chaim Mendelsohn, who helped make this book possible in all kinds of ways.

Three people became involved in the last stages of production: Frank H. Scheme, a good friend and a brilliant professional photographer, who provided the beautiful picture on the cover of this book; and Genevieve Hone, a friend who happened by, read the manuscript, and was greatly moved by it. She worked diligently to prepare the manuscript for publication. Thank you to publisher Matthew Miller of The Toby Press for bringing this book to completion, as well as to Reuven Ziegler, Caryn Meltz, Aryeh Grossman, Tomi Mager, Tani Bayer, Leah Goldstein, and Rachel Miskin.

Many other people have contributed in the thoughtful ways of friendship, each in their own manner. Thank you all for your encouragement and help.

Introduction

These days, I enjoy sitting by the large living room window in our comfortable Sandy Hill apartment in Ottawa, staring out over the rushing Rideau River. I have come to appreciate, and maybe even identify, with this meandering river, which is right in back of my building, across a partially landscaped yard, and down a small embankment. The Rideau, which I've learned is about one hundred kilometers long, looks like it should flow in the opposite direction. But it travels north, bubbling and splashing, to finally empty into the mighty Ottawa River not too far from where I live.

As I gaze, I also reflect. I spent a lifetime singing, and I loved almost every minute of it. As a child prodigy, singing came easily to me. My talent gave me an exhilarating career as a ḥazan, or cantor, and it took me all over the world. It was a fulfilling profession that I still cannot quite believe is over.

Since I am 100 years old, I am probably living in the last home I will know, but I am happy. My beautiful wife Rivka and I – married 71 years – have resided in this building for over forty peaceful years. Our apartment is small enough that Rivka can still do the housework, which she does so attentively each week. Every Thursday, the apartment is immaculately cleaned in preparation for Shabbat, the Jewish Sabbath. And it sparkles, like her eyes.

I am grateful. Sometimes I wonder which comes first, the blessings or the gratitude. Of all the lessons life has taught me, a very big one is that the more thankful I am for the good and positive experiences God has given me, the more of them He continues to give me. Is He proud of me? Does He expect more gratitude from me even at my old age? I often wonder about these things as I watch the river flow.

My thoughts wander so much these days. Maybe it is time to organize them and write them down. I speak six languages: Yiddish, Hebrew, Hungarian, Czech, German, and, of course, English. I taught myself English from scratch. I have never had a lesson. It is the last language I learned, and it is still sometimes a bit challenging. But for some strange reason, I now actually think in English when I think of my past. Why? Maybe because when I talk to people these days about my history, I speak their language, English.

Different episodes of my life will sometimes fly into my mind too quickly. I hope to get all the important information written out properly. I will have to be patient and let the thoughts come clearly and wistfully. I survived great pain and horror in my youthful years. I was in Bor, a labor camp in Yugoslavia, and in Bergen-Belsen, a concentration camp in Germany, for nine and eleven months respectively between 1943 and 1945. I almost died more than once during that time. By the grace of *HaKadosh Barukh Hu*, the Almighty God, and thanks to the strong British army, I was liberated instead. I am still bursting with gratitude for my freedom after so much terror.

Bergen-Belsen is long over I know, but, especially since I retired a few years ago, the experiences somehow manage to rise up in my mind and grip my soul when I am least prepared. It seems to happen most often when I am alone in our home, when Rivka goes shopping or to the apartment swimming pool. She comes home and finds me sitting on the couch or by the window watching the river, and crying. I can't seem to numb completely those horrendous feelings from the Holocaust. I just can't believe it still hurts after all these years. There is no answer as to why. If somebody gives you an answer, tell him he's a liar. There is no answer.

I am no stranger to crying. Though I have always been a stable person, and though I am almost always happy and contented, since World War II, crying has come easily to me on sad occasions, and even on very joyous ones. In fact, I cry easily during exceptionally moving situations, including deeply spiritual moments. I can't help it. Shedding tears is one way I express myself. I have even been referred to as the crying ḥazan.

Since my time in Bergen-Belsen, I have a very hard time remembering exactly when certain events took place. Sometimes, for instance, I cannot remember when I was in Mexico City, yet I lived there for part of the 1970s. When I think quickly about an experience in Mexico, I wonder if it took place three years ago or three months ago. The very best psychiatrist in South Africa tried to help me. He couldn't. He told me to live with it. That is what I have done.

Fortunately, there has been much laughter in my life, too. I am pleased that I cultivated a cheerful personality, which has manifested itself most of the time. For my cheeriness, God has rewarded me with much peace of mind. Thankfully, this positive attitude also helped me to share some sparks of happiness and joyful songs, even in the darkest places.

It is difficult sometimes to believe that my life has been so long already. Watching the endless flow of water reminds me of the steady harmony we, my dear Rivka and I, have enjoyed; that quiet calm and serenity we have achieved for ourselves for the greater part of our lives. When I stare at the Rideau, at its fresh

The Life of Moshele Der Zinger

white-capped rapids continuously moving, sometimes I am carried back to times I thought I had forgotten forever. But I can't forget. I must try hard not to forget.

I was a professional *ḥazan* for more than seventy years. Can you imagine that? During those years, I sang at religious services, concerts, and *smaḥot*, the last being happy Jewish celebrations such as marriages and bar mitzvas. Fortunately, I was also able to bring comfort to many, many crying souls, at funerals, *shivas* – those weeklong mourning periods after cemetery burials of close Jewish relatives – and even in the Nazi labor and concentration camps. After the war, it continued to be important for me to try hard to ease the pain of people who were hurting, particularly those in mourning. I remember exactly the moment I decided to never take financial advantage of the bereaved. I made this important decision when I was younger than thirteen, maybe only eleven.

As a child singing sensation, maybe 75 percent of my time was given to travel for *Shabbatot* (the plural for Shabbat) in different towns throughout Eastern Europe in order to sing for congregations during religious services. Arriving early one week, on a Thursday afternoon, I was at the home of the community's cantor, when he came running into the kitchen and bellowed to his wife, "You can go now to the market and buy a duck! I had a fat funeral today." I remember listening with all the attention a young boy can muster. For some strange reason, I recall what I was eating at that moment: a flaky *borekas* with tea. Why do I remember that? I have no idea. Maybe because I compared it to duck, the most luxurious dinner item a person could buy at that time. "A fat funeral," I thought. I had never heard this expression, but I was no fool, and I understood what he meant. My host meant that he had been generously compensated at the funeral where he had just sung.

In truth, I was mortified. I asked myself privately, so no one could hear, "Am I supposed to make my living from people's fat funerals? Not a chance." I made a *neder*, a promise, an oath, that when I became an adult *ḥazan*, I would never, ever, take money for funerals. I never did, not a penny, not for funerals or even *shivas*. I would get checks in the mail from people who did not know this policy of mine, and I would send the checks back with a letter: "As much as I appreciate your kind gesture, I am returning your gift in the hope that you will receive it in the spirit in which it is meant. I do not accept gifts from people in their times of sorrow. I hope to meet you at *smaḥot*."

In my long career, I never met another *ḥazan* who did this. In fact, the other cantors and rabbis who heard about my policy did not like it at all, because it cast them in a dim light. While I am on the subject of career-long self-commitments, let me mention here that I sang as a *ḥazan* every single Shabbat, every single weekend, when I had a contract. It is not uncommon for *ḥazanim* (the plural of *ḥazan*) to take off the Shabbat the week before each of the six major *yom tovim* (religious holidays), to rest their vocal cords and maybe practice a little. I never did this in my life. I believed if my job was to *daven* (pray) and sing for Shabbat and the *yom tovim*, then that meant all of them. My singing voice never suffered from this commitment.

Okay, it is decided. I am going to record my life in a book, this book. I want people to know what I went through and suffered, and then to see that I overcame the dreadful devastations of the Nazis and managed to live a full and wonderful life. The Nazis murdered almost my entire family: my two parents, five of my eight siblings, about twenty of my uncles and aunts, and almost one hundred cousins – cousins who never had a chance to know the joy of adulthood and marriage. I hope my experiences will help people understand that suffering does not have to exclude the possibility of a good and positive survival, a rich and happy life. I want people to know that I came to have a blessed and wonderful life, despite the past.

***

Now I would like to give the first of a few history lessons. It is important, before I begin relating my personal journey, to write a bit about Hasidism. The hasidic movement – into which I am proud to have been born – is often referred to as ultra-Orthodox Judaism. To me it is just Judaism, but that is neither here nor there. Hasidism started in the 1700s in Eastern Europe, when poor, uneducated, young Jews were drifting away from Judaism at a rapid pace. It is not hard to understand why they did that. Judaism is very wonderful in every way, but it is also a complicated and intellectual religion, requiring a focused and curious mind. Judaism is, in fact, a system of law not totally unlike British Common Law, though one major difference is that Jewish law dates back a few thousand years further than the eight hundred-year-old English Magna Carta.

The destruction of the Second *Beit HaMikdash* (Holy Temple) – which took place in Jerusalem in 70 CE – has meant that for two thousand years, a good portion of Jewish learning has not been practiced or conspicuously relevant. But that does not mean that Jews do not learn it intensely, like all serious law students. Jewish learning has the added beneficial effect of continually refining an individual's character in every kind of positive way. All Orthodox Jews, including hasidic Jews, believe that when *Moshiaḥ*, the Messiah, comes to save humankind, the Temple will be rebuilt and all Jewish law will be practiced again. The main point here is that Jewish law requires a very engaged mind to study and follow it. These uninformed young individuals who were fleeing from Judaism didn't even understand what was being said at the *tisch* (lit. "table," joyous and public celebrations around the rabbi's table). The unschooled youth hardly knew what was going on in the synagogues.

The first Hasid ever, the great Rabbi Israel ben Eliezer, known as the Baal Shem Tov, explained to many of these untaught men that performing any mitzva – any commandment from God – is as important as the most imperative mitzva of learning Torah. For example, he taught that the mitzvot (the plural of mitzva) of lighting Shabbat candles and eating kosher food were significant individually and on their own. This concept brought many poor, illiterate Jews running back to their religion. That soon led them to study Torah and for many of them to become *talmidei ḥakhamim*, Jewish scholars. Before long, the hasidic *talmidei ḥakhamim* equaled no less in number than the *mitnagdim ḥakhamim*, the non-hasidic Jewish scholars.

The number of hasidic Jews in the world today is hard to estimate, but it is surely more than half a million, which is many, many fewer than the number of Hasidism – maybe 2.5 million – wiped out by the Nazis in their genocidal madness. Each hasidic Jew belongs to a specific hasidic group, or sect, with its own special name, for example, Lubavitcher. There are so many groups: Bubov, Belz, Ger, Satmar, and Bostoner Hasidism, to name but a few of the hundreds still surviving. I grew up a member of Munkatcher Hasidim. Most groups derive their title from the Eastern European city in which they started. It goes without saying that the vast majority of members within each hasidic group at one time lived in the same community, though today in many cases there is more than one community for a particular group.

The present-day number of hasidic sects remains high, perhaps as high as four hundred, despite the fact that hundreds of individual sects were totally annihilated by the Nazis during the Holocaust. Most are now headquartered in Israel or the United States, though they still retain the name of the Eastern European towns from which they originated. A unique characteristic of each hasidic group is that it virtually always has a leader for life: a *rebbe*, who is like a sovereign to his followers. When that *rebbe* dies, he is succeeded by another *rebbe*, usually a blood relative, but not always. The oldest of these hasidic dynasties reaches back to the 1750s.

The Life of Moshele Der Zinger

As an example, the current Munkatcher Rebbe, Rabbi Moshe Leib Rabinovich, is the seventh *rebbe* since the dynasty started in the town of Munkacs, Hungary, in the early 1800s. His father preceded him as *rebbe*, and his father's predecessor was his father-in-law, who himself was preceded by his own father. The largest Munkatcher community is in Borough Park, Brooklyn, where Rabbi Rabinovich himself lives. But there are other major Munkatcher communities in and around other areas of New York, such as in Williamsburg and Monsey. There are also Munkatcher communities in Israel and Australia.

A word about titles. In the book you will see *rav*, rabbi, *rebbe*, *reb* and *tzaddik*. They are not exactly interchangeable, but they all refer to the great leaders and teachers of the Jewish faith.

Another thing to know about Hasidism is that they love to tell stories; they always have, and no doubt always will. It is a major part of hasidic culture. Hasidic tales comprise a collection of stories, many told since the beginning of Hasidim. It is true that the people who tell them and create new ones are at various levels of religious observance, but everyone who does relate them is motivated and inspired by the hasidic tradition of transmitting our values and moral philosophy through stories. Hasidic tales were made for and are passed on as part of the concept of *Raah maaseh yizkor halakha shiru laHashem ki gamal alai*. This roughly means, "Seeing is believing, and I will sing praises to the Lord that He has protected and saved me." My *melamed* (teacher) in *ḥeder* (primary school) explained that *gamal* here means "protects like an umbrella."

Why am I telling you all this? To explain why this book has many hasidic tales, and why I have frequently told them. Every part of my life has been influenced by *ḥazanut*, Jewish songs, but also by hasidic culture and stories. My father was a great storyteller, like my *zaide* – my grandfather – and also like my *zaide*'s father. This goes even farther back. Thus, I am a storyteller. A great one? I am not sure "great" describes me in this line of work. But I have been told by many that I am certainly not bad at it, though being a *ḥazan* has always been my career and my central focus.

Let me tell a quick story about the Baal Shem Tov, since I just introduced him, and you can decide how well I am doing. It is very painful to bury a wife with whom you've shared a harmonious life for forty years. The Baal Shem Tov – may his merit protect us – went through this. He lost his *rebbetzen*, his wife, after forty glorious years. He was walking silently with his pupil Rav Josef Kitzes after her funeral. Suddenly, he stopped, turned to Rav Kitzes and said, "I want you to know that everything I achieved, everything I accomplished, everything I am, is thanks to the *rebbetzen* whom I just left behind in the cemetery." The two moved on. The Baal Shem Tov stopped again, turned to his pupil and said, "I want you to know, Rav Josef, that I never let a day pass in our forty years of marriage without telling her my grateful thoughts about her." When we consider that the great Baal Shem Tov, who dealt all day in the higher spheres with holy thoughts, found every day the time to come down from his spiritual heights in order to pay tribute to his *rebbetzen* and thank her for her devotion, shouldn't we do the same?

Something else I must explain is the writing style of this book. As you can already see, I have chosen to write at the level of non-Jewish readers who know virtually nothing about Judaism. And I have also chosen to explain Yiddish and Hebrew phrases within the text, rather than in footnotes, which I feel can interrupt the flow of the content. Forgive me if I slip into Hebrew or Yiddish phrases that some readers will not understand. As far as possible, I translate them immediately after writing them.

Also, the way particular words are displayed – for example, italicized non-English nouns and verbs, or non-italicized non-English proper nouns – may seem complicated and even lacking uniformity, but as much as possible this is not the case. Please do not dwell on this aspect of the style, but know that the book's wording style has a simple internal consistency. Any errors in this area of the writing are completely my own fault.

This brings me to one more literary "device" that is indispensable for me in this lifetime project: my assistant writer. If words seem to come directly from my lips and my mind and yet do so in a coherent and structured fashion, it is due to the extraordinary efforts of professional writer Lynne Cohen.

The content in the chapters that follow is primarily arranged in chronological order. However, the book is not perfect in this regard, either. Chapter One focuses on my early life, until age eight when my singing voice was discovered. Chapter Two details the years roughly between 1930 and 1942, presenting my youthful singing tours around Eastern Europe, along with my early exposure to Nazism. This chapter also mentions the great *tzaddikim* (righteous persons) and *rebbes* I was privileged to meet in my life, and describes these brief fortunate encounters. My experiences before, during, and right after my time in the Bor and Bergen-Belsen concentration camps are the topic of Chapter Three.

Chapter Four focuses on my initial stay in Israel, my position as Chief Cantor for the Israeli Defense Forces, and my unforgettable wedding. Chapter Five is about Rivka and my six years from 1952 in Antwerp, Belgium. Chapter Six describes our years in Johannesburg, South Africa, from 1958 to 1970, and our return to Israel for eighteen months. Chapter Seven is about our life in Mexico City, from 1973 – when the Yom Kippur War broke out – to 1976. Chapter Eight chronicles my life in Ottawa, Ontario, Canada. Following the conclusion is a chapter entitled, "Tales My Father Told Me." Here, I have written down the original stories that have been passed on orally in my family from parent to child for generations, but have not been included elsewhere in the book.

I sincerely hope and believe you will enjoy your reading.

Chapter One
Uzhhorod

I was born August 15 in either 1922 or 1923 – I will explain this confusing statement later – in a tiny hospital in the city of Uzhhorod. I came out small and I came out screaming, a sound totally unlike the beautiful, captivating voice that would later define my life. I must have been pleased to join the world, if you can believe my mother, of blessed memory. She took me home after a few days in the hospital and gazed in wonder at me for what seemed like hours, or so she told me years later. She often reminded me that I was almost always a contented baby. I was her first of nine children.

It was easy to be happy growing up in Uzhhorod, a largely peaceful and enchanting place. Its history, though, is another story: a confusing one to be sure, and more than a little bumpy, but also fascinating overall. You might even say this: If Uzhhorod had been a child, it would have been very unhappy, that is if you believe stability is best for children! For most of the time while I was young, Uzhhorod was in Czechoslovakia, which was in those years thankfully democratic. Located currently in Ukraine,

The Life of Moshele Der Zinger

it is near the borders of Hungary – another country to which it belonged in recent history – and Slovakia. Uzhhorod felt like a big city to a little boy, but the population in 1910 was only seventeen thousand, so the "city" was actually quite small. It was a capital city, though. In fact, in 1919, a few years before I was born, part of the region of Subcarpathia was officially assigned to Czechoslovakia, and Uzhhorod authoritatively and proudly became its administrative center.

I remember Uzhhorod as a Jewish city, a fantastic hasidic city. Everyone spoke Yiddish, at least the Jews did, at home and in the streets. Uzhhorod was full of synagogues and other Jewish organizations. We had *mikvaot,* ritual baths; a *beit din,* a court that deals in matters of Jewish law; and a *ḥevra Kaddisha,* the Jewish burial society. To be part of the *ḥevra Kaddisha* in Uzhhorod was a special honor. In 1904, a majestic central synagogue had been built. Around the same time, a Jewish hospital and a home for the aged had also been established. There were of course *ḥederim* and yeshivot, both Jewish schools, the latter for older boys and more intensive learning. My *ḥeder,* or Jewish elementary school, had opened in 1890, and soon after, at least two more Jewish schools, including a *Talmud Torah* afternoon Hebrew school and another yeshiva, were opened.

As a boy, I certainly remember there were non-Jewish children in the town, but we experienced virtually no antisemitism on normal days. We formed school groups with non-Jews for certain activities. We sometimes played soccer together with them. I do not remember any bad things being said to Jews. There was no cheating us, ever, not in games and not in business. The only time we experienced violent behavior by non-Jews was on Christmas Eve. Early in the day every Christmas Eve, hours before the local priest's inflammatory sermon about how the Jews had killed Christ, my father would nail thick wood over the windows and doors. At midnight, my parents would wake me and all my siblings and

Chapter One: Uzhhorod

instruct us to sit very still, and not to cry or scream. Suddenly, there was riotous shouting and running outside: "Death to the Jews! Kill all the Jews! Beat the Jews!" Stones and bricks were thrown at the homes where Jews lived. I always heard my mother crying softly, though we children sat quietly, terrorized. The next morning, when my father, brothers and I walked to *shul* (synagogue), we saw burned houses and broken windows. We were very, very fortunate that our home was never vandalized during these rampages, but we ached for our friends, and of course helped repair their damaged property.

We had brilliant and famous rabbis in Uzhhorod. The one I remember best is Rabbi Elimelech Kahane. There was also a chief rabbi, Rabbi Shlomo Ganzfried, who was a *dayan*, one of the judges in the *beit din*. This rabbi, in the mid-nineteenth century, wrote the *Kitzur Shulḥan Arukh*, a universally-known shortened version of the Code of Jewish Law. These two outstanding rabbis worked side by side for several years before I was born. Besides Rabbis Kahane and Ganzfried, other phenomenal rabbis came from Uzhhorod, including Rabbi Meir Eisenstadter who, in the 1850s, exerted enormous spiritual sway on the Hungarian Jews; and Rabbi M. Klein, who famously translated Rabbi Moshe Maimonides' twelfth-century book *Guide for the Perplexed* from Arabic into Hungarian.

Then there was Rabbi Myron Shapira, whose last *derasha* (sermon), was simply brilliant. He gave it on the night of *Kol Nidrei*, which is the service named after the alluring prayer recited at the beginning of Yom Kippur, the Day of Atonement. Rav Shapira arrived at the *shul*, and we could all tell he was quite sick. Still, thousands were packed into the synagogue, they so badly wanted to hear him. He slowly walked up to the *Aron Kodesh*, the Holy Ark that holds the Torah scrolls. He opened the *Aron Kodesh* and said, "*Yidden, siz tzeit tsui vinen,*" Jews, it is the time to cry. And the crying poured out. I will never forget that. Where have you ever heard a rabbi give such a *derasha*? He closed the *Aron Kodesh* and he began *Kol Nidrei*, as tears streamed down our faces.

***

Uzhhorod's Jewish community dates back to about the sixteenth century, developing significantly at the end of the eighteenth century, and expanding further in the second half of the 1800s. A former stronghold of Orthodox Jews, including Hasidim, Uzhhorod was at different times named differently, including Ungvar, Hungvar, and Unguyvar. Uzhhorod's current name, not surprisingly, comes from the Uzh River, which slices the city into two parts. *Horod* means "city" in Rusyn, an East Slavic language of the Rusyns, an Eastern European ethnic minority. Today, Uzhhorod – though small – is only a somewhat famous city to the world, but for Jews, it has always had great significance. As mentioned, historically, Uzhhorod has been bounced around, metaphorically speaking, belonging to at least four different countries even in my lifetime, including Czechoslovakia, Hungary, the Soviet Union, and now Ukraine. It has been ruled by many different leaders, and types of leaders, going all the way back to the sixth century.

In 2010, I wanted to make a brief visit to my hometown, but a funny thing happened on my way to Uzhhorod: I could not get in because I did not have a visa. Stopped at the Ukrainian border, my wife Rivka and I were told we would need the proper documents to visit the town of my birth. I laughed because it seemed ridiculous to need a visa to visit the town in which I was born and grew up. I showed the border official my passport and explained that we were only going to stop in Uzhhorod for about an hour, just to see some of the old places I knew. Thankfully, I did not have to bribe the official. (That is a joke; I never bribe authorities.) The guard decided to let us in either because he agreed it was stupid

Chapter One: Uzhhorod

to require a visa for a one-hour visit to a hometown, or because he took pity on us, since we looked exhausted.

Anyway, he let us in after all, and we had a wonderful last visit to my hometown. It was great to see that Uzhhorod – after the Holocaust – still had some strong Jewish life, a community center, a *shul*, and at least one Jewish school. We also heard there was a local magazine called *Gut Shabbos* – which focuses on Jewish activities and events in the Carpathian Mountain region – but we didn't find a copy. We were told that the Uzhhorod Jewish community currently oversees the nearby Jewish communities of Munkacs, Khust, Vinogradova, and Rachov.

My parents – who had seven siblings each – were Myer and Henya Kraus. They both came from families of prominent European rabbis. Myer – who was born in Szmotor, Hungary – had a father who was both a *dayan* and *shohet*, a ritual slaughterer. My mother's maiden name was Nuchomulvitch, her father was Rabbi Wolf Nuchomulvitch, and her family lived in Kish Dubrony, a tiny village near Uzhhorod. Like Uzhhorod, Kish Dubrony was in Czechoslovakia when I was growing up, and is today in Ukraine.

With God's constant help, my parents made sure my siblings and I grew up in a close and happy family. As mentioned, I was the oldest of nine children: five boys and four girls. We were all about one to three years apart in age. Only one sister is alive today in 2022, the year 5782 in the Jewish calendar.

I was born in 1922, but my papers are wrong. They say 1923. Why? It's a funny story. After WWII, I was kicked out of the Displaced Persons hospital after liberation because the doctors said, "You are not sick. You are only weak. You have to leave." So, I wanted to join the group that was getting the best food. The distributors there asked my age. My English was not very good. I said I was born in 1922, but they wrote it down wrong. They wrote 1923. Soon thereafter, I decided to go home to get some identification documents, including my birth certificate. I traveled to Uzhhorod, only to discover that its city hall had burned to the ground and all the records were lost. I had to get witnesses to swear I was born in 1922, not a year later. But for some reason, my official papers still say 1923. I accept that it does not matter one little bit, not anymore. Maybe when I turn one hundred it will matter!

My family lived in a neat and tidy apartment on the first floor of a three-story building on Foe Street, a main street in Uzhhorod. The apartment had three large rooms, plus a kitchen, which had a bed in it. That's right. One of the children slept in the kitchen, but we moved the bed out during the day. My parents had a bedroom, and there was a large dining/living room. There was one other bedroom for the children. Except for the lucky child who got to sleep in the kitchen, all the children, boys and girls alike, slept together in the same room, even with the babies.

As children, we were incredibly close. I used to bring my siblings gifts when I was older after traveling around Eastern Europe to sing as a ḥazan and give concerts. And no, they were not jealous of me at all. The opposite in fact. They were very happy for me. All the younger kids tried to copy my singing. It was so cute. We were such a close family. We loved each other. There was no fighting. We all helped our parents. We all made meals. We were a nice, happy family. We children had so much respect for each other and our parents. As the oldest child, I had to help my mother a lot. I had to clean. And I, of course, had to help with the younger children. There were always young ones who needed to be cared for, bathed, dressed, rocked, fed – you name it. I enjoyed helping, because my mother was grateful. When they grew older, my sisters always helped my mother, too.

It was well known in Uzhhorod that our house was exceptionally clean. In fact, one day, the mayor visited our house. I do not remember how it came about that he was there, but he was in the house. A few days later during a public speech, he said, "No one should say, 'I am poor, and that is why I don't clean.' I know a family with nine children whose house is immaculate. You must go and see their home, how clean it is. And they are certainly not rich people." That was what the mayor said.

Once in a while I made the *ḥallot*, the special bread for Shabbat. It was my mother's habit to make *ḥallot* every Friday morning for Shabbat, which started later in the day at sundown. Early one Friday, I changed the clock in my parents' bedroom so she could sleep longer. I set it back one hour. Then I made the *ḥallot* myself. When she got up, she screamed, "It is so late! The *ḥallot*! They won't be ready!" But they were already baking in the oven. My mother was incredibly happy.

My father – whom we children called Tatty, Yiddish for father – was an officer in the Czechoslovakian army in World War I. I was very proud of him for that. He was very busy earning a living, but he also helped my mother whenever he could. None of that macho "it's women's work" for my father. He was happy to roll up his sleeves and help with the babies and children, whatever needed doing. He set a great example for his sons. It was hard to make money for his family. He had several jobs. He began working as a *shoḥet*, like his father, but my tatty was a gentle man and this work was hard for him to carry out. So, he needed to do something else. As it turned out, besides being a fantastic storyteller, my father had beautiful handwriting. He decided to change jobs and become a *sofer*, a scribe, a job for which he was much in demand. While he did that, he also became a *melamed*, a teacher, and his students loved him.

Another job he sometimes did was selling matza – unleavened bread – which is eaten on Pesaḥ (Passover). When I was very young, I sometimes went with him as he made his deliveries. I remember clearly once a small Gypsy boy – whom I knew from around the neighborhood and who was about four years old – followed us saying, "matza, matza, matza!" I was laughing, but my tatty told me this little boy had probably been born and raised as

Jewish for a few years, until he was taken by the Gypsies. I later learned my father was right. But the boy – when he was much older – ultimately found his way back to Judaism. I met him in Israel many years later, when we were both adults.

My father's brand of Hasidism was Spinka. Tatty actually began as a Ziditshov Hasid; however, after the death of the Zidichover Rebbe, he had a choice to consider. He could either continue to make the arduous journey across the Czechoslovakian border to visit his deceased *rebbe*'s successor and son, or he could start to follow the late *rebbe*'s son-in-law, Rabbi Yitzchak Isaac Weiss (the Chakal Yitzchak) of Spinka, who lived closer (in fact, in the same country as we did). Partly for convenience, he ultimately picked the latter option.

***

I do not think we were poor. As a child I never thought we were, but what do children know? I remember for the longest time my mother had only one dress for Shabbat. This seems underprivileged, yet she took such good care of it. It always looked brand new to me. During the week, she pressed it between two clean sheets. I used to say I had two mothers. One during the regular week, when she ran after nine energetic children, and one on Shabbat, when she wore the beautiful dress and she looked like a queen, relaxed and smiling. On Shabbat, when all the children were dressed up in their nicest clothes, my father, in his finest suit, would take five perfectly behaved boys to *shul*, while my unruffled mother in her gorgeous dress would come later with the four angelic girls.

I think my father made a good living. We were probably middle class for the times. Things were especially good after I started making a lot of money as a child singer. As I will describe in more detail in Chapter Two, I became very popular in Eastern Europe when I was quite young. I gave concerts. I traveled very far

Chapter One: Uzhhorod

frequently, and I came home with my pockets full of coins, since back then there were no simple checks. I would dump all the coins on the kitchen table. I didn't really understand money very well. All I knew was that it made my parents happy, so I was happy. I know my family's life improved when I started to sing.

Back to my father. Tatty was not the best at construction jobs around the house. He rarely did even the lightest "men's work." For instance, everyone – Jews and non-Jews, at least during peaceful times – used to cut the grass with their hands, but my father never did this. He was asked why he didn't join the men in the common social setting of sitting on the ground, chatting and pulling off the top of the grass. He said "If I get used to it I will forget and do it on Shabbat, which is forbidden, and that's why I never do it." I believed him of course, but I also thought that when it came to unpleasant men's work, he preferred not to do it.

As the oldest child, I got some extra time alone with my tatty, which I treasured. Sometimes, just the two of us ventured into the countryside, where we would visit Jewish farmers. These rural folks were admirable and interesting, but they had quite different experiences than Jews who lived in town. For instance, they had almost no exposure to yeshivot or *bokherim*, yeshiva students. Jewish children growing up on farms generally learned about Judaism from their parents, at home. Once, when my tatty and I were visiting a Jewish farm, the farmer was really impressed with my *payot*, my sideburns, that were long for religious reasons. They fell almost to my shoulders. He asked me to test his son, to ask him what he knew about Judaism. So, I asked the youngster, "What do you know?" Shyly, he mentioned that he knew his *Alef-Beit*, which meant he knew all twenty-two letters of the Hebrew alphabet. His father wanted to have *naḥat*, pride, so he urged me to go ahead and tell his boy to say all the letters. I did what the farmer asked, and his son recited the *Alef-Beit* perfectly. Then I wondered what else I could ask the child to do. After some thought an idea came to me. "Now say the *Alef-Beit* backward," I prompted. He turned around and said it again while standing with his back to us. We all laughed so hard, the sheep started bleating.

As a family, we sometimes went to my uncle's farm for a holiday in Debrecen, which I am pretty sure was in Hungary when I was little. We would go for a brief summer-holiday break. My uncle was not just a farmer, but also a *shoḥet*, so we were able to get some free kosher meat to bring home when we visited him and his family. Later, when I was older and in yeshiva, and spending a great deal of my time singing as well as learning, I would go to that farm by myself. It was a holiday for me alone. My parents recognized that I needed to get away. I went by myself every summer when I was seven, eight, nine, ten, and eleven years old to get a break from everything, even my siblings. I was so much in demand for my singing, I needed time away from everyone. But when I visited the farm, I would of course sing for my uncle and auntie and their many children.

One summer I was there, when my auntie gave birth to her thirteenth child. The midwife yelled at me to go to the *shul* where my uncle was studying and tell him that his wife had had another boy. They already had twelve boys! I ran to the nearby *shul* and told my uncle "*Mazal tov!* Congratulations! You have a baby boy." My uncle stood up slowly and walked over to the window. He looked out, and up, and yelled to the *Ribono Shel Olam,* to God: "We will see who will get tired first!" In case it is not obvious to you what he meant, he was telling God he would not stop having children until he had a girl, and he was daring God to give up first, to get tired first, creating only boys for his family. After that baby, his wife gave birth to three girls. On a horrific note, this entire extraordinary family of sixteen children and their loving parents were murdered in Auschwitz.

This uncle, father of sixteen children, had a vast, colorful garden in his yard where he enjoyed sitting and learning. At the

Chapter One: Uzhhorod

same time, all his boys would do their learning inside the house. In fact, it was quite normal for Jewish children to be relatively pale – compared to their non-Jewish counterparts – because they spent so much time learning indoors. When I was visiting my uncle's farm one time, I decided to join my uncle outside instead of sitting in the house with all my cousins. I sat with him in the garden for a few hours each day for about a week. If I may say so, I got an attractive tan on my face. When I arrived home, my surprised mother stared at me. After a moment she gasped and screamed: "My God, you look like a *goy* (non-Jew)!" A touch of Jewish humor from the old country.

***

With all my chores and jobs and learning, growing up could be difficult sometimes, but the difficulty was unimportant compared to the love I felt for every baby sibling that came along. After me came Rivka, Gittel, Yoel Hershel, Chaim, Yitzchak, Pinchas, Shideleh and finally little Chana Pesal. I can never mention my sisters and brothers without remembering that five of them, the youngest five, lost their precious lives in Auschwitz, the biggest Nazi death camp. I still tear up when I think of them. My loving parents were lost at that horrific death camp, too.

As I mentioned, before the Holocaust, all of us children and our parents formed a close family, very affectionate, very loving, very caring. My parents set an excellent example. They never fought or screamed at each other, so we never did either, at least not too much. You know how siblings can be. But we never rebelled in any kind of serious way. We never even thought of rebelling against our parents.

That is not to say I was always perfectly behaved. In case it is not obvious yet, I have always had a great sense of humor. And since a young age, I have had a fondness for pulling pranks. Here

I will tell an inspiring story about my tatty, of blessed memory, and how he handled me after a naughty episode at the local *heder*. The principal had come to our home and told my tatty about my uncharacteristic bad behavior. I was a young boy. I do not remember the bad act or my exact age, but I think I was no more than seven. I thought my father would be really upset with me. He called me into his room. He told me to sit down. He said, "I want to tell you a story. The story goes like this. There was a family with just one son, a son who was awfully spoiled. He misbehaved constantly. He was bad. He did all the wrong things. His father tried to teach him. His mother tried to teach him. Nothing helped. So, one day his father said, 'Listen son, whenever you do something wrong, I will put a nail in this wall. Each time.' So, he started. He put in one nail then another nail, then another, until the wall was full of nails. One day years later when the boy was sixteen, he came into his father's study and he saw all the nails. He thought, 'My God, that is ugly. What will I do? I think I am going to change my ways. I am going to behave, because this is hideous.' After that, not only did he do the right thing, but whenever he did something positive, and when he listened to his father and mother, his father took out a nail. A few years later there were no nails left.

"One day, when the boy had become a young man, he came into the study and he saw the wall. There were no nails, but it was full of holes. He looked at it, recalled the past, and burst out crying. So, his father asked him, 'Why are you crying? When the nails were being put in you didn't react. But now when the nails are gone, you cry.' All the young man said to his father, philosophically, was: 'The nails are gone, but the holes remain.'"

***

Education was always easy for me. When I was five years old, my father first took me to *heder*. The *melamed* showed me the letters, *alef, beit,* etc., from a book on the Hebrew alphabet. He asked me to read them. Then he closed the book, paused, opened it again, then asked me to show and name for him as many letters as I could. I was able to name all 22 letters, with no problem. As I recited each letter correctly, candy fell from above. The *melamed* was holding a broom over my head with candy resting at its top. He would shake the broom to make the candy fall. I was so happy. It was candy from heaven!

In *ḥeder* at seven years old, I was number one in the class. In fact, I was usually the only one who had *kushiot* – questions – for the *rebbe*. I was an inquisitive child, and I asked good *kushiot*. The *rebbe* really liked my questions. One day, when we were discussing marriage in class, I asked him what *shelo kedarko* meant, because he had mentioned the term. I didn't know then – but I learned years later – that I was asking him about sex. He hit me, and said, "And *kedarko* you know already?" *Kedarko* is the heterosexual way to have sex and *shelo kedarko* is the homosexual way. Very soon after, he apologized for hitting me, realizing that I was too young to understand the topic or what I was even asking.

When I was a young child, it was *ḥeder, ḥeder, ḥeder* almost all the time. I also spent many hours at home and in the synagogue studying. Indeed, I spent most of my waking hours learning from the Torah and other sacred texts appropriate to my age. Sometimes I would get up at 4 a.m. to learn. Then I would go to Shaḥarit, the morning religious service, at 6 a.m., then have breakfast, and then go to public school from 8 a.m. until noon. I came home for lunch, and then I went to *ḥeder* until 6 p.m. I seemed to be always busy learning.

I had lots of friends at *ḥeder*. Many of them were older than I. As children, we would sit and learn together in the yeshiva or the synagogue. We had no television, no movies, no organized sports, no video games, no baseball. We really did not play much, as we were always learning. When we found a little time for play, it was often the game called marbles. But instead of using glass marbles, we used nuts, and when you won a round, or hit another player's nut, you got to keep and eat it. Sometimes, we would run and play in the grass in the fields at the edge of the neighborhood, but only until we were discovered by the adults. Then it was back to the books. I rarely took time off school, but visiting my grandparents was important, so sometimes the family would go on a weekday. When I was perhaps six or seven years old, my *zaide* died during one of those visits. I was alone with him while he was resting in bed. He said to me, "I am not feeling well," so I brought him some water. I helped him to wash his hands and his beard. I said, "I love you," and then I left him alone. He died right at that moment. He closed his eyes and that was it. I have always felt honored to have been the last person to speak to him and to help him.

When I was only eleven years old, during the weekdays, I went to live in Munkacs, the town of my hasidic *rebbe*, and attended his yeshiva. While there, I received important lessons in helping the poor. Every week, the other *bokherim*, who happened to be a few years older than I – would take the school wagon and the horse around to the local villages to collect food both for the yeshiva and also for the poor people in town. The *bokherim* would visit storekeepers and wealthy farmers who were happy to donate food – potatoes, corn, milk, vegetables – and sometimes even money. Though it was always the older boys who were allowed to go, I desperately wanted to join them. Why? It looked like such an adventure! I begged the *rosh yeshiva*, the head of the school, that I be allowed to go with the older boys. He said I could go if I passed a test on the material we had learned already that week. Of course, I passed with flying colors, and therefore earned permission. When the time came, we all went off with the horse and wagon.

At some point, we arrived at a farm where we were invited in for lunch. The nice farm lady was serving some kind of beans, which I hated. I didn't even like the smell. In those days, many people – including my family – ate beans frequently as they constituted the most inexpensive yet healthy meal to make. For some reason, I could never get used to eating them. My taste buds rejected them even before my stomach did. When the really kind farm lady left the kitchen for a moment or two, I took the beans off my plate and slipped them into my pants pocket. She came back and screamed, "Oh! You love the lunch! You are already finished. You want more!" She was so happy. It was hard for me to disappoint her, but I coughed and sputtered, "No thank you, I am much too full."

***

In yeshiva in Munkacs I had a *ḥevruta*, a partner with whom to study Torah. The son of a well-known chief rabbi in Hungary, he was brilliant, a first-rate partner. In some ways, he was a better learner than I. We used to get up at four in the morning some days and sit on the windowsill to study together. One day, I noticed he wasn't himself. I asked him what was wrong, but he said nothing. For the next few days I noticed his bad feelings again, yet he kept telling me he was fine. Finally, he broke down and told me he was having a recurring dream. In the dream, a milkman was complaining, saying, "I miss your *Kaddish*," the prayer said by family members when a close relative passes away. "I don't understand this vision," he said. There were no phones, so he couldn't just call home for family support. I told him to go home and tell his father what was happening. He took my advice right away. His father told him to forget it, it was just a dream. But interestingly, he learned the town's milkman had died. He continued to have the dream while visiting his parents, and he complained again about the problem to his father. Finally, his father took him to see the milkman's widow, and she broke down crying. She told a story that would change his life. "When I was pregnant, your mother was also pregnant, and we both had boys at the same time. But your mother could not produce milk, so I had to nurse both her baby and my baby, which I was happy to do, of course. Your mother would bring her baby to me during the day and the night, but it became too difficult, so she decided to leave her baby son with me during the nights. One night, when he was only a few days old, her baby died. My husband and I were distraught beyond words. We discussed what we should do. Because we were poor, humble people, we knew we could never give our son a great life. But with the rabbi and *rebbetzen*, our child would have everything he could ever need or want. He would grow up in a wonderful home and have the best education. We decided to tell the rabbi and *rebbetzen* that *our* child died. We gave them our child to raise as their own. That child was you."

Now he understood. He came back to Munkacs and said *Kaddish* for his biological father, but he never told anyone, not a single soul, besides me. To this day, I am the only person with whom he shared this information. I do not want to write his name because his family, now living in America, still does not know about his real birth parents.

***

You might say that, when I was growing up in Uzhhorod, things were a little backward, or old-fashioned, and my family was no exception. In fact, the first time I saw a bus when I was a young boy, I ran to my mother and I said, "Mommy, Mommy, there is an apartment moving on wheels!" We never read newspapers or listened to the radio. Not at all. Instead of newspapers we got the *Munkatcher* newsletters, which were all about Torah, Jewish values, and Jewish rituals. Other than sacred religious books, just about all that was read by Jews were these hasidic papers.

Chapter One: Uzhhorod

Sometimes, for secular news, bulletins were stapled to a board on a wall outside city hall. People, but not many Jews, would gather round to read about local ordinances or other information.

One other important form of communication was shouting. A trumpeter would come to the middle of town and blow his instrument loudly. When lots of people had gathered around him, he or another man with him would announce the news of the day, such as where the Germans were advancing in the war. There was an ancient joke about the trumpeters, which I must tell. The trumpeter announced: "We killed two thousand Russians!" The crowd shouted back, "How many of our men were killed?" The trumpeter responded, "That is being announced in Moscow!"

On a more serious note, a trumpeter in Sevlush – a hasidic town before World War II, and the hometown of famous nineteenth-century composer Bela Bartok – once saved the Jews from a deadly pogrom. From my understanding, this town experienced more than its share of pogroms right up into the twentieth century. During riotous pogroms in Sevlush, the bad *goyim* would break into Jews' homes, kill them, and then steal their silverware, candelabras, and other precious belongings. Once, the day before Yom Kippur, the town's rabbi was learning in his office when he heard a loud rapping on his window. He looked up and saw the town trumpeter. He let him in. "What can I do for you?" asked the rabbi. "The bad *goyim* of this town are planning to burn down the synagogue with all the Jews in it on the night of *Kol Nidrei*," the trumpeter replied. "They know this is the one time in the year when entire families come to the synagogue to hear the opening prayer of Yom Kippur. You won't be able to escape. They plan to lock everyone in. Then they are scheming to steal from all the Jews' empty homes, take their silver and anything else they want. I am taking a huge risk telling you. If they knew I was here with you, they would kill me."

The stunned rabbi asked, "How do you know this? And when exactly are they coming? I thought relations with the gentiles in

Sevlush were improving." The trumpeter answered, "They are planning to attack the synagogue when you are about to sing *Ki hinei kaḥomer.*" The rabbi was surprised to learn that the non-Jewish trumpeter knew the prayer that begins with "Behold, as the clay is in the hand of the potter." "When you are about to sing those words," continued the trumpeter, "they aim to launch the attack. But I will warn you by blaring my instrument just as I see they are gathering together. I know where they propose to meet. You will have enough time to announce to the congregation what the *goyim* intend to do, and to lead your people into the hills behind the town where you can all hide." This is exactly what happened. Two Jews stayed close by the *shul* to let the others know when the disappointed *goyim* had disbanded. Once alerted, the Jews returned to the *shul* and continued the service to the end.

Days later, the rabbi went to the trumpeter to ask why he had risked his life to warn him. The trumpeter told this story, "When I was a little boy I had a cruel stepmother. She used to give me bagels she had baked to sell in the town market. She knew exactly the amount of money I was to return home with. One day, I stumbled and lost a coin. I was terrified to go home. I sat and cried by the side of the road. The *rebbe* of the town was passing by, and he stopped to ask me why I was crying. I told him. He reached into his pocket and gave me the exact coin I needed. I never forgot his kind gesture, and that is why I warned you."

The other popular place to learn word-of-mouth news and gossip was the town *mikve*, the ritual Jewish bath. When Polish or other Jews would come to our town during World War II, they would come to the *mikve* and tell us horror stories about the Nazis. But we didn't believe them. They would describe unimaginable atrocities being perpetrated against Jews in Poland and elsewhere, but we could not accept their words as truth. I remember bathing, sitting, and talking in the *mikve* before Shabbat with the newcomers in town, and listening carefully to learn what was happening outside our little world. But we – the simple, naive, devout Jews of Uzhhorod – thought the visitors were lying. We thought they were making up false tales because they wanted *raḥmanut,* pity. "Yes," we said amongst ourselves out of their earshot, "they want us to feel sorry for them." We wanted to help them, but we didn't know how because we just did not believe them.

Chapter Two

Childhood

I was recognized as a *wunderkind*, a singing child sensation, one Shabbat afternoon at shul during *shaleshudis,* the late Saturday afternoon meal. As usual, all the men and boys were singing *zmirot,* Shabbat songs, and I was contentedly joining in with the others. All of a sudden, everyone fell silent. I was singing alone and the rest were all staring at me, their mouths slightly open. I didn't know whether to be embarrassed or proud, but I noticed my father smiling, so I just continued to sing by myself. At one point, one of the men lifted me onto a table so I could be better heard. I was almost nine years old, and my amazing alto singing voice had been discovered.

After that, for a few years anyway, my father would not allow me to sing in the Uzhhorod boys' choir, mainly so I could develop as a soloist, which I certainly did. Later, even when I was permitted to rejoin the choir, I was too often away to lend much consistent vocal support. From the moment I was discovered, word spread around Eastern Europe like wildfire. From age eight to thirteen and beyond, I was booked all over a large area to sing on Shabbat, give concerts, and perform as a soloist during High Holy Days. I went to Vilna, Lodz, Nitra, Klausenberg, Warsaw, and Poshtan, to name just some of the better-known places where I was invited to sing. It has been said that before World War II, I traveled more than any other *ḥazan* in the world. Indeed, I traveled to places where *ḥazanim* had never been before.

***

The Jews have always loved and embraced music to their very souls. In fact, I have met people who told me they converted to Judaism just for the music. With help from the "My Jewish Learning" (MJL) website, which assists my fading memory and facilitates my being brief, I want to give you a short lesson in Jewish musical history.

Music has been integral to Jewish life since the early days of the Jewish nation. When the people of Israel were led out of Egypt, the Torah tells us, Moses led them in a song of heavenly praise. Music was later an important part of the Temple services in Jerusalem, during both worshiping and sacrifices. In future years, music became part of synagogue prayers as well as religious observance at home. It is hard to find children anywhere who do not love to sing with their father, mother, and siblings around the Shabbat table. Music generates joy and brings families together.

Besides cantorial, which is the music of the professional prayer leader like myself, Jewish religious music includes other forms. There is *nusakh*, which refers to the different tunes to which traditional prayers are sung or chanted; modern liturgical music, in which songwriters set passages of prayers to choral harmony or even to other music that may actually not be Jewish; cantillation, which describes the note system for singing or chanting public readings of the Torah and other sacred texts, including the *haftara*, which is taken from the book of Prophets; and *nigunim*, which are, in effect, wordless melodies.

Not surprisingly, throughout the world, and throughout history, different observant Jewish communities have created their own unique musical sounds for their prayers and other religious expressions. But as the world has shrunk, and the global community has become ever more interconnected, each individual Jewish community has become increasingly less distinct – in music styles, yes, but also in other areas, such as clothing and speech. You could call it cross-pollination across the many Jewish communities in different countries.

According to the MJL website, of all the different types of Jewish music, *ḥazanut*, or cantorial music, may be the most difficult to appreciate. I partially agree with this assessment, especially if you consider that *ḥazanut* is the Jewish equivalent of classical music. Just as classical pieces and composers are often hard to decipher and learn about, and as classical music can be an acquired taste, so, too, cantorial music may require much time and attention to be well understood. But that does not mean it cannot be enjoyed even right out of the gate. The songs of the *ḥazan* do, in places, soar with astounding elegance as they praise God the Almighty. The music reaches right down into your heart and soul, where God resides, and the glorious sound can make you weep with joy and awe at the same time. No former or formal lessons required. Just an open mind and a pure heart.

Interestingly, before there was such a thing as recorded music, before there was instantaneous access to the very latest entertainment, concerts and other performances by *ḥazanim* and their choirs were the main type of leisure distractions for Jewish people. At some point in recent history, that somewhat hazy line between entertainment and *davening*, praying, became even blurrier. *Ḥazanim* commenced to sing many intricate and complex songs right there in *shul* during Shabbat services. Religious congregations generally love the weekly performances – why wouldn't they? – but many of the musical pieces were actually and originally created just for entertainment.

Singing and chanting Jewish liturgy is not for the faint of heart. In truth, proper Jewish learning of any kind is both intense and complex, including the requirement to study at least two new languages, Hebrew and Aramaic. Moreover, the difficulty and concentration required in learning Jewish religious texts cannot be overstated. Limits to Jewish knowledge don't exist; there is always more to learn and to re-learn. In case it is not obvious yet, I will say it right out: Education is as integral to Judaism as the Torah. Education through the study of Torah – and through the examination of innumerable other venerable Jewish volumes, including the sixty-three densely written tractates of the Talmud – has helped bind the Jewish people and generations together since biblical times. Jews believe that learning serves God, and, as such, Jewish children as young as three are taught to begin to read Hebrew. By age six, all Orthodox Jewish children are profoundly steeped in learning about their religion.

I am explaining this because I want the reader who does not know about Orthodox Judaism to understand how much time and energy I devoted to learning even as a young child. I did much extra work outside school and yeshiva to prepare to sing expertly and elegantly for services and congregations throughout Eastern Europe. I do not want to brag, but I was a quick learner. It is simply a fact that the vast majority of Jewish children do not study as much or prepare for services the way I did. Of course, all those hours and hours of learning every week were worth it. I always enjoyed the learning, and I deeply loved the *davening* and the performing.

***

Chapter Two: Childhood

It is the absolute truth that the golden age of ḥazanut happened during the first half of the last century. It is also the absolute truth that I was graced by the Almighty with the good fortune to be part of that most engaging time period. It was God's desire that I share that exulted era with a dozen famous ḥazanim, all of whom will go down in history as the greatest ḥazanim of all time. Could I have asked to be in better company? I humbly admit I owe much of my success and my style to some of these talented older contemporaries. One was a world-famous ḥazan by the name of Yossele Rosenblatt, of blessed memory. I was ten years old when he died in 1933.

Rosenblatt was one of the very first great European ḥazanim to move across the ocean to live in the United States, though in truth he was not the only ḥazan of his time to make such a major transition. And while there were dozens and dozens of highly qualified American-born ḥazanim leading the *davening* in synagogues in major cities across America, from New York to Los Angeles, Rosenblatt set himself apart. It was the time when there were a plethora of recordings and concerts by many cantors. In fact, many of the most famous ḥazanut, cantorial melodies, were written during that era. But Rosenblatt himself was truly one in a generation. Many of his experiences were later undertaken – in a remarkably similar fashion – by me.

Born in Russia, Rosenblatt, who ultimately invented some magnificent and now widely-used cantorial techniques, came from a long and distinguished line of cantors. Like me, his devoutly religious childhood prohibited him from getting early formal musical training at one of the reputable and distinguished European music schools of the day. Like me, he began his career as a member of the local synagogue choir, though, as mentioned, I left the choir for years as soon as I was discovered. And like me, he was highly praised as a child prodigy before he was ten years old. Like me, in his mid-teens, Rosenblatt traveled to Vienna for a few months. While there, he led prayers at one of the largest synagogues in the city. Informally, he worked with accomplished singer, musician, and businessman Jacob Maerz. After Vienna, he toured widely among the Jewish communities of the Austro-Hungarian empire, including Budapest. I toured many of the same communities a decade later, and I eventually worked as the chief ḥazan of Budapest.

Unlike me, Rosenblatt fortunately never experienced the Holocaust. Instead, he married at eighteen, following which he accepted his first full-time position in the hasidic community of Munkacs, Hungary, where I later went to yeshiva.

***

Another singing genius in my lifetime was Yosef Schmidt. He was simply an amazing tenor, the greatest in the world in his time. Not only his music, but also his *neshama,* soul, was extremely important to me during the war. Schmidt – who spoke five languages: German, French, Yiddish, Hebrew and Romanian – unfortunately died of a heart attack at the end of 1942 in Switzerland, aged thirty-eight. He was in a refugee camp, and reportedly the harsh conditions there and his already weakened health contributed to his untimely death.

Schmidt was born not too far away from where I grew up, in a village in Davideni (Davydivka) in the province of Bukovina, which was part of Austria-Hungary at the time. He received his original voice lessons when he was very young, while he sang as an alto in the choir of the famous and former Czernowitz Synagogue, a place he returned to sing as an adult. He performed his military service with Romania in the 1920s. Like Rosenblatt, he shared a couple of my traits and experiences. For one, Schmidt was short, in fact even shorter than myself, since he did not even

Chapter Two: Childhood

reach five feet, and I am about five feet. Also, he was recognized early, at maybe seven or eight years old, and he was performing recitals by age ten. In 1924, he gave his first solo performance in Czernowitz, during which he sang traditional Jewish songs and also beautiful arias by Verdi, Puccini, Rossini, and Bizet. I cannot say I have ever sung the works of any of these composers, at least not publicly or professionally. He was very impressive.

Before returning to Romania for his military service, Schmidt moved to Germany, where he took piano and singing lessons at the *Königliche Musikschule* in Munich. This historic venue is one of the most highly regarded, long-established professional universities in Germany teaching music and theater arts. It has gone through more than a few name changes, and was actually moved and rebuilt for the Nazis. It is infamous for being the building in which Britain's Prime Minister Neville Chamberlain and Adolf Hitler drew up the deceptive Munich Agreement in 1938. In 1929, Schmidt returned to Berlin, where his career really took off. Unfortunately, I never met Yosef Schmidt, who died just before I was sent to Bor, but his voice lives on to this day. One of the reasons I liked Schmidt so much was because he sang softly, which the Germans appreciated. They call it the *"musk"* in German, which means the voice is coming from the forehead. And no one did the *musk* better than he did. I was desirous to copy his ability to take extremely deep breaths. Pavarotti was twenty-five years younger than me but he, more than I, had to take in air while singing. You could see him breathe in the middle of a phrase because he couldn't inhale deeply enough. By listening to Schmidt, I learned how to take a deep, deep breath, and hold a note or notes for an extended time.

It is a great irony of history that Yosef Schmidt's best professional years were during the 1930s, when the Nazi Party was frantically building up Germany's armed forces and consolidating its power. These were also the years of the early and ominous decrees against the Jews, including the one that forbade Jewish artists or writers to work. Many German leaders did not know, or want to believe, that Schmidt was Jewish. Some Germans who knew he was Jewish dared to call him an "honorary Aryan." I never met Schmidt, but I know he would have been so pleased with himself after I told him how he inadvertently saved my life in the Holocaust, a hair-raising story related in the next chapter.

When I heard Yosef Schmidt for the first time, I said to my parents that his was the technique I wanted to learn. But it was not until a few years later that I was able to receive such professional training. It happened like this. One day, when I was sixteen years old – not long after my voice had switched overnight to a tenor – I was sitting studying a difficult part of the Talmud, in Munkacs. Two men aged around twenty sat down on either side of me, looked at me, and smiled. They knew me well, because their parents used to invite me for meals on Shabbat, and I'd sing for their wealthy families, which they greatly appreciated. I remember they especially enjoyed it when I performed Havdala, the special candle-and-wine ceremony marking the symbolic end of Shabbat every week, as well as the conclusion of holidays. I stopped my learning, and asked the two what I could do for them. They handed me a train ticket to Vienna and one hundred American dollars. They told me I was to study music at the Vienna Conservatory. "You can become something special," one of the young men said to me. I was so excited that I jumped up and almost knocked the sacred book I was studying off the table. I thanked them, and could not wait to travel to Uzhhorod to tell my father. Sadly, my tatty did not share my excitement, because he knew he'd see me even less. I left for Vienna within a few days.

When I arrived at the music academy, I was enrolled with Schmidt's teacher, Werner Wolff. Professor Wolff taught me a wealth of musical information, including a treasured song written by Yehuda Meir Shapiro. Shapiro is famous for being the founder of *Daf Yomi*. This well-known and widely accepted system of learning – now used by tens of thousands of busy Jews in a wide range of professions all over the world – involves studying one page of the 2,711 pages of the Babylonian Talmud a day. It takes more than seven years to complete a cycle, after which there is traditionally a celebration, and then the studying begins again on page one, and lasts another seven plus years. Many Jewish individuals are known to read their page-a-day while taking public transportation to their jobs. Shapiro's song was in Yiddish, and I sang it after I'd heard it only a few times. Professor Wolff cried and kissed me on my forehead when I sang it. I'll never forget that. He was very sensitive and emotional. Wolff, who was also Jewish and ultimately fled to the US to escape the Nazis, was so famous that he couldn't walk down the street in Germany without being recognized by admiring Germans. I once saw a woman throw herself in front of his car to get him to stop so she could get his autograph.

***

Sometimes, I used to make up tunes myself to the prayers I was saying. In my childhood career, one *ḥazan* in a nearby town taught me that I should keep the meaning of the words in my mind when coming up with a tune. That was excellent advice. For the rest of my career, for more than seventy years, I tried to remember to do this every time I made up a tune. What I was essentially doing was interpreting the words in order to make up the *nigun*. Even when I was not creating my own tunes, I still tried very hard to concentrate on word connotations. When I did this, when I was focusing carefully on the meanings of the words I was singing, my voice gained a richer, more passionate sound. In fact, I got this exact same advice from Professor Wolff when I took lessons from him in Vienna.

Part of my musical education was singing to children at their *ḥederim* and during Shabbat afternoons. I would sing songs like

Zara ḥaya vikayama, which conveys the message that children live, and all the while they continue learning and developing. I sang this in Yiddish, and the children loved it. I continued to sing for children for many years. I came to see that they make fantastic audiences, especially because they love to laugh.

As a young ḥazan, I was sometimes called a *baal tefilla*, which means a prayer leader, especially when I *davened* in hasidic places. Jews in hasidic communities would sometimes come right out and say to me, emphatically, "You are not a ḥazan. You are a *baal tefilla!*" What's the difference? There is a striking difference. As a ḥazan, you are acrobatic. You use a lot of color, so to speak. There is some volume, and much entertaining. A *baal tefilla davens* for the *Ribono Shel Olam*, not for the people.

One other thing I learned early in my singing career was to dress impeccably. From a very young age when I started performing, until I retired more than seventy years later in Ottawa, the capital of Canada, I dressed the part. My perfectly fitting shirts were always pressed. I wore suits that contoured my body flawlessly, and that were often tailored. I never went anywhere without a matching and fashionable tie. I wore a black bowler hat when I dressed up, instead of a *kippa* (skullcap). And before, during, and after I served in the Israeli army, my shoes were polished to a spit shine. You cannot put a price on being dressed for success. As for my beard and mustache – if I had one, the other, or both – they were neatly trimmed before every show. I am not saying my clothes and superb grooming earned me my living, but I am saying they did not hurt. I have been complimented on my wardrobe many more times than I can count.

***

As well as meeting and being influenced by great ḥazanim in my life, I have been blessed to meet and share words of Torah with

Chapter Two: Childhood

many of the finest *rabbonim*, the most venerable rabbis in the world. I am going to write about them here – in this chapter about my boyhood singing – putting the majority of them together in one place, though many I met much later in life.

One was Rav Chaim Ozer Grodzinsky, son of Rav David Shlomo Grodzinsky, the latter being, for forty years, the Rav of Vilna's suburb Ivye. Rav Chaim Ozer was a child prodigy with an unbelievable memory and who, at fifteen years old, was specially admitted to the exceptional *shiurim*, classes or lessons, of the world-renowned Rav Chaim Soloveitchik in Volozhin, at the time the most prestigious Lithuanian yeshiva. Rav Ozer, who was considered particularly adroit in answering halakhic (Jewish legal) questions from all over the world, was also highly influential in retaining the Lithuanian yeshivot during the Communist years. He married the daughter of an eminent Vilna *rav* and *dayan*, after whose death in 1887 Rav Ozer was appointed to his place on the Vilna Beit Din. The Vilna Gaon – a brilliant non-hasidic *talmid ḥakham* of the late 1700s – was said to be Rav Ozer's archetype. Rav Ozer, who was opposed to the formation of a Jewish state in the absence of the messiah, served the European Jewish community with love and dedication for more than fifty years.

Surprisingly, I cannot recall exactly where I met Rav Ozer, but it was during my prewar travels as a young *ḥazan*. We ended up at the same small place at the same time. Lucky for me, as he graced me with his words, and he even praised my singing.

Before he moved to Boston in 1932, I had the enormous honor when I was still a child to meet a descendant of the above-mentioned Rabbi Chaim Soloveitchik, that descendant being Rabbi Joseph Ber Soloveitchik, who was born in Pruzhany, Russia in 1903. Without exaggeration, he turned out to be probably the most seminal figure in modern Orthodox Judaism. Referred to sometimes as a modern Jewish philosopher, he served as *rosh yeshiva* of the revered Rabbi Isaac Elchanan Theological Seminary

The Life of Moshele Der Zinger

at New York City's esteemed Yeshiva University. Before his death in 1993, this giant of Judaism – who did foment some controversy within the Orthodox community – guided, taught, counseled, and advised tens of thousands of Jews, both students and followers. He earned the exalted title *rav*, as he ordained almost two thousand rabbis in fifty years.

I was similarly honored to meet Rabbi Avraham Dovber Shapira, son of the great Zalman Sender Kahana Shapira. Born in 1871, the younger Shapira studied in the world famous Volozhin Yeshiva. In 1913, he became the cherished Chief Rabbi of Kovno, Lithuania. Tragically, he died in 1943 in the Kovno ghetto, ten years after I met him.

It was also a great honor to meet Rav Yosef Rosen, known as the Rogatchover Gaon, the genius of Rogatchev, a city in Belarus. I met him in Dvinsk – (since 1920, known as Daugavpils), which is in Latvia. We were seated beside each other at a breakfast, but we did not converse much as he was learning Talmud throughout the entire meal. Rav Rosen is known for his photographic memory. It has been said that he was very likely the foremost Talmudic genius of his time.

I received a *brakha* – a blessing – when I was a mere youngster from the pious and sinless Ḥafetz Ḥaim, whose real name was Rabbi Yisrael Meir Kagan. He was standing at a train station surrounded by many Jews each trying to get a *brakha*. I elbowed my way in, politely of course, and got mine, to my eternal gratitude. He is famous for writing his eponymous book, the definitive amalgamation of the severe laws of *lashon hara*. *Lashon hara* means evil speech, but it only constitutes gossip about a person that is actually *true*.

Another great *rebbe* I had the honor to meet was the Baal Shem Tov's descendant Ahavas Yisroel Hager, the firstborn son of Rabbi Boruch Hager, the latter being the second *rebbe* of Vizhnitz Hasidim. Boruch had eight sons in total, almost all of whom became the beloved *rebbes* of small Eastern European towns. Yisroel – the *rebbe* I met – took over from his father to lead the Vizhnitz hasidic dynasty, which started in the Polish town of Vyzhnytsia, today located in Ukraine. Yisroel took on the exulted *rebbe* position following his father's early death after only eight years at the helm. Only eight years, yet Boruch, and then Yisroel, presided over many thousands of followers. I met Yisroel in Grosswardein, the former Hungarian city currently in Romania, where I sang *zemirot*, Shabbat songs, with his son Reb Chaim Meir Hager, the future Vizhnitz Rebbe.

Then there was the Lubliner Rebbe, Rav Meir Shapiro, the above-mentioned creator of the page-a-day *Daf Yomi*. He was also Lublin, Poland's, treasured and adored *rosh yeshiva*. He started the famous boys' school Yeshiva of Ḥakhmei Lublin, which had the aim of enhancing Hasidim in future Poland. More specifically, the goal of Ḥakhmei Lublin was to train hasidic rabbis to guide the next generations of Polish Jews. We know what happened to that goal, since Polish Jewry suffered staggering losses under the Nazis. Situated in a mammoth structure – for which the 1924 groundbreaking attracted some twenty thousand people – the school taught hundreds of boys at a time. Fashioned mainly on the Lithuanian Volozhin model, the school owned an impressive hundred thousand-volume book collection.

I met this great *rav* when I was visiting Lublin to sing in the city's Great Synagogue. I sang a piece that Rav Meir Shapiro himself composed. As a kind of reward, I was invited the next day to sing for him and his *rebbetzen*. The *rav* cried when I got to the Yiddish parts. Is it any surprise that I loved this sensitive and brilliant *tzaddik*?

I wish to relate another story about him, which occurred earlier, in 1931, when he was first appointed Chief Rabbi of Lublin. He gave a *derasha* on the first Shabbat in his new job. To begin, he said, "Ladies and gentlemen, before I give you my *derasha*, I would like to expand on some words of the Talmud. *Bimkom gedolim al taamod.* This means, don't stand in the place of the Torah giants. You won't understand them. They are too high. But I am changing that to say, no, of course don't stand in their places, try to grow bigger, try to be greater. I promise you, I will try to measure up to these giants, I will try to be as high. I will try to attain their greatness." He was also telling his listeners that they, too, should not stand in one place but always try to grow. Finally, he said, "Who am I to take this position? I will give you an answer. A man can think, 'Meir, you are already the Chief Rabbi of Lublin. This is the greatest position in the world. It is enough. Have a good time.' But of course, it is not enough. All *talmidim* must not stand still. They must go up, try to be higher."

Another famous rabbi I was very fortunate to meet was Rabbi Yitzḥak HaLevi Herzog, the Ashkenazi Chief Rabbi of the British Mandate of Palestine and then of Israel from 1936 until his death in 1959. Before going to the Land of Israel, he was a rabbi in Belfast from 1916 to 1919, after which time he got a job as a rabbi in Dublin. During the Irish War of Independence between 1919 and 1921, he was a staunch supporter of the republican cause. In fact, he got the nickname, "The Sinn Fein Rabbi." Between 1922 and the time he went to Mandatory Palestine, he served as Chief Rabbi of Ireland.

Rabbi Herzog is famous for the Catholic/Jewish story he called, "We'll talk at your wedding." It goes like this. When he became Israel's first Ashkenazi Chief Rabbi, the Republic of Ireland invited him back for an official visit. He was treated like royalty, with great honors bestowed on him by high representatives in the government. After he spoke in Parliament, Rabbi Herzog was given more accolades at the state dinner, where he was seated next to an Irish cardinal. Worried about *kashrut,* the rabbi ate only fresh fruits and vegetables at the meal. Noticing this behavior, the Catholic priest beside him sighed and then asked him, "Why, after all these centuries, can you not allow yourself as a Jew to eat the excellent food that everyone else enjoys, such as the delicious meats and cheeses being served here? Why can't you just take pleasure in eating the scrumptious cuisine?" Rabbi Herzog laughed uproariously, thought for a few moments, then retorted, "I cannot answer that question now. But I will definitely be able to give you a response at your wedding."

Acknowledged as an eminent rabbinical scholar, Rabbi Herzog authored many books and articles that focused on Jewish law and the issues involving the Torah and the State of Israel. He is credited with helping to mold new perspectives on Religious Zionism.

Because I mentioned this immediately above, I should quickly explain the two main ethnic Jewish categories, Ashkenazic and Sephardic. Sephardic Jews established communities around Spain and Portugal more than ten centuries ago. Ashkenazic Jews descended from ancestors who inhabited the Roman Empire around the year 1000 CE. Members of this latter category put down roots throughout eastern and central Europe, and they spoke Yiddish. The Land of Israel has always had both a chief Ashkenazic and a chief Sephardic rabbi, dating backing several hundred years.

I was also deeply honored to meet Rabbi Herzog's son, Major-General Chaim Herzog. Though Chaim was not a rabbi, he was influential, brave, and extremely important to the State of Israel's beginnings, serving as an early Israeli politician, an IDF general, a lawyer, an author, and ultimately as the country's sixth president.

About 27 years after World War II, when I was in New York on a vacation, I was honored to meet and talk with Bobover Rebbe Shlomo Halberstam in Manhattan. We talked about the war and we both cried. He was only the third *rebbe* of his dynasty, which started in Bobowa, Galacia, now Poland. Thousands upon thousands of members of the Bobover sect, including the second *rebbe*, Reb Shlomo's father, were annihilated by Hitler. With barely three hundred members, Reb Shlomo Halberstam – who had the same name as the first Bobover Rebbe, his grandfather – moved to the United States to start over. He eventually moved the headquarters to Brooklyn. When it came to building, this *rebbe* was unstoppable. Besides the famous yeshiva in Brooklyn, for more than fifty years, he constructed a vast number of *shuls*, *ḥederim*, yeshivot, *mesivtot* (high schools), *batei midrash* (study halls), summer camps, and other institutions all over the world.

I was blessed and honored to have met the Satmar Rebbe Yoel Teitelbaum, in Israel of all places. I say this because Satmar Hasidim are notoriously anti-Zionist, against the State of Israel, but here he was visiting the Jewish state. I spent an inspiring hour with him and Reb Boruch Hager. Reb Hager belonged to the great hasidic movement of Seret, a city currently straddling Ukraine and Romania. Seret Hasidim were eradicated in the Holocaust. I want to re-emphasize here that the Nazis completely annihilated hundreds of hasidic groups. The Seret sect was among those entire hasidic bodies that ceased to exist. Reb Hager – who was a grandson of the above-mentioned Boruch Hager – was living in Haifa, where he set up a community, and he became known as the Seret-Vizhnitzer Rebbe. During the hour with the two *tzaddikim*, I certainly enjoyed their banter. Reb Hagar teased the Satmar Rebbe for setting up his Satmar headquarters in America – in Williamsburg, New York City – as opposed to Israel.

During that same car ride the two rabbis discussed an ancient debate that happened to be going on yet again in Israel: Where was King David's tomb? Scientists and Bible experts were arguing among themselves whether the grave site was on Mount Zion in Jerusalem or in Bethlehem. In his most sarcastic tone, Reb Hager said to Reb Teitelbaum, "We aren't sure about either of those cities, but we are absolutely positive King David was not buried in Williamsburg."

Chapter Two: Childhood

One more quick story about the great Satmar Rebbe. He once took time out of his full schedule to hear me sing. When I was in Satmar as a young boy, Reb Teitelbaum came into the synagogue I was visiting to listen to me for about ten minutes, before he left to go on his way to his own *shul*. A profound compliment to me.

***

What follows here is the lengthy and important story of my experience with Rebbe Yekutiel Yehudah Halberstam, sometimes referred to as the Sanz-Klausenburg Rebbe. I was blessed and honored to *daven* – as well as to sob uncontrollably – in his esteemed company. His leadership lasted until his death in 1994, after which the movement split into two separate hasidic groups, the Sanz-Klausenburger Hasidim, located in New York, and Sanz Hasidim based in Netanya, Israel. Netanya is where this great *rebbe* ultimately lived and died. He was a child prodigy, a top scholar, and the grandson of Rabbi Chaim of Sanz who founded Sanz Hasidim. Rabbi Halberstam himself founded Transylvania's Klausenberger Hasidim in 1927, the same year that he took the title of Rav of Klausenburg. He attracted large and increasing numbers of followers until World War II, which saw 85 percent of his sect die in the Holocaust. The *rebbe* lost his wife and eleven children. A natural leader, even in his profound grief, he created the functional organization "She'erit Hapleitah" in nineteen Displaced Persons camps, where the group conducted services and where it operated Jewish schools, including yeshivot.

It was during this time, right after the war, that I was humbled to meet Rabbi Yekutiel Yehudah Halberstam. At the time, I was working for the Joint, short for the American-Jewish Joint Distribution Committee, an organization that helped feed and provide resources for Jews who survived the Holocaust. Dr. Joseph Schwartz, the Joint's European chief and my boss, asked me to travel to DP camps to give concerts. Once he sent me to Fernwald, a camp in Germany where thousands of refugees were receiving aid. I was put in a guest room – in the former home of a German – when I arrived on Thursday afternoon. I dropped my bag, and went outside to hear what people were talking about, to see if I could hear the names of my family. I heard someone mention Shalom Eliyahu Felberbaum, my cousin. I asked, "Where is he?" I went to the apartment I was told he had been given, and I found him there, with another cousin, Chaim Alter Roth. We all cried and kissed and talked, for hours.

"Why are you staying at the guest room?" Chaim asked. "Come and stay with us." I went and got my things and moved in with my cousins. On Friday, they told me we were all going to the *mikve* before Shabbat. I didn't really want to go. Though I was religious after the war, I was not as observant as I had been before the genocide. But I did not want to be rude, so I accompanied them. After that, we went to the synagogue. While I was standing at the door about to enter, I saw Rebbe Halberstam, the Klausenberger Rebbe. In a word, I was terrified. I no longer had a beard, I was wearing a beaver hat instead of a kippa, and my tzitzit – those ritual tassels attached to a special undershirt worn by Orthodox Jewish men – were tucked inside my pants so they could not be seen. I was embarrassed. My cousins urged me to go inside. There were about two thousand people, so I hoped I could stay hidden in the crowd. I went to the back of the sanctuary, got a siddur, a prayer book, and started to look inside. I felt a hand on my shoulder.

"Moshele," the *rebbe* said, "*Kabbalat Shabbat.*" In his quiet, unassuming way, he was telling me to lead the congregation in the prayer service to usher in the Sabbath. "*Rebbe,*" I replied, "Look how I am dressed and how I look. I am not for you tonight." "Moshele, *Kabbalat Shabbat,*" he repeated. I had no choice. I went up to the front and performed the service. After, I went home, had a hot meal, and then left again to go to the *rebbe's tisch*. Hundreds

Chapter Two: Childhood

of people were gathered for the discussion. He asked me to sing song after song, which everyone seemed to enjoy.

For the services the next day, I thought I would be clever and arrive late so the *rebbe* would forget about me and not ask me to lead in *davening*. When I arrived, some people were screaming *Kol haneshomo tehalail Yoh Halleluya* – let every soul praise God. This is part of Shaḥarit, which had not formally begun. I grabbed a siddur, stood at the back of the *shul*, and started to say Shaḥarit quietly. I quickly moved ahead in the long prayer. Soon, I felt a hand on my shoulder and heard the words: "Moshele, Shaḥarit and Hallel," the latter being the prayer said only on holidays or Shabbat Rosh Ḥodesh, which is any Shabbat on which a new month begins. "But *rebbe*," I moaned, "look where I already am in the prayer. I've gone so far." He repeated, "Moshele, Shaḥarit and Hallel." I went to the front to do as I was told, and the *rebbe* followed.

I led all of Shaḥarit and began to sing Hallel. I noticed that during *davening*, this great *rebbe*, the Klausenberger Rebbe, would actually talk in Yiddish to God, right in the middle of prayers. I was standing quite close to him. During Hallel, I heard, "*Yasor yisrane Yoh velamo-ves lo nesononi.*" The original translation for these words of King David is, "God has punished me but he did not let me die." As I listened, the *rebbe* translated the verse differently: "God, you punished me so bitterly. You took away my dear wife and my dear children. Why didn't you also let me die?" When I heard him say these words quietly, I broke down crying. I was so upset, I could not continue on with Hallel. After a few moments, I managed to collect myself and I started to sing again. But I could not finish. I was again overcome with grief and tears. The *rebbe* turned to me and gestured with his hands for me to calm down. I cleared my throat and started to sing once more. It was no use. I could not stop sobbing.

The *rebbe* came over to me and gently directed me to his spot on the *bima*, the special raised platform in Orthodox synagogues for leaders of the service. After we traded positions, he finished Hallel. The only thing left to say about this sad occurrence is that it was the only time in 74 years as a *hazan* that I was unable to finish a song.

Later that evening, I went to Havdala. After that, the *rebbe* invited me into his private room to talk. He began to tell me about how he went to yeshiva with my father, when all of a sudden, he asked me why I did not take off my hat. "Because I have no *kippa* underneath," I replied. He handed me one. At that moment, he also took off his hat and revealed his *kippa*. Then he did something unusual in the extreme: he walked behind me, picked up a pair of scissors, and cut my hair off in the middle and on top of my head. "You will take off the rest," he said. The following night was the first time in my career I gave my concert with a hat on, instead of only a *kippa*. I got a haircut the very next day.

Spending time that weekend with Rebbe Halberstam had a major impact on my religious observance. As you will read in detail in the next chapter, the Holocaust made me question my beliefs, be angry with God, and even want to stop serving Him. By the time I was sent by my Joint boss to give the concert in Fernwald, where I met the great Rebbe Halberstam, I was basically religious, but no longer hasidic. Thankfully, this incredible *rebbe* helped me return back to hasidic practice, which I have never again left. His faith and spirituality were inspiring and contagious. He told me: "Regarding the Holocaust, we have lots of questions and no answers. But the answer is, there are no answers."

Rebbe Halberstam went to New York in 1947, where his sway and leadership seemed to know no bounds. In the Williamsburg section of Brooklyn, he expended seemingly unlimited energy to increase religious observance, influence that reached to Israel, Mexico, and Canada. He left to work his magic in Israel in 1957. That year he set up Kiryat Sanz, a community in Netanya, where eventually he established *hederim*, yeshivot, a hospital, a nursing

Chapter Two: Childhood

home, and even an orphanage. In the 1960s, he set up another Sanz community in New Jersey. There he spent time when he wasn't home in Netanya, where he eventually was buried.

***

Now, to get back to my early career. The first time I ever traveled by myself was a couple of months before the High Holy Days, when I was just nine years old. I remember my father putting me on the train, alone. I was to travel to a Jewish community in a strange city. I was to arrive with much time to prepare with the rabbi and local cantor. When I was seated on the train and my father was standing on the platform by my window, I said, "Tatty, I am going out into the world all alone and I don't know anything." He answered me, "I don't know what to tell you, Moshele, except that when you are invited to people's tables to eat because they love your singing voice, sing as well as you can, so you are effectively paying for your dinner. Also, what you see the other people do, you do, too." Ah, wise words from my tatty, that you will see came in very handy.

That trip was the first of so many I took that I cannot even hazard a guess as to the number. Some things I learned early, and never forgot. For instance, there are stark differences between hasidic and non-hasidic congregations, especially where excited children are concerned and particularly on the night of *Kol Nidrei*. In a non-hasidic synagogue – where I occasionally sang for the High Holy Days – the noise and chaos were over the top. I could end up waiting for up to a half hour for the sanctuary to be quiet enough for me to begin, yet even then it was not perfectly silent before I started singing. Sometimes the noise would increase so much again that the rabbi would not be able to give his *derasha*. In hasidic *shuls*, on the other hand, you could hear a pin drop almost from the start.

The Life of Moshele Der Zinger

When I was away, I got used to writing to my parents and siblings. Sometimes, although not often, I would telephone them, but it was nothing like it is today. Almost no-one had a home phone. I would go to the post office, telephone the post office in Uzhhorod, and tell the clerk there to pass a message to my parents to come to the post office at exactly 4 pm. I would call back at that hour and we would have a brief chat.

For most of my childhood, many of my friends were much older than I, some twice my age. I have always enjoyed the company of older people. And I credit my singing voice for helping me make more mature friends. Almost invariably, these friends appreciated and praised me for my voice. Having older friends helped build my confidence.

Here is a story of how I made an older friend. When I was about ten years old, I knew about a *ḥazan*, Reuven Chaim Rosenberg, who lived in the nearby town of Sevlush. He had a son-in-law who lived for a while in Uzhhorod. Every morning, this son-in-law arose from his bed, got dressed, and walked to our *shul*. He liked our *shul* because there were new minyanim – groups of at least ten men for the prayer quorum (minyan) – every thirty minutes until 10 a.m., so he could go at later times, when he needed or wanted to. Almost every day when he passed by our house on the way to a later minyan, he would hear me through the window. My mother had a *tiḥel* (scarf), that I used as a make-believe tallit (prayer shawl), something males don't use until they are bar mitzva. I would don the pretend tallit and sing. After hearing me sing for a week or so, this man stopped and knocked on our door. He was very distinguished, and asked my mother where was the boy who was singing. She corrected him, laughing, and said, "You mean who is screaming." She often said this about my voice.

Then my tatty arrived. The man offered him one thousand kronen, the type of money we used, to allow me to stay with him at his home in Sevlush for one month to help him prepare for *Seliḥot*,

Chapter Two: Childhood

some of the prayers and poems said in the days leading up to the High Holy Days. My father agreed, but only if I would be staying with his father-in-law Ḥazan Rosenberg, because, my father said, Rosenberg's house would be an excellent environment for me. The young man agreed. I should remember his name, but I don't. I know we remained friends for several years after that.

***

Once I was invited to *daven* in the city of Nove Zamky, today a proud city in Slovakia, but then a small town in Czechoslovakia before it became part of Hungary during World War II. The synagogue where I sang is now a historic landmark, but that isn't part of this story. I actually made it safely to Nove Zamky two years in a row for the High Holy Days without being kidnapped, an accomplishment I explain below.

The first year, before I sang as a soloist at the synagogue, I was invited to the elegant home of a rich family, the Roths. I was so happy to eat their delicious food, after which I sang some *zemirot* for the family at the table. Out of the corner of my eye, I saw Mr. Roth take out a small stick and rub it in his mouth between his teeth. Of course, it was a toothpick, but I had never seen a toothpick before. So, remembering my father's advice to follow and do what I see, I picked up a toothpick and did the same. When Mr. Roth saw me, he smacked his seventeen-year-old son across the back of his head and said, "You see how this youngster knows how to clean his teeth? And you still don't do it. You eat so sloppily, like a pig." I know this does not sound kind or nice, but the father was joking and the smack was pretty light. Everyone at the table laughed.

The third year I went to Nove Zamky, when I was maybe twelve – it must have been 1934 – I was to be the *ḥazan* soloist again. I arrived on the train. As I was standing and talking with the local cantor who had come to pick me up, a strange man approached. He had also just arrived from another town – for some reason I forget which – and he walked up to me and politely begged my pardon. He said he wanted to speak to me privately for a few minutes. Remembering my manners, I unthinkingly and trustingly walked a few meters away with him to hear what he wanted to say. He mumbled something about needing help with a package, with which I was happy to assist. Instead, as soon as we rounded a post, he grabbed my hand and quickly brought me onto a waiting train.

There is nothing else to say but that he kidnapped me. There is no other word for what he did. Without my permission – or anyone else's permission for that matter, for instance, my parents' – he dragged me onto the train and held me there until it left the station. We arrived shortly at his home town. Though I cannot remember the place's name, people there knew me well. I was already a big star, a *wunderkind*. So, for those holidays I was the soloist in their city, and I even stayed for a few weeks after.

While there, I sang at a few weddings and at a couple of small, late-afternoon concerts, the type given when a rich man leads the *davening* of Maariv, the evening prayer. There, I would stand beside the man leading the prayers at the lectern, in front of many people. I would sing a few lines before each *berakha* of Maariv, after which the adult would *daven* the rest. At the end of Maariv, I would continue to stand in front of the audience and sing four or five *shirei kodesh*, religious songs.

My parents ended up not being too angry about the kidnapping, because I was safe and well paid, but it was a few years before the town of Nove Zamky asked me back again. Oh, and interestingly, I met the kidnapper many years later in Israel. He was such a sweet, nice man, a good musician. He said he felt bad about what he'd done. I forgave him.

At one point in the mid-1930s, I was invited to Frankfurt, Germany, to a *ḥevra Kaddisha seuda* (burial society meal) on the seventh of Adar. For this organization to have a special meal on the seventh of Adar is common. The date is very significant, in that Moshe, who most people know as Moses, was both born and died on that day. In a quirk of our faith, there are two Adars in a leap year, and Moshe happened to be born on the seventh of the first Adar and to die on the seventh of Adar II. It was an honor for me to be invited to the *seuda*, since a well-known rabbi was also going to give a talk. His name was Rabbi Dr. Joseph Breuer, the grandson of the famous but controversial Rabbi Samson Raphael Hirsch. Rabbi Hirsch, who died in the late-nineteenth century, is often credited with being a main founder of modern Orthodox Judaism. Rabbi Breuer helped establish the German K'hal Adath Jeshurun shul in Manhattan, thus creating a congregation that is basically a direct transplant of the pre-war Jewish community of Frankfurt, the very community I was visiting.

After the Tuesday night *seuda* was over, a man from Hamburg walked up to talk to me. I was looking forward to leaving Germany and heading home, as Hitler was already the chancellor and I did not want to stay any longer than I had to. This man took my hand and brought me to the lady's flat where I had been boarding. He helped me gather my luggage, and explained to me that he desperately needed me in Hamburg. Still a young child of eleven or so, I agreed, because he was an adult and very polite. We spent one night at a hotel, and the next morning, Wednesday, he took me to Hamburg. He asked me to wait for six or seven days for a wedding, and I agreed. On Shabbat, I led the Friday night service, but only until *Barekhu*, the part that serves as the call to prayer, because I wasn't yet bar mitzva. I led *Lekha dodi*, the sweet song to usher in the Sabbath. I sang it the special hasidic way, the Munkatcher hasidic style, and everyone loved it. *Lekha dodi* means "Come, my beloved," but in the song the beloved is the Sabbath. I sang at the *ufruf*, which is the Shabbat morning service before the wedding during which the *ḥatan*, groom, usually reads from the Torah. On Saturday night, the *ḥatan* came to *shul* again, and I sang more songs. The wedding was on Sunday, when I sang even more. The nice man paid me well, and I happily went home after almost an entire week.

***

When I was eleven, my father took me to meet the famous Munkatcher Rebbe, my *rebbe*, Chaim Elazar Spira, a man who came to love me almost as much as I loved him. He was only a few towns away, in Munkacs of course, and I was very excited. It was the first time I would meet him. We didn't have a car, so we went by train and walked. The rule according to the *rebbe* was that a boy had to be thirteen years old to stay and learn with him full time at his yeshiva in Munkacs. But my father begged: "Try my little Moshele out. He is such a smart boy. He learns at the yeshiva in Uzhhorod with the older boys," many of whom actually came from Munkacs! The *rebbe* agreed to try me. He asked me a few questions and I knew the answer to every single one. After that, he took me in to learn with him full time, even though it was before I was bar mitzva. The Munkatcher Rebbe had never, ever done that before.

So, at the age of only eleven, I went away to yeshiva in Munkacs to study with my *rebbe*, my adored Munkatcher Rebbe. This may sound strange, but hasidic parents, even today, almost always send their children away when they are old enough to sit patiently and learn. Not often, but sometimes, children even as young as eight are sent to faraway cities to study Torah in yeshivot. The reasons for doing this are sound. The Mishna – the core part of the Talmud – says, "*Havei gola lemakom Torah*," a person should exile himself to a place of Torah. In other words, if the children are too close to home, they will want to run to see their parents all the time. In their hometown, there will be many distractions. Their mother may even fetch them to help at home. But

Chapter Two: Childhood

when they are in a different town, those distractions are kept to a minimum. Even young Orthodox girls today are sent many miles from home so they can have long, quiet stretches of time to study. It is believed that sending children away to learn is also a great way to help them develop their own personalities. It was not a coincidence that children from Munkacs came to Uzhhorod to study, as Munkacs had the same distractions for them as Uzhhorod had for me and others from my town who studied in Munkacs. You could call it a student exchange program. Indeed, being away helped me learn not only Torah, but also Talmud, Tanakh, Mishna and *Shulḥan Arukh*, all sacred Jewish texts.

In those days in my home town, there were no cars or buses or taxis. In order to get back to my yeshiva in Munkacs after Shabbat each week I would start to walk there from my home in Uzhhorod. Jews, and frequently even non-Jews, would offer rides on their wagons with their horses. It usually took me two hours to get to Munkacs.

The Munkatcher Rebbe Chaim Elazar Spira was the man I respected most in the world when it came to Jewish learning. He impressed me so much, it was unbelievable. I have never met a man like him, not before I went to his yeshiva, and not since he died in 1937. There has never been a better speaker. There has never been a better singer. There has never been a better leader. There has never been a better-looking man. He was extremely handsome. Whenever I speak at universities – which I have done numerous times in my adult life – I always talk about Rebbe Chaim Elazar Spira, and life before the war.

***

Bar mitzva refers to the Jewish coming of age ritual for a thirteen-year-old boy. Mine was very unlike the bar mitzvas you see today. Typically, even for boys from middle-class Jewish families, thousands upon thousands of dollars are spent to celebrate with lavish parties after the boy's first experience reading from the Torah in the synagogue. By comparison, mine was quiet, though my parents and siblings were proud of me. I had studied my *parasha*, the specific section of the Torah read on a particular day, but in all honesty, I pretty much knew how to read all the Torah *parashot* by then. Nevertheless, I spent hours chanting and preparing with the help of my father and my *rebbe*.

My bar mitzva was not celebrated on a Saturday, as many are, which meant we were able to have a photograph taken of my father and me, the only picture commemorating the day. One other picture was taken the day before by the same photographer for my passport. These two pictures were prized possessions and they went with me everywhere. However, by the time I was liberated from the concentration camp at Bergen-Belsen in 1945, I had lost them, a fact that had made me cry often in the camp. Indeed, I came out of the war as naked as the day I was born. I came out with my life, nothing more. Years later, while I was Chief Cantor of Antwerp in the 1950s, I received a letter from a man in Gary, Indiana, containing the two photographs. I was overjoyed to receive them. There was also a letter explaining that the writer was originally from Uzhhorod. When he was already living in America, he remembered the child prodigy that I was and he wanted to bring me and my father to the United States to do a tour. So, he wrote to my father and asked for photographs. My father sent copies of the two pictures and a letter, but the concert tour never happened because the war broke out. After the war, the man who eventually wrote to us first asked one of the four *ḥazan* Koussevitzky brothers – I cannot remember which one – to get my address when he was on tour in Europe. Mr. Koussevitzky found my address when I was living in Antwerp and gave it to the Uzhhorod-born American, who kindly sent me back the treasured photographs.

Chapter Two: Childhood

Getting back to my bar mitzva: On that day, for the first time in my life during *davening* at *shul*, I wore tefillin, which, as described nicely and succinctly by Wikipedia, "are a set of small black leather boxes containing scrolls of parchment inscribed with verses from the Torah, [and] which are worn by observant Jews during weekday morning prayers." I then gave a well-prepared *derasha*. After *sheheḥianu*, a prayer to celebrate special occasions, we returned home for an extra nice breakfast with a few friends and the rabbi. Both the rabbi and I said some words of Torah after the meal. Then the professional photographer we hired took that memorable picture, which I have always loved.

As I said, the day before the celebration, the same photographer took my picture for my passport, which I needed to visit my *bubbe*, my grandmother, in Kerestir, Hungary, during the afternoon of my bar mitzva. After the breakfast was finished, my father grabbed my hand and we ran to the station so we would not miss the train. I was to get a *berakha* from her. Kerestir is the Yiddish name of the Hungarian town of Bodrogkeresztur. But far more fascinating is the fact that my *bubbe* was the *rebbetzen* of Rebbe Yeshaya Steiner, the well-known founder of Kerestir Hasidim. Some have called him one of the greatest Hungarian hasidic rabbis of all time. Sadly, he died long before my bar mitzva. But visiting just my *bubbe* was still a great honor.

Rebbe Yeshaya Steiner was actually my *tatty*'s stepfather, and the man who raised my *tatty*, since his biological father had died when he was very young. Reb Steiner was my *bubbe*'s second husband.

We arrived in Kerestir at 3 p.m., only to discover that my *bubbe* was sleeping. So, we waited in the room where the *rebbe*, my *zaide* – my grandfather – of blessed memory, used to sit and counsel the people who came for his advice and to get his blessing. My *bubbe* awoke at four and she came out to see us. She gave us cake and something to drink and said *leḥaim, a* Hebrew toast meaning "to life." She then put her hand on my head and blessed me. I kissed her hand.

Before we left, she told us a story, as Hasidim are wont to do on any occasion, even right before wedding ceremonies. On the day of her *huppa*, the canopy under which Jewish couples marry, her *hatan*, her husband-to-be, came into the room where she, as the *kalla*, the bride, was waiting with all the female relatives and guests. Yeshaya came to her from another room where all the male family members and guests had gathered earlier. They steered him and followed him and danced and sang with joy as they all moved to the *kalla's* room. Before everyone joined together to go to the *huppa*, which was set up outdoors, Yeshaya insisted on first telling his *kalla* a hasidic tale. Just before he told her the story, he reminded her that a hasidic tale does not have to be true, but it must have a moral. He told her the following story:

> One day when I was walking around in heaven, before I was born, I was enjoying watching the angels running around doing God's will. It was beautiful. Suddenly I heard, "*Panu makom haRav haGaon baSinai ve'oker harim arzai haTorah!*" Make room for the great rabbi, he is coming through! The *neshama* of this rabbi was coming before God's court, and the angels were carrying many books. I must see this, I thought. I followed them and saw them put the books on the scale, which broke. On the scale's other side were just a few sins. The judges were about to pronounce that he go to *Gan Eden*, to heaven. Then I heard a voice saying, 'Wait, wait!' A little angel ran over and explained that the Torah learning that this man did was not *lishma*. In other words, he did not study Torah for its own sake, but rather so he would be honored and respected. To prove it, the angel made a blowing sound and the books tumbled down off the scales. Without pause, the judges then pronounced *Gehenem*, hell.

When I saw this, I went crazy. I said, 'God, what will be with me?' I wanted to ask an angel to explain everything, but out of the blue I heard another voice saying *panu makom*, make room, someone else is coming.

It was an innkeeper, a man who would always give food and drink to travelers before they left his premises. He would give each person free bread to take for the road because often they had miles and miles of walking ahead of them. For this innkeeper, the angels piled the bread he gave away on the scale. There was so much bread that the sins on the other side flew away.

Now remember, my *kalla*, bread, bread, bread. Bread is what everyone needs to live, physically, but also spiritually. We must always remember to be generous with our hearts and our bread. Now, my *kalla*, let's go to the *ḥuppa*.

The *mussar haskeil*, the moral, of this charming hasidic tale is to always help poor people. Moreover, Rebbe Yeshaya Steiner wanted his *kalla* to know that, like the patriarch Abraham, it was important for him to have a home that offered constant *hakhnasat orḥim*, hospitality. Indeed, during their marriage, dozens of travelers, walkers mainly, came to their home every day for free food and drink as well as for rest, company, and spiritual refreshment. Since hearing this tale on my bar mitzva, I have always remembered, throughout my life, to give to those less fortunate. Giving *tzedaka*, charity, is an important mitzva. Hearing about the mitzva in this story told by my *bubbe* made giving *tzedaka* even more special for me because, whenever I gave, I remembered her and her inspiring words.

Within a few days of my bar mitzva, everything returned to normal. My father took me back to Munkacs, and I continued to learn with my *rebbe*.

***

The Life of Moshele Der Zinger

When I was thirteen, I wanted to start *davening* Shabbat as *ḥazan* in a particular *shul* in the Hungarian town of Kosice, sometimes called Kassa, which has as fascinating, pot-holed, and diverse a history as Uzhhorod, but I won't go into that now. For this specific job – at the city's main synagogue, which comprised two *shuls*, a smaller one and a larger one – I had to get a permit. I went to the large *shul* to meet with the president. I explained to him what I wanted to do. He just glared at me. Though I was thirteen, I was not big. Even my mother said I looked like I was only ten. To get rid of me without disappointing me, the president told me to go ask Rabbi Shaul Brach, who would do the difficult job of letting me down.

I went to see Rabbi Brach. As predicted, he, too, said it was impossible. He added: "If you go to the big *shul* you'll see in the entrance there is a large announcement that says an unmarried man cannot *daven* as *ḥazan*. I had seen the sign, and agreed that it was very specific. But I also pointed out that it was not a Torah law. I further answered back: "If you will not allow me to *daven* here, no other *shul* in this region will allow me to *daven*, either. You will be a *Mesia lidvar avera*, which roughly translates as, you will enable me to do a sin. Rabbi Brach got visibly upset. His face turned red with anger. "How dare you talk to me that way?" he shouted. "What do you mean? Where is your *derekh eretz?*" He was asking me what had happened to my respect.

He was right. Even at my young age, I had the *ḥutzpa*, or audacity, to speak up for myself, which sometimes sounded rude. I didn't mean to be rude. "God gave me a gift," I answered. "I have a voice. I want to sing. I want to use my voice for holiness, to pray to God. If you don't allow me to *daven*, no one in the vicinity will let me, and I will have to go to the non-Jewish world. Then you will be a *Mesia lidvar avera*. If I go to the non-Jewish world, who knows what will happen to me?" Rabbi Brach calmed a little, and he searched my face. He softened completely, and then relented:

Chapter Two: Childhood

"You know, you are right." He reached for a pen and paper and he wrote a permission letter. I took the letter back to the president, who almost fell off his chair. He couldn't believe his eyes. To say he was surprised is an understatement.

So that Friday night, as directed by the *shul* president, I *davened* in the small *shul*. It was a trial so the congregation could try me out. The plan was that if I was successful on Friday night, the next morning I would sing in the big *shul*. Was I a success? Don't you know it? Here is what happened. When I arrived at the bigger *shul* Saturday morning, there were so many people, they couldn't all fit inside. There was a huge crowd around the door, and I overheard that they were there to hear the new, young *ḥazan* sing. I said as loudly as possible, "I am that *ḥazan!* Move aside so I can enter." Not hearing me, they shoved me away. One man even said, "Get lost, kid." I started to cry. Just at the last minute, I saw the president, who immediately identified the problem. He hoisted me onto his shoulders and brought me into the sanctuary. It turned out the congregants were not expecting a boy at all. They thought the new *ḥazan* would be a young man.

***

At age thirteen, I was deeply honored to superficially meet – with three hundred other students – the daughter of Queen Wilhelmina of the Netherlands. I was a *yeshiva bokher* in Munkacs, and it turns out hasidic Jews were not the only people to love Munkatcher Rebbe Chaim Elazar Spira, who, by the way, spoke eight languages. One day, as we were studying, a messenger – there were few phones in the town then – from Czechoslovakian President Thomas Garrigue Masaryk came to the door. He told the *rebbe* that Princess Juliana from the Netherlands wanted to meet "The Wonder Rebbe," as he was known throughout Eastern Europe. The *rebbe* agreed, but he wanted to obey a Jewish law forbidding a man and a woman from different families to be alone together. Therefore, though he did not really need one, he requested a translator. My cousin happened to be chosen as translator. When the princess arrived, the three hundred students formed two lines, between which she walked, then climbed the stairs to the *rebbe's* room, where he was waiting for her with my cousin, the translator. She extended her hand, and the *rebbe* apologized, saying, "I cannot shake your hand." She was completely accepting. Then she told him that she was pregnant and she desperately wanted a son who could eventually be monarch. She requested a blessing from the *rebbe* to ensure that that happened. He politely explained to her that it was too late. "It is what it is," he said. "It cannot be changed now, since he already exists. If you'd come to me earlier I might have been able to help." She said she understood, and then she got up to leave. Before she turned to go, she asked him, "Why did you not shake my hand?" He said, "My mother taught me not to touch something that belongs to someone else." She said she understood, and gracefully said thank-you and goodbye.

It was not until almost sixty years later that I finally understood how it came about that Princess Juliana, the daughter of Queen Wilhelmina of Holland, had visited my *rebbe*. I was in Toronto, Canada, where I had gone to visit old friends from Munkacs, Shalom Estreicher and Shimon Fehrner. "For some reason I never asked my cousin, the translator, why she came to see our *rebbe*," I told them. "Can you please explain, if you know, why the princess visited our *rebbe*?" Fehrner knew, and he told me. "One day, Queen Wilhelmina was visiting the same town as was the former Munkatcher Rebbe, Reb Zvi Hirsh Spira. She could see out her window that he was in the park across the road with about sixty students, who were listening intensely to every word he said. The queen ordered her adjutant to go outside and find out what was happening. He did as he was told, and discovered that the *rebbe* from Munkacs was visiting. She asked her adjutant

Chapter Two: Childhood

to again go out and find out if the *rebbe* would receive her, meet with her, if she came to the park. The task was performed and the *rebbe* agreed. When she came down, she told him that she had been unable to have children from the time she'd been married, nine long years. The *rebbe* closed his eyes and made the special blessing for royalty. He also said in one year you will have a child, and this came to pass, and the child was Juliana. And that is why Princess Juliana of the Netherlands visited the next Munkatcher Rebbe, our *rebbe*, in 1935."

At age fourteen, I again traveled to the town of Sevlush, staying as usual with the local *ḥazan,* Reuven Chaim Rosenberg. During that stay, people would visit his house and I would sing for them. On *Seliḥot* night, when everyone was to sing pre-Rosh HaShana (Jewish New Year) songs and prayers in *shul,* unbeknownst to me, my father was visiting the same town. He stayed with his other friends, the Rosenbaums.

During services, my sneaky father sat at the back of the *shul* to hear me lead the *Seliḥot* service. It wasn't until about forty years later that I learned what he had done. I was visiting my mother's relative in New York City, and she told me. I was stunned to learn about my father's presence at that place and time, so long ago. The synagogue where I sang had 1,500 congregants, many of whom were there for *Seliḥot* that night. Apparently, when I finished my solo, my father asked Mr. Rosenbaum who the boy was who had just sung so richly and beautifully. Of course he knew, but he was curious to see what his friend would say. Rosenbaum answered, "That is Moshele. He is an amazing prodigy." My dad broke down crying with happiness. He confessed to Rosenbaum that he knew it was his son, but added, "At home he sometimes sings so wildly, whereas here, he sounds like a professional."

It is impossible to forget my one and only visit to Stropkov, a very small town now in Slovakia that has endured horrible antisemitism throughout most of its history. People always flocked

The Life of Moshele Der Zinger

to Stropkov to hear the great Rebbe Menachem Mendel Halberstam – yes, another great Rabbi Halberstam – who, after the war, moved to New York, where he established the venerable Stropkover Yeshiva in Williamsburg, Brooklyn. When I went with my tatty to Stropkov in Europe to see and hear this rabbi, space was so limited, many people had to listen from outside the window of the *beit midrash*, the study hall, where the *tisch* was held. Literally hundreds of the *rebbe*'s followers were standing outside. We were lucky that we arrived early enough to get seats near him. He put on a comprehensive show, if you dare to call it that. He sang Shabbat songs and prayers, including: *Shalom Aleikhem,* a song sung before the first Shabbat meal; *Ribon kol olamim,* a prayer said after *shul* on Friday night; *Eishet ḥayil,* which means Woman of Valor, and is sung in honor of the Jewish woman before the Friday night meal; *Kiddush,* which specifically means sanctification, and is said over wine or grape juice to sanctify Shabbat or holidays; and *Hamotzi,* the prayer said over bread. Then he gave a *shiur*; ate his soup; gave another *shiur*; sang the Shabbat song *Kol mekadesh*; ate the main meat meal; and sang *Ma yedidut menuḥatekh,* "How Beloved is Your Rest."

After that my father nudged me, and told me to sing. "Moshe, stand up and sing," he said quietly. "No," I whispered back to him. "I want to wait until the *rebbe* asks me to. Remember the young boy who sang too early, when his *zaide* told him to, instead of waiting to be asked by the *rebbe*? He lost his voice? We were pretty sure it was a spiritual punishment because he sang too early, when his *zaide* told him to, during a *rebbe*'s *tisch*." My father nodded knowingly. The *rebbe* continued with his program. He said words of Torah; then, a *posek*, adjudicator, answered some questions about the *Ḥumash* – the Torah in printed form – with commentaries from Rashi, the great Torah scholar of the Middle Ages; sang three more songs; learned more *Ḥumash*; and then everyone *benched,* that is, we sang Grace after Meals. Partaking in a common ritual among

Chapter Two: Childhood

Hasidim, Rebbe Halberstam left a small part of his meal on his plate, then passed the plate to the crowd so some of his followers could eat the leftovers and feel a part of him.

Then the great Stropkov Rebbe gave a *Devar Torah*, a lesson based on the *parasha*, or Torah portion of the week. It is so strange, but I clearly remember the Torah portion, *Miketz*, which, like many *parashot*, is both the name of the Torah portion and the first word or two of the Torah section. *Miketz* concerns the end of exactly two years of imprisonment for Joseph in Egypt, and describes Joseph's grieving. *Miketz* is a hint that *tzarot*, troubles, are coming. The *rebbe* wanted to talk instead about the end of *tzarot*. Some people began to leave, because they thought they saw the *rebbe* throw an apple, a hasidic ritual to indicate the end of a holiday (even though this day was not that holiday). But suddenly, he began to tell another story. Finally, the *rebbe* said some very complimentary words about me and my father, and he finally asked me to sing, which I did with great pleasure.

***

Malavei malka, post-Shabbat parties, are always enjoyable, and sometimes challenging. I used to attend a regular *malave malka* at the home of the great-great-great-great-great-grandchild of Yechezkel ben Yehuda Landau, who traced his lineage back to Rashi, a medieval French rabbi and one of the seminal biblical commentators of the Middle Ages. The Landau of the eighteenth century was a famous *dayan* of Yampil, now located in Ukraine, who wrote the *Noda Biyehuda*, one of the principal sources of Jewish law at that time. His five times great-grandson, also named Landau, used to offer a thousand pengers, about two hundred dollars, to anyone who could come up with a relevant story that was not in the sacred book *Noda Biyehuda*, a title that also applied to Yechezkel ben Yehuda Landau himself.

The Life of Moshele Der Zinger

Naturally, I wanted to take up the challenge. When the time came I told this story, which I had heard in Kosice the previous week. I had sung there on Friday night. At first, it was very boisterous and hectic in the sanctuary. The *gabbai* (beadle) instructed me to wait five minutes until everyone settled down. I did that, and began to sing *Lekha Dodi*. When services were over, I saw one of the Landau relatives, who told me the following story:

"When Yechezkel ben Yehuda Landau was the Chief Rabbi of Prague, he was still a young man. He was the colleague of a rabbi known as Tzop, which means braid in Yiddish. Tzop was called this, because he always wore his long hair in a braid. The reason he wore it in a braid was to help him stay up all night learning. He would always stand to learn, and he would tie his braid to the top of a chair behind him so if he started to fall asleep, his head falling forward would pull his hair tied to the chair, startle him, and wake him up, so he could continue learning. Tzop was widely respected, well off, and a scholar. When Yechezkel ben Yehuda Landau became chief rabbi, he got all the votes, except one. He did not get the vote from Tzop. Landau, also called Noda Biyehuda, was disappointed, but graciously and maturely accepted not getting the one vote.

"Landau's oldest son Shmuel then was eight years old. It was around that time that Tzop adopted the custom of visiting Talmud Torah schools every Thursday afternoon to check and see if the *melamdim* (teachers) were doing a good job. One day, Tzop came to Shmuel's school with the two candidates whom Landau had beaten, as well as some congregants of the local *shuls*. Tzop asked Shmuel, 'What are you learning?' Shmuel answered, 'The names and ways of all the rabbis.' Tzop was upset, and smacked Shmuel across the back of the head, obviously unhappy with the reply. 'First you learn, and then you become a rabbi,' Tzop said, angrily. 'Not like your father, who became a rabbi first, then he learned.' Shmuel went home crying, and told his father what happened and

Chapter Two: Childhood

what Tzop had said. 'Don't worry, my son,' he said to his boy. 'At the Monday meeting of the *shul*'s leaders I will resign. I do not want to make trouble. I have lots of other offers from places to work.'

"On Monday at the meeting, his resignation was met with rejections. 'Just because one man, Tzop, does not like you is no reason to resign,' he was told by a *shul* president. 'Everyone else loves you.' The president also went to Tzop and said, 'You are crazy. We might have the greatest rabbi in the world in Noda Biyehuda.' Tzop said this was not good enough, adding, 'I am willing to change my negative opinion if you, Landau, will answer one question by Thursday.' Noda Biyehuda said he already knew the answer, and he explained how: 'On Wednesday last week, a book fell in the library from a desk. I picked it up and put it back, but I noticed it was from the *Masekhet Soferim*, a non-biblical Talmudic section dealing mainly with the rules relating to the preparation of the holy books, as well as with the regulations for the reading of the Law. So, I checked it over carefully until midnight. Then I tried, but I could not sleep. I knew there was a question to be answered the next night, Thursday, and I was worried about being embarrassed. I thought maybe I did not know the answer. I finally fell asleep and had a dream. The dream told me that Tzop was a *tzaddik nistar*, a hidden, righteous person. Tzop said in the dream that there never was an answer to the question, but even if there was an answer, it was only for Tzop to know. Always remember to respect a great man. I awoke after that.'

"The next day, Tuesday, after *shul*, when Tzop and Landau met, Landau announced the answer: 'Always remember to respect a great man.' Tzop closed his eyes for a few seconds, and then opened them. He said: 'I wanted to test you, and you passed. From now on *shalom*, peace.'"

I was given the thousand pengers from the five times great grandson of Yechezkel ben Yehuda Landau for the original story, and I was happy.

The Life of Moshele Der Zinger

***

My *rebbe*, Chaim Elazar Spira, died on May 13, 1937. I was crushed. But I was honored to officiate at his funeral. I was only in my mid-teens, but I remember it clearly. He had a daughter, Freema, who was married to the next Munkatcher Rebbe Baruch Yehoshua Yerachmiel Rabinowicz. Freema and Baruch had only one son, and the doctor had told her she could not have any more children. This upset her more than anything, but it was at the funeral that she let out all her anguish. Once the dirt was placed on the grave and most people had left the cemetery, she threw herself on top of the mound. She began to cry and cry, loudly. "I won't leave until you promise me more children!" she screamed at her deceased father. "I refuse to move!" Everyone tried to console her, but it was impossible. All the visiting *rebbes* – from Spinka, Koson, etc. – tried to calm her down and reassure her. She would not budge. Finally, her husband, who had become the Munkatcher Rebbe instantly upon her father's death, came to his distraught wife's side and gently spoke to her. "I promise," he said, "that we will have more children." They subsequently had two more boys and a girl.

At his *shiva*, a quirk of the Munkatcher Rebbe was explained to me and his other followers. He always wore his collar open, and never put on a scarf. When the weather was thirty degrees below zero for three months straight, he still never wore a scarf or pulled closed his collar. His *gabbai*, who happened to be at the *shiva* at the same time as me and some other of his pupils, told the story of why he did this. As is a *shiva* custom, some people, including me, who were very close to the *rebbe* had on a garment with a deliberate tear. When everyone was quiet, the *gabbai* began to talk about our beloved *rebbe*. "When Chaim was a boy, he went on a walking trek with his father, Reb Zvi Hersh Spira, to visit the Sanzer Rebbe Shulem Lazer Halberstam. The distance was far so they stopped for two different nights at pre-arranged homes. When they finally arrived in Sanz, the air was freezing. The Sanzer Rebbe welcomed them with hot tea, which Reb Hersh drank right away and warmed up. Chaim found the tea way too hot to drink, so he sat there, staring at it. Reb Halberstam asked why he was not drinking his tea, and the boy answered, "Because it is too hot," to which Reb Halberstam replied, "Drink this tea and you will never have a cold." In order to demonstrate that the *rebbe*'s blessing worked, he never wore a scarf. Of course, he eventually learned that weather does not cause colds, germs do, but nevertheless he never wore a scarf and he never caught a cold.

I remember wandering around Munkacs about two weeks after the funeral and feeling so depressed. I happened to walk past the office of a local rabbi, and I heard voices inside. When I entered, I saw a group of *bokherim* listening to stories about Reb Spira. This was the story I heard the rabbi say, and to my surprise, I was in it.

"Near Munkacs is a small town where the *shul* president and the *rav* have been in a long-time fight. The president is scholarly about Jewish law, so one day he told his wife to no longer take halakhic questions to the *rav*, but rather to let him, her husband, answer them. It so happened that the following Erev Shabbat, Friday, the day before Shabbat, the wife was forced to ask the *rav* a question about an imperfection in the chicken she had started cooking. Her husband was working, and could not be reached in time. 'The chicken is kosher,' the *rav* said, with his usual certainty. On the way home, she ran into her husband who was curious about where she had been. She explained, after which he studied the chicken. '*Treif!*' he asserted. 'Not kosher.' The chicken was replaced for Shabbat dinner, and the old one put in the icebox. On Sunday, the president grabbed the chicken and rode in his horse-drawn coach to pick up the *rav*. 'Get in,' he said. 'We are taking the chicken to Munkacs.'

"Once in Munkacs," the rabbi continued, "they stopped at the *rebbe*'s place, just when I happened to be up on a ladder shelving some of his books. I watched the events unfold." The storytelling rabbi continued: "The president unwrapped the chicken and explained to the Munkatcher Rebbe what had taken place, how the *rav* had mislabeled the chicken kosher. The Munkatcher Rebbe looked closely at the fowl. Then he pulled a small piece off the partially-cooked chicken, made a *brakha*, and ate it. This was a punch in the stomach to the president, who walked out of the room shaking his head, humiliated. One of the *rebbe*'s nearby students was shocked also, but only because the *rebbe* had eaten chicken that had been the subject of a *sheila*, a question, which makes the particular food no longer *glatt* kosher, a higher standard of kosher that many Hasidim follow. He asked the *rebbe* why he had done this. The *rebbe* pounded his fist on the desk, hard, and shouted in Yiddish: 'And human flesh is permitted for one to eat?!'" To make this crystal clear, in Yiddish, to eat someone's flesh is a saying that means to insult him or her, or to rub in an insult.

At the time of the incident I was confused, but now, hearing the story retold, I understood everything. The president had been rude and arrogant, prepared to dishonor his *rav* in front of the Munkatcher Rebbe and others. That was wrong. The *rebbe* preferred to eat sub-standard – though still kosher – chicken over allowing the "meat" of the *rav* to be eaten, or the feelings and pride of the *rav* to be crushed.

***

When I was sixteen, a remarkable thing happened overnight. As a child prodigy, I was warned by more than one person, including music experts, that when I went through puberty my voice would change, and then maybe I would no longer have a professional singing voice. I worried a little, but there was nothing I could do. What in fact happened was that I went from an alto to a tenor overnight.

Chapter Two: Childhood

One day I was an alto, as I had been for about seven years; the next I was a tenor, but no less talented than I had been the day before.

Before Rosh HaShana in 1941, Jewish leaders in Sighet were trying to find a *baal tefilla* for the services on *yamim noraim*, the High Holy Days. They picked me, and from that year on until retirement, I never missed *davening* at the *amud*, the lectern, on *yamim noraim*, even during the remaining years of the Holocaust. I was only eighteen. It was a huge deal to land this leadership job in Sighet, even if it was only for the High Holy Days. But before long, I was *shtot ḥazan*, the city cantor. To be only eighteen and a *shtot ḥazan* was unheard of. Never in the history of *ḥazanim* had this ever happened. I was very proud of myself. As city cantor, I had to attend every Jewish event that took place – every bar mitzva, every wedding, every funeral, every *brit mila* (ceremonial circumcision) – no matter what synagogue was involved, and there were more than five *shuls* in Sighet. As exciting as this job was, because of the war, it only lasted a matter of months.

There are two main reasons Sighet – a city that was at different times part of Hungary and Yugoslavia, and that is currently part of Romania – is famous to this day. One, it is the home town of the late Elie Wiesel, the world-renowned Holocaust survivor who wrote the brief memoir *Night*, which relates his World War II experiences. The winner of the 1986 Nobel Peace Prize, Prof. Wiesel was the author of many books, as well as an acclaimed international speaker and activist. While I was working in Sighet, I got to know him, years before anyone outside his town had ever heard of him. In fact, he sang in my choir, and we became close friends. Up to the day of his death, whenever he saw me he called me his *rebbe*. We visited each other when we were in each other's cities. When not, he phoned me, I phoned him.

The second reason is that it is the original town of Satmar Hasidim, which started sometime in the middle of the nineteenth century. Indeed, Sighet was the quintessential hasidic Jewish community before World War II. It was the biggest Jewish city in the world at that time, except for maybe Munkacs. Sighet had five large synagogues, including the Central Synagogue, which was built in 1836. There were a dozen *batei midrash*, and they were connected with various hasidic courts in other cities. Tragically, very few of Sighet's Jews survived the Holocaust; most of them were murdered in Auschwitz. Once they were gone, their non-Jewish neighbors took over their property, and casually continued on with their lives. If this sounds surreal, a local newspaper headline on July 16, 1944, captured the mood. It read simply, "Without Jews."

Satmar Jews are a breed apart, and I mean that in the nicest of ways. This sect of Hasidim was founded by Rabbi Hillel Lichtenstein and his son-in-law Rabbi Akiva Yosef Schlesinger, right before there was a major schism among Hungarian Jews around 1860. When he saw the decline in religious observance in the community, Rabbi Lichtenstein took to sermonizing against modernity, completely. Rabbi Schlesinger bestowed on Yiddish as well as on traditional Jewish clothing a new and higher status in Judaism, insisting these old cultural elements were an effective way to separate the community from the outside world. Both men did everything they could to prevent secular society from "infecting" hasidic life and culture, including by virtually banning non-Jewish education. Rav Lichtenstein's successors have been no less harsh; the leader between the two world wars even demanding total political passivity.

"Both the demeanor and principles of Satmar today reflect Yoel Teitelbaum's adherence to the Hungarian Ultra-Orthodox school of thought," says the ubiquitous Wikipedia, helping me out with brevity yet again. "Teitelbaum began referring to himself as the 'Rebbe of Satmar' in 1905, shortly after leaving Sighet and settling in Satu Mare, Yiddish for Satmar." His father, Rabbi Tov Lipa Teitelbaum, had been the *rebbe* of the Sighet dynasty until 1904, when he died. Leadership was passed to Yoel's older brother,

Chaim Tzvi. But a tiny number of Sighet Hasidim regarded Yoel as the proper heir.

Today, next to Lubavitch, Satmar comprises the largest number of Jews of any hasidic sect, with more than 120,000 in New York State alone. They mix with their host countries as little as is humanly possible, usually only in order to make a *parnasa*, a living. Satmar Jews are also legendary for their fierce opposition to Zionism and the State of Israel, despite there being Satmar communities within the borders of Israel.

It was while I was working in Sighet that I finally accepted the truth about what was happening to my people, the Jewish people. Because of this knowledge I had a relatively brief and private war with God. I rebelled against my religion because, though I knew intellectually that understanding all the ways of God is beyond human ability, I nevertheless was angry at Him for allowing so much suffering to happen, especially to little children. I continued to sing and work as a *ḥazan*, but for a time I stopped putting on tefillin. I all but stopped praying three times a day. My faith was being severely tested.

I got a real taste of Nazi brutality in Sighet. One Friday, the Hungarian police had closed the street because they were rounding up as many Jewish men as they could find and taking them to the police station. Naively, when they approached me, I told them I was the Chief Cantor of Sighet, and needed to get to the synagogue in order to get ready to lead the Shabbat services. The policeman made fun of me: "Oh, you're a very important Jew, eh? We'll show you how important you are." The police in Hungary were known for their size and strength. They were illiterate, but big and strong. One policeman hit me and I was knocked out. After I fell, I am pretty sure a few of the policemen proceeded to kick and punch me. I have no idea how I got home, but I do remember waking up on my bed where a few friends were sitting by my side and applying cold cloths to my head. I was burning

The Life of Moshele Der Zinger

up with fever. When I was finally well enough to stand and look in the mirror, I was shocked at how swollen my eyes were; they looked like mere slits.

Something incredible happened to me while I was working in Sighet, an event that ended up inducing me to completely return to *yiddishkeit,* or Jewish observance. Succeeding my beloved *rebbe* Chaim Elazar Spira, of blessed memory, as Munkatcher Rebbe, was his son-in-law Rabbi Baruch Yehoshua Yerachmiel Rabinovich. I am very proud that I helped to save Rabbi Rabinovich's life and, in a spiritual way, he helped to save mine. While I was the Chief Cantor in Sighet, the president of the synagogue came to me one weekday and told me, "Moshe, everyone wants to hear the eighteen-year-old Chief *Ḥazan* of Sighet sing. You must travel. You must go to Satmar and *daven* there for this Shabbat. A month from tomorrow, you must go to Khust," which at that time was part of Hungary, and is now in Ukraine. The *shul* president continued: "The following week you have to go to Yurvish. For a minimum once a month, you must travel to different cities and towns."

This idea did not sound too good to me. I didn't really feel in the mood to travel so much these days, which were filled with my struggles with God and my thoughts of Jews dying. But because I was being paid extra money, I could not refuse. The week I arrived in Khust, while I was sitting with the chief rabbi and eating Shabbat lunch, Shakur Rosenfeld, the local book binder, came in. Tears were running down his cheeks. He did not say a word, but the rabbi knew exactly the cause of his despair. He got Rosenfeld a chair and he poured him some Slivovitz, apricot brandy. Rosenfeld finally began to talk. He said, "Rabbi, I have very bad news. Rebbe Baruch Rabinovich and his son are on the train going to the death camp in Kamenetz-Podolsk. Anyone who goes to this camp does not come back alive. You must do something to save them." He was referring to the apparently first "bad load" that the Hungarians agreed to deport as required by their German ally at

Chapter Two: Childhood

that time. The agreement was that every Jew who was not from Hungary, was not born in Hungary, would be forced to leave the country. They were to be taken away, and, according to the Nazis, it did not matter where the alien Jews were dumped, but in the end, most were sent to death camps.

When Rosenfeld stopped crying, the rabbi handed him one thousand dollars. He told Rosenfeld to sew five hundred dollars in each side of a large book's cover. "But Rabbi, it is *Shabbat*!" cried Rosenfeld, confused that he would be told by the rabbi to break the Sabbath. The rabbi responded: "This is a situation of *pikuah nefesh* (the principle in Jewish law that saving life overrides all other laws, even the most restrictive laws of Shabbat)." Rosenfeld immediately understood, and he ran away to do the work. In quick order he came back with the book. "Who will take this book to Rabbi Rabinovich?" the rabbi asked. No one raised their hand or made a peep. Why? Because to get to the train station one had to run through a kind of no-man's land that was very dangerous; in that section of the city, murders and robberies occurred regularly. I thought quickly to myself that I was alone, I had no children, and I could afford to do it. Before anyone could stop me, I grabbed the book and ran to the door. "No!" yelled the rabbi. "We are responsible for you!" I continued running anyway, and made it through the dangerous section safely and without a problem.

At the station I saw the train, which seemed extremely long. I started walking beside each car yelling, "Rabbi Rabinovich! Rabbi Rabinovich!" No-one answered. But I heard a lot of people screaming for water. I felt so terrible because I could not help them. Finally, I got to the very last car, the only one where the doors were open, and where I found Rabbi Rabinovich. He was with his six-year-old son. I handed him the book.

"*Rebbe*, I must go," I said, as I stood by the door. "But I have one question, *rebbe*. Why does the *Ribono Shel Olam* need so much *kiddush Hashem* – so much sanctification of His name by having so many of our people die?" He answered by saying, first of all, that he and I and his son would survive the war. Then he said, "Moshele, there is no *kiddush Hashem* here. *Kiddush Hashem* is only when you have a *brera*, a choice. In Spain during the Inquisition, Jews had a choice: kiss the cross or burn. Many Jews chose to be burned. They would not kneel for the cross. That is a *kiddush Hashem*. You know, Moshele, when there will be *kiddush Hashem* again? When the war is over, when you remain alive and you keep Shabbat, you eat kosher, and you behave the way a Jew is supposed to behave. That will be a *kiddush Hashem*." I was mesmerized. After this, I came back to *yiddishkeit*, and I have never left it again, though – as I explained above – it took some time, in fact until after the war, before I returned to the more stringent hasidic practice.

***

From Sighet, I was stolen away to Budapest. I won't say kidnapped, but it was pretty darn close. A strange man came up to me during the week at synagogue and said he wanted to speak with me. He asked me to accompany him to the train station, where he had to wait thirty minutes before his train left. When we got there, he said, "Why should we wait outside? Come onto the train, sit down and we'll talk." I was only a young lad of eighteen, well-traveled, but still naive. When we sat, he announced, "I have everything you need in this train car. All you have to do is take the train with me to Budapest, and you can sing and work there." Before I could decide, the train started. I could not jump off, so I went to Budapest, where I became the chief cantor of Hungary's capital and biggest city. In truth, I did not get the job immediately. I had to pass a singing trial on Yom Kippur Katan, the so-called Minor Day of Atonement. It is observed on the day before each new Jewish calendar month, known as Rosh Ḥodesh. There is some fasting, but it is not as difficult as the fasting done on the real Yom Kippur.

Chapter Two: Childhood

The *nusakh* is very difficult on Yom Kippur Katan, but I passed the trial without a problem.

Compared to Sighet, Budapest was already modern. Some Orthodox Jews didn't even have beards. One uplifting thing about Budapest was that every day, most of the Jews *davened* in *shul*. During the weekdays, the synagogues were full, just like on Shabbat. I had never seen that before. And when I was *davening*, it was considered special, so people came just to listen to me.

The way I became Budapest's chief cantor has always bothered me. Sometime in 1942, the Nazis took away Michael Shpiegel, the chief cantor of the city, to a labor camp. He happened to work at a different *shul* than I. I was working at the city's big synagogue, known as the Shomrei Shabbat Synagogue. Shpiegel's absence caused a local religious crisis. There were only a few weeks to go before the *yamim noraim*. His *shul* could not find a ḥazan. An emergency meeting was called, during which the city's chief rabbi said, "Let's talk about this young man from Shomrei Shabbos," referring to me. Since I was actually employed by the same *kehilla* (congregation) as Shpiegel had been – in fact about twenty rabbis and ḥazanim from all the *shuls* were paid by the same *kehilla* – it was not such a difficult shift. From then on, I became the chief ḥazan.

Not long after I attained that lofty role, I attended a meeting chaired by Adolf Eichmann. Yes, *that* Adolf Eichmann, one of Hitler's main coordinators of the Holocaust. Hungary was still an Axis power at the time, and he was in Budapest to enforce some anti-Jewish laws. I was at the meeting, as were all important rabbis and ḥazanim in the city. We were members of the Jewish committee, kind of a *Judenrat*, or Jewish council, a popular mechanism imposed by the Nazis to control Jews in ghettos. As members of this committee, we imparted information to the Jews in Budapest on what they could and could not do. I sat totally silent and rather dumbfounded during the meeting, which discussed restrictions on where Jews could walk and how their yellow stars had to be worn on their outer garments.

The last Purim holiday before my father was taken away to the Uzhhorod ghetto, I came home from Budapest, taking a break from my job as chief cantor. I was nineteen years old, and I couldn't wait to see Tatty. Because it was Purim, my father performed the mitzva of drinking enough alcohol in order to not recognize the difference – in the reading aloud of the *Megillat Esther,* the Book of Esther – between the name of the evil Haman and the name of the hero Mordekhai. I always enjoyed Purim, because my father made sure to drink according to this halakha (Jewish law), which meant he loosened up and spoke more than usual. In a tipsy state of mind, he liked to talk about the past, which I usually enjoyed hearing about. On our last Purim together, he seemed particularly nostalgic. He spoke a lot, not all of it news to me. "You know Moshele," he intoned, repeating a story I had heard many times. "I married your mother in a place called Telek, not far from Uzhhorod. At first, I didn't have a profession, so I opened a small grocery store, the only one in the village. But we would visit Uzhhorod every Shabbat, so that I could *daven* in a minyan."

He then told me a story I had never heard him relate: "One night when I was in bed sleeping beside your mother, I was woken up by a noise. I was startled to see three men, three gentiles, standing at the foot of the bed. One had a knife, one had a stick, and the third man had something else which I could not make out. You know, I was a strong man. I was formerly an officer in the Austro-Hungarian army. But here I was helpless in bed, and scared senseless for my small family. There were three of them with weapons. You were but two or three years old Moshele, but you got out of your bed in the corner of the room, came over to our bed, and you put your little hand over my eyes. Somehow these three men must have been spooked when they saw you. I guess they did not realize you were there. They walked out quickly. I think you saved my life."

Chapter Two: Childhood

That same night of Purim he said, "You know Moshele, *miyom omdi al daati tikkun ḥatzot*." He was saying, from the day I had understanding I never missed the ritual of midnight mourning. Midnight mourning is a prayer said every night after midnight to express sadness and longing for the destroyed Holy Temples. My father then held a lit candle in his hand and we both wept. I was an adult, and I was crying with my father. After this visit, I never saw him again.

My job as chief ḥazan in Budapest did not last long. The Nazis finally came for me too, in 1943, and they sent me to the Bor labor camp. I davened *yamim noraim* in Bor that year, and in Bergen-Belsen the next.

The Life of Moshele Der Zinger

Moshe with his father

Chapter Two: Childhood

Moshe at age thirteen as a cantor

The Life of Moshele Der Zinger

Moshe in the middle as a soloist

Chapter Three

Bergen-Belsen

I was twenty years old in 1943, when I was forced into the first of two concentration camps. Because I was young and strong, I survived. That, and by the grace of *HaKadosh Barukh Hu*, the Almighty God, and the fierce British army. Since surviving the Holocaust, I have rarely gone one week without remembering some horrible part of those bloody, deadly years. It has been a huge challenge to live a normal life sometimes, but as the decades have melted away since the day of liberation, the pain has subsided and the memories have become more distant. I am going to recall as much of the war as possible in this chapter.

November 9, 1938, was the *Kristallnacht* pogrom, the Night of Broken Glass. It was a large-scale synchronized attack on Jews and Jewish businesses throughout the German Reich. At the time, I was living in a gentile home in Vienna, Austria. The family members were very kind to me, and they told me I always would have a bed in their home. Their place was not big. They had a kitchen, one bedroom, a sitting room, and a dining room. Sometimes they'd set up a bed in the dining room and take in a student, but the student was away all day so he or she didn't disturb the family.

The family had an eighteen-year-old daughter, Inga, who slept with her parents in their bedroom. I slept in a special corner in the sitting room, which had a window. From that window, I could see the main Vienna synagogue. One night at around 10:30 p.m., not long after *Kristallnacht*, I heard screaming and shootings. I looked out the window and saw the *shul* burning. I saw Nazis taking away Torahs and *sefarim*, religious books, and burning them outside in a big fire. My hosts came and stood beside me and were looking out also. We saw Inga standing outside near a young Nazi, talking. All of a sudden, he shot her. I could hardly breathe. Her parents went crazy when they saw her fall. They called the police. An ambulance also came and took her away.

Her frantic parents asked me to stay behind to guard the apartment while they went to the hospital. They wanted to make sure no one would come in and steal anything from them. They returned home quite quickly, after their daughter was declared dead. Her body was placed in the morgue, and her funeral was the next day. Of course, I went, as did many of her family's friends. The police came to the home three or four days later to tell Inga's parents that they had the killer in custody. They asked the three of us to write down what we had seen. Within a month, we all testified in court. What we learned there was that the killer had believed Inga was a Jew. "If I'd known she wasn't Jewish, I would not have shot her," the murderer told the court. "She had asked me to stop the burning of books." The judge then said the killer was free to go because "He didn't know she wasn't Jewish."

For me this was a game changer. After leaving court, I told Inga's parents, "God bless you. I am going straight to the train and not even returning to your home to pick up my things." I took the last train leaving for Prague that day.

Chapter Three: Bergen-Belsen

***

For most of eighteen months before I was taken away in 1943, the Jews of Uzhhorod had been hearing that Jews were being slaughtered indiscriminately in far-off places. As I mentioned, we absolutely did not believe this. Every time we heard this from a stranger in town, we totally dismissed it. We did not think such atrocities could ever be committed, even by Nazis. We knew they were brutal. We knew they meant nasty business. But the Hasidim and other Jews I spent time with in my hometown and surrounding villages simply could not believe the "rumors." Was this willful blindness, or were our hearts and minds too frightened to accept the truth? I will probably never know. But I clearly remember the disbelief. I recall exactly how it felt to hear about the mass killings and to completely disregard the information as hogwash. That is why we never considered running away. And even if we had thought about fleeing, where would we have gone?

Sometimes, my father invited to our home Jewish refugees from Poland whom he met at *shul*. He would ask them to come and eat breakfast or another meal, but he was almost alone in offering this charity. No-one really wanted these strangers in their homes, because they were usually dirty. Yes, there was the *mikve* that had showers, and many local Jewish men went in the mornings and before Shabbat, but it cost money. The foreigners could sometimes afford it, but not often. My family tried to help the refugees by giving them meals and money. We tried to help them by introducing them to other people who would donate money. But we didn't believe their crazy stories about mass murder.

We, of course, knew that from 1939 Poland was occupied by Germany and the Soviet Union. It was divided, but were we in serious trouble? In the beginning, we did not think so, but we were not absolutely sure what was going on. In 1940, while I was

The Life of Moshele Der Zinger

still attending the Munkacs yeshiva, a couple of young Hasidim decided to go to Belz in Poland to see the Beltzer Rebbe, and to find out how Poland was faring. I decided to go with them. We took one train, and then we had to change to the Polish train system, which was already controlled by the Germans. We had to wait two hours for the second train to take us to Belz. During the wait, we walked into the adjacent little Polish town to see if there was anything interesting. A few Polish gentiles walked up and surrounded us. I could see they were angry, ready to hit us. Poles were known for their antisemitism. Afraid, we did not know what to do. There were three of us, two sixteen-year-olds and a fourteen-year-old, who happened to be the strongest. His last name was Halperin.

As we stood there wondering what to do, all of a sudden one of the *goyim* (non-Jews) prepared to hit Halperin. But Halperin was quicker and he hit the stranger first, and very hard. Another of the *goyim* seemed to get ready to help his friend by fighting, too, but the third said in Polish, "No! No! Do not do anything! You must respect such a strong punch." We were relieved. In the meantime, two police officers arrived on bicycles. They asked what was going on. We took out our passports and showed them. "Hmm," one policeman said to the other. "We cannot touch them because they are not Polish Jews." The police took us to the station and sat with us until the train to Belz arrived. When we came home from Belz three days later, our friends in Munkacs teased us and called us the three "Behaim," after a highly successful and tough German explorer who lived in the fifteenth century.

***

Despite having every apparent reason to abandon God during my time in the Nazi concentration camps, I never did. Yes, I had had that serious fight with God while I worked in Budapest. But once I spoke to Rabbi Baruch Rabinovich, to whom I had given the book with the thousand dollars sewn inside while he waited on the train with his son to be deported, I was committed again to my faith. It never again occurred to me to stop accepting what I'd been taught, what my parents had been taught, what their parents and ancestors had been taught. I never again questioned God's role in the Holocaust. I completely accepted that as humans we are totally unable to understand His methods.

Throughout my suffering, I frequently recalled the story of Job. I remembered that Job had beseeched God to tell him why he had lost everything in his life, including his family, his health, and his wealth; to tell him why God had punished him so harshly even though he, Job, had always been a righteous and kind man. God was adamant, and even a little sarcastic: "Where were you when I created the universe?" The implications of this short question are powerful. First, God acknowledges that Job's hardships were caused by Him, thereby confirming that pain and suffering are not by necessity a punishment for any visible wrongdoing. God also confirms that punishment is nevertheless part of His master plan. Finally, and perhaps most tellingly, God asserts that His master plan – including the role of pain and suffering in that plan – is beyond the understanding of mere mortals who are themselves integral to that plan.

Though many, many Jews went to their deaths still loving and believing in God, not every Jew did. Many who survived the Holocaust lost their love of God. Once, not too many years ago, I met a man on a plane donning tefillin, which are attached to parts of the body of observant Jews during weekday morning prayers. I noticed another man nearby watching the first man. "Before the war, I used to wear my tefillin every day, too," the second man said to me, "until Hitler came and killed my wife and my little Pinchas." I knew what he meant.

***

After the Munich Agreement was signed in 1938, the beautiful town of Uzhhorod, my birthplace and hometown, was taken over by Hungary. Immediately, laws against Jews were passed and enforced. Not that Hungary was alien to Jews. Not at all. Indeed, Jews have been in that region since before 900 CE, and they have suffered dearly for living there, even being blamed and expelled for the Black Death c. 1350. The lives of Jews did not get much better through the Middle Ages. Not until Queen Maria Theresa's oldest son Joseph II took the reins of power in the 1700s were the oppressive decrees against the Jews finally rescinded. Joseph II, who died in 1790, set the stage for the eventual emancipation of the Jews, which was approved by the national assembly some sixty years later.

By World War I, the Jews of Hungary were quite favorably integrated into Hungarian society. Around that time, the community had swelled to about 5 percent of the country's total population, and almost 25 percent of the capital Budapest's population. With their freedom, Jews tended to lead in the areas of science, the arts, and business. But they were not appreciated for their success, and pervasive bitterness against these achievements set in among non-Jews. With the fall of the Austro-Hungarian Empire at the end of World War I, Hungary's elite – determined to regain swaths of lost land, Hapsburg Lands – held their collective noses and made alliances with the fascist states of Germany and Italy. Though regent and head of state Nicolas Horthy hoped to keep Hungary out of any European battles – he agreed to get militarily involved only if Germany proper was attacked – he honestly thought that Germany and Italy would be the likeliest to help with Hungary's land reclamation desires. Thus, beginning in 1938, Horthy, who had been an admiral in World War I, presided over anti-Jewish policies in Hungary that became increasingly repressive, and they happened to look a lot like Germany's Nuremberg Laws.

Chapter Three: Bergen-Belsen

The Nuremburg Laws were instituted first in 1935 during the Nazi Party's annual rally in Nuremberg. They incorporated many of the racial theories of Nazi ideology. Jews were denied Reich citizenship, and were forbidden from marrying or even being intimate with anyone who had "German or related blood." Disenfranchised, Jews were soon denied almost all political rights. The Nuremberg Laws defined "Jew" specifically as anyone who had three or four Jewish grandparents, even if that individual had never identified him or herself as a Jew. Even Jews who had converted to Christianity were snared and terrorized by these laws.

The Berlin Olympic Games of 1936 – which banned Jewish athletes – prompted the Nazis to temporarily lift some of the more odious rules and to remove the most obvious racist images, such as public signs that said "No Jews Welcome." This was done to improve the regime's international image while the world was focused on the Games. But in 1937 and 1938, the regime set out to virtually bankrupt Jews by several measures. For one, they had to register all their property. Then Jewish businesses were "Aryanized," which meant Jewish employees were fired and Jewish businesses had to be sold to non-Jewish Germans at basement prices assessed by the Nazis. Jewish doctors could no longer treat non-Jews, and Jewish lawyers were forbidden from plying their trade. And on and on. Jews had to carry special identity cards with a "J" stamped on them, and if their names were not Jewish sounding enough, they were given new middle names to rectify the "problem."

***

Hungary's desire to stay out of the violence was not met. In 1939, having joined the Anti-Comintern Pact, the international anti-communist treaty – which Germany, Japan, and Italy had also signed – meant that Hungary was committed to fight in 1941, after Hungary and Germany declared war on the Soviet Union. Like a kitten trying to roar like a lion, Hungary also declared war that year on both Great Britain and the United States. But by early 1943, Hungary's entire war machine was in fact neutralized by the Soviets in the Battle of Voronezh. Seeing the writing on the wall, Hungary made quiet proposals to the Allies, offering to switch sides in exchange for defense assistance against Germany and the Soviets. When he learned about this offer in October 1944, Hitler moved to occupy Hungary. The puppet regime Hitler installed followed his orders until December 1944, at which time it was overthrown by the Soviets. On the last day of the year, the communist government of Hungary declared war on Germany.

It has always been a gut-wrenching fact of history for the international Jewish community that the Jews of Hungary – who were for the most part not forced into ghettos – were deported to Nazi death camps so late in the war. They were sent to Auschwitz starting in May 1944 and continuing even as Soviet troops were approaching. It has been estimated that a Jew who resided in the Hungarian countryside in March 1944 had a less than ten percent chance of being alive a year later. In Budapest, a Jew's chance of survival during the same time period was about 50 percent. Overall, some six hundred thousand Hungarian Jews lost their lives in the Holocaust.

For three weeks encompassing Pesaḥ of April 1944, all the Jews of Uzhhorod – at this point part of Hungary – and the surrounding areas, a total of about twenty-five thousand people, were squeezed into a ghetto: a brick factory and lumber yard on the outside of the city. During this very difficult time, my father somehow managed to write one letter to me. In it he told me that a very clever man, a gentile, outside the walls of the brick factory, brought potatoes to a hole in the ghetto wall, and shoved them through to my father. This man saved many lives as the Jews had very little food. At the end of three weeks, all the Uzhhorod Jews were deported to Auschwitz. Among them were my ten family

Chapter Three: Bergen-Belsen

members, of which only the three eldest children survived. I also survived, but at a different camp.

Just a few words about Auschwitz, a term that now rightly conjures up the notion of pure evil. Formally known as Auschwitz-Birkenau, it actually stood for a network of Nazi death, concentration, and labor camps. Established in Poland, they represented the biggest of all similar facilities across Europe. Auschwitz could hold some 150,000 inmates at a time. Between 2.1 and 4 million people were killed there – mostly in gas chambers, but also from forced labor, shootings, starvation, and medical experiments – the vast majority of them Jews. It is now a macabre museum. To date, more than thirty million people have visited the camp. Auschwitz was one of a staggering number of camps, some twenty thousand, established by the Nazis between 1933 and 1945.

***

I was already living and working in Budapest when the Nazis got nasty there, but this didn't affect me too much at first. They wronged other Jews more in that they were forced to wear yellow stars on their clothes, and they couldn't walk on the sidewalk nor on the side of the road. I was exempted from these rules, because I was the city's chief cantor. The chief rabbi, in fact all the rabbis and all the other cantors, were also treated a little better than the general Jewish population. But life was terrible anyway. I did not feel more important because I had better treatment in these small ways. I ached for my fellow Jews. It was also while I was in Budapest that I received a letter from my father, who was in the ghetto in Uzhhorod. I was shocked to get the letter, and very happy to hear from him, though I was distraught to learn of the terrible things going on in my hometown. I treasured this letter, but I lost it when I was in Bergen-Belsen. I believe it was burned along with my two treasured photos.

After *davening* in the morning, often my friends and I from the Budapest *shul* would go eat at a restaurant called Taichernok, which only served breakfast and could seat about six hundred people. Though it was not certified kosher, there was some supervision over the milk products, so the rabbis determined that we could eat there. One morning, I heard some men talking at the table beside ours. One man said, "I do not remember the name of the king." I answered for him, "Aḥashverosh," an ancient king of Persia. "Ah, yes, thank you," the man said. Ten minutes later when the men at the other table got up to leave, I noticed they were all priests. After our table had *benched*, I went outside and met the young priest to whom I had spoken. His last name was Attila, and he said, "I liked how you remembered the king's name. I'd like to meet with you for an hour a week to learn the Bible." We ended up fantastic friends and we met frequently, one hour every weekday. We didn't meet on Saturdays and Sundays, our respective Sabbaths. The study sessions, usually about the Talmud, went like this: Attila would ask questions and I'd either answer them or bring the answers the next day, after I'd done research or asked a rabbi. Attila preached to his congregation to be good to Jews, saying things like, "They gave us light," and "Jesus was a Jew."

The time came when I was forced on a cattle car train with other Jews to go to a labor camp. While I was standing, waiting on the train with the others, I heard, "Max Kraus. Max Kraus." Max was my legal name at birth since Moshe was rejected by the authorities, but I almost never used it. But I recognized "Kraus," of course, so I yelled back. Attila banged on the closed train door and said, "Get down. You do not have to go." A Hungarian guard opened the door and screamed at me, "What are you doing here, Max? Go with your priest." I told Attila no, I had to go with my friends, my Jewish friends and community, to wherever we were being sent to work. After liberation I tried to locate Attila, but he had been murdered. I learned this when I stopped at his Budapest church. An old lady there told me he had been killed by the Nazis because he used to preach that people should try and help save the Jews. I wept for my friend.

The living nightmare got worse for me when I was deported from Budapest to Bor, a forced labor camp in chopped-up Yugoslavia. When taken off the train, about the first thing I noticed was that the inmates' heads were shaved completely. I was quickly introduced to the order of things. As the enemy leaders, the Germans were in charge of the Hungarian Nazis, or *Neroshes* as they were known, who did pretty much all the dirty work. For instance, as I soon learned, the *Neroshes* would go with us into the mining tunnels to supervise and watch us work. They would also routinely kick us and beat us with bottles. The *Neroshes* were not entirely unlike the *Sonderkommandos,* who constituted camp work units comprised almost completely of Jews. These Jews, of course, were prisoners who were coerced – on threat of death – to help with the dumping or burning of the victims of gas chambers in Auschwitz and other death camps.

Among all the naked heads, only one man walked around wearing a *kippa*. His name was Rabbi Meir Leifer, a grandson of the Nadvorna Rebbe. The Nadvorna hasidic group had been located, no surprise, in the town of Nadvorna, which was in the East Galicia province in the Austro-Hungarian Empire. After World War I, the town was in Poland. I associated with Rabbi Meir because we were both from Hasidim. We had our religious backgrounds in common, but we were not able to even partially embrace them, as most religious observance was not allowed in the camp. We conducted services from time to time, but we had no tefillin and no tallitot. Sometimes, we got up early and made a minyan. That was not difficult to do because, firstly, there were hundreds of Jewish men in every barrack, and secondly, most of them were awake and out of bed, as the sleeping conditions were too uncomfortable.

One day Rabbi Meir came up to me and said excitedly, "I have good news, I have permission to make a minyan for Rosh HaShana and I will give the *derasha*." It was wonderful, for a while. About two thousand inmates came to hear the services. They stood outside, while Rabbi Meir and I were under a tent. Almost everyone had to stand as there were only a few chairs. Of course, I *davened* as the *ḥazan*. I had no *maḥzor*, holiday prayer book, but I sang every word by heart. It was sweet, at least as sweet as anything could be in that hellhole. A couple of German Nazis stood nearby enjoying the music. Ten days later, on Yom Kippur, Rabbi Meir gave a pre-service *derasha*, but it was very hard to hear him. Then I began *Kol Nidrei*. In the middle of singing the prayer, I heard a loud noise. The *Neroshes*, in brown shirts, were advancing fast on our religious service, yelling and screaming orders. There must have been about a hundred of them. Everyone attending the service was terrified and ran away, while the German Nazis just stood there laughing and watching.

After most people had fled, I alone was left standing there. One Hungarian *Neroshe* stared at me and blurted out, "Huh, a proud Jew! I will show you. You will have a court case at 8 a.m. tomorrow." I was afraid, and believed I would be put to death after the court case, but so many Jews had already died at this labor camp that I was somehow sadly accepting that my time was probably up. The next morning at eight, all the Jews, about five hundred, from my barrack were standing at the *appel*, the roll call. It was still Yom Kippur. I was taken out of the *appel* and brought before a table with three Nazi officers serving as judges. Two other youngsters were standing there too, but I cannot remember what they had done to be brought before this kangaroo court. The ruling was: *Kikabesh*. What is *Kikabesh*? The prisoner's hands are tied together behind his back; the attached rope is thrown over a horizontal beam and pulled until the prisoner's feet are off the ground. The two others were to hang for eight hours and I was to hang for ten.

Chapter Three: Bergen-Belsen

The hanging began, outside so everyone could see. The pain was excruciating. The Nazis would let us down periodically when we fainted from the pain. They would give us water and hang us again. Things improved after about ninety minutes, when our wrists became numb. In the last five or six hours we were hanging nonstop because of the numbness, and we didn't faint. The Nazis wanted all the other prisoners to see us as they passed by as a lesson to them. People passing by were crying and giving me quiet encouragement.

When I was finally let down, it was late evening. Then I was locked in a room where I sat on the floor. It was dark, except for light from the moon coming through a small window. I assumed the other two were in different rooms. An hour later, a *Neroshe* entered and gave me porridge. I was very hungry so I tried to grab the bowl but I couldn't. Even though my arms could move, I could not control them. So, I stuck my face in the bowl, intending to eat like a dog. I tried to hold myself up with my hands but they didn't work. My face sank in the porridge and for a few seconds I was suffocating. Luckily my arms gained a little strength and I was able to push my face back up, and sideways. I ate awkwardly for awhile. When I stopped, my face was covered in porridge. At least I could lick a little of what was on my face. Then I fell asleep against the wall.

At one or two o'clock in the morning, I was awakened by someone having difficulty trying to open the door. When it finally opened, I saw that it was Rabbi Meir. He cried, and said, "Moshele, I am so sorry. Everything is my fault. I was supposed to *shlep* you, carry you, and hide you with me, but you had this trouble." My trouble was that I could not move my hands and could not eat properly. I forgave him, and I asked him to feed me, and he did. Then for the next two nights, he visited me in the room and fed me. On the third night, I told him not to return because, I said, "You will be killed if they catch you." After a total ten days in this solitary confinement, the door opened at about 10 am and the German commandant came in. "*Du leptz noch* – Are you still alive?" he asked in German, rhetorically, but in disbelief. That is when he told me the other two young men had died. I believe to this day that they died because they did not have Rabbi Meir Leifer to feed them.

The commandant kicked my back with his military shoes, which must have severely bruised my spine because it left me with excruciating pain for three days. During this time, kind people massaged me and encouraged me, which helped a little. They would even try to help by hitting me in other places on my body, to diminish the feeling of pain in my back. I was crying endlessly from the agony, keeping my bunkmates from sleeping at night.

Against all odds, we celebrated Pesaḥ in 1944. I remember having a *seder* with some others in my barrack. For some reason I forget, it was held very late in the night, when the Nazis patrolled most. When the guards came around, we made sure we were sitting instead of standing – the latter position being required for parts of the *seder*. How we got eggs for the *seder*, I do not remember. We also had greens. We had a potato. It was not complete, but it was still a Pesaḥ *seder*, and we were proud. Rabbi Aaron Davidi, from my understanding once the Chief Rabbi of Rotterdam, conducted the service. He started by apologizing for not having everything we needed and for not being able to celebrate Pesaḥ perfectly. "But," he continued, "thank God we are still alive and we are still here in this world. Please redeem us quickly that we shall be able to observe Your laws and do Your will with a complete heart." Unbelievably, we all sang and danced. Where did we get the strength to believe and the will to sing and dance? Only Jews could do this. Referring to our constant companion, hunger, Rabbi Davidi said we'd done a lifetime of *viddui*, which refers to a prayer of confessions and atonement said on Yom Kippur, when Jews fast for twenty-five hours.

Chapter Three: Bergen-Belsen

Eventually, after nine months in Bor, I was transported to a coal-mining camp in the city of Katowice in southwestern Poland. Sometimes my job in Katowice – where I stayed a matter of weeks – was to walk up a long hill and hold up a flag to signal when the coal trains were coming. While doing this work, I would often sing arias and Hungarian songs. Some guards took a liking to my singing and to me. One young lieutenant asked me many questions, like how and where did I learn to sing. I told him I was born with a talent. One day, I learned that a train was returning to Budapest, so I plucked up the courage to ask him to put me on that transport, and he agreed to do it. He told me, "Tomorrow your train will take you to Budapest, where you can work at something you like instead of here in the coal mines." I was relieved and I dared to be a little excited.

The next day I was put in the last cattle car of many. Each was packed with probably 150 people. The train ride was horrifying and tragic. I remember being really tired, thirsty, and hungry. We traveled two or three days with no food or water or heat. Many people died during the trip. They had to be stretched out on the floor, to the eternal discomfort of the live prisoners. We decided to stack the dead bodies on top of each other. It helped, but not enough. We could not even sit; we had to stand all the time. We used to trade places so we could take turns doing a little stretching against the wall. Most of the time I was somewhere in the middle, so I could not peek between the boards and see where the train was going. We all had to relieve ourselves in one place. It was unpleasant in the extreme.

We stopped somewhere after an unknown number of hours, probably about thirty. At that point they broke off the last car, my car, and connected it to another train, which returned to the coal mines. When I got out, I was informed that not one person on the formerly attached train cars remained alive. All the Jews had been told to get off at some point and to enter a stable, where they were shot to death by machine guns. More Holocaust horror. The train never even went to Budapest. It turned out to be a huge personal gift from God that I was not returned to that city as it suffered tremendously. In 1944, Budapest was partially destroyed by British and American air raids. For fifty days, during the Battle of Budapest, it was besieged by encircling Soviet forces. Some thirty-eight thousand non-combatants died during the clashes. The Germans destroyed all the city's bridges, though by some miracle, some treasured statues remained standing.

Within days I was sent to Bergen-Belsen, a Nazi concentration camp in northwest Germany between the villages of Bergen and Belsen. Built in 1940, it began as a prisoner-of-war camp for captured French and Belgians. One year later, after Germany invaded the USSR, it was renamed Stalag 311. At that time, it held some twenty thousand Russian prisoners. The POW section of Bergen-Belsen continued to be active until early 1945. The camp's name was changed to Bergen-Belsen in 1943, when it was converted into a concentration camp for Jews. A critical part of its mandate – though it was not implemented very often – was to exchange Jews with foreign passports for German nationals in prison in other countries. In this vein, about 1,500 Hungarian Jews from the camp were permitted to move to Switzerland, and about two hundred Jews were allowed to immigrate to British Mandatory Palestine.

Constructed to house only ten thousand prisoners, Bergen-Belsen was eventually divided into eight sub-camps, including a detention camp, two women's camps, a tent camp, and a Hungarian camp. By 1945, it was holding more than sixty thousand prisoners, in part because of evacuations from other camps, including Auschwitz. Tens of thousands of starving inmates arrived after the infamous and inhuman death marches. As the Germans retreated and the Allies advanced, the death marchers completely overwhelmed what few feeble facilities the camp had, such as food, water, and

Chapter Three: Bergen-Belsen

sanitation services. The result was epidemics such as typhus, which killed thousands, including Anne Frank and her sister Margot.

***

Though some historians say conditions at Bergen-Belsen were "good" compared to other concentration camps, it was still worse than a living nightmare. At one point, Bergen-Belsen was redesignated as a "recovery facility," a place to bring sick prisoners from other camps. Despite the nice label, there were no medical treatments to help them, and most died. And while it is true that Bergen-Belsen had no gas chamber, approximately fifty thousand people starved to death, were worked to death, or died of disease, Nazi beatings, or perverse medical experiments. Prisoners were also thrown in pit fires. It is apparently difficult to find written records of this most horrifying of practices, but I remember clearly that the Nazis selected precisely one thousand people per day to burn to death in the pit fires. Some of these daily allotments were sent to Auschwitz, where they were immediately gassed. Any time fewer than one thousand arrived by transport, the Nazis would take inmates already at the camp to make up the one thousand-body quota. When I arrived at Bergen-Belsen, I was one of 1,012 persons on the train. I was also one of the twelve who remained alive.

Understandably, pretty much everyone was out for themselves. The only time prisoners helped others was when trains first arrived and were unloaded. They would grab the younger-looking children and whisper to them to try and look older, and they would grab the older-looking Jews and tell them to try and look younger. Otherwise, they were told, you will be part of that, pointing to the smoke rising from the crematorium. But people generally did not help others. They were happy if they had a *shmata*, a rag, and a tiny piece of rotten bread. People would fight over a little crumb.

The food was often rotten. It was mixed with whatever was available, old stuff, stuff that fell on the ground. I think they used to put human feces in the bread and more than once I was sure I ate it.

Any work assigned at the concentration camp was random and painful. It was incredibly difficult to perform tasks when you were constantly hungry and weak.

Sweeping streets, peeling potatoes – it was all drudgery. But worst of all was when the sadistic guards made us perform irrelevant tasks. I recall being told to carry heavy rocks to the other side of the road. I thought it was to build a wall or something. When I was told to pick them up and return them to where I first found them, I could barely find the energy. While doing this useless task, I tripped and fell several times. Of course, when I did, I was kicked and beaten. Doing work for no reason was somehow even worse, if possible, than doing real jobs for the Nazis.

I was put in the Holland barrack which held Dutch Jews, even though I spoke no Dutch; however, I could understand it a little when I heard it. Friends and acquaintances, such as Shmuel Greenberg-Shaver – his father was the biggest *shohet* in and around Uzhhorod – whom I knew from home and from yeshiva, were put in other barracks. At first, I was so depressed about not being with familiar people that I didn't socialize at all. Then, one day, three Polish prisoners originally from Warsaw visited my barracks, where they sang Yiddish songs to entertain the people. I remember they sang "My Yiddishe Mama." People cried so hard when they heard the songs, because they felt so much nostalgia and sadness. When the singing was finished and I realized how much the already depressed prisoners cried more, I knew what I had to do. I had to sing happy songs, make people smile, even if just for a few seconds. It was my only opportunity, my only way, to give *tzedaka*. Giving *tzedaka* is every able Jew's obligation. Right away, I jumped up and yelled, "I am the Chief Cantor of Budapest, and I will sing too!" I sang *"Der rebbe Elimelekh,"* which is Old King

Chapter Three: Bergen-Belsen

Cole, using a rabbi instead of a king, and all sorts of other well-known ditties. Soon, I was going from barrack to barrack singing for the inmates. I got to be known as Moshele *der Zinger,* Moshele the Singer.

***

One day when I was singing at a barrack, I met a heroic Jew. I knew him from before the war, in Uzhhorod. Near the *shul* I attended in my hometown, there was a gentile who seemed to always be hanging out. When I was older, I learned that he converted to Judaism. This is the hero I bumped into in Bergen-Belsen. After my singing, he came up to me and hugged me. I asked him if he regretted converting. He responded, "I am the happiest man in the world. I'm happy I belong to the murdered and not the murderers." When it was his turn to be murdered, I remember him walking and screaming that he was on his way to sanctify God's name. He was a rare victim indeed.

Another day, I met a courageous man who heard me speak Hungarian. I came into the barrack and accidentally hit my head on the bed when I lay down. I cursed myself for being stupid, "*agyilag zokni!*" A man yelled, "You speak Hungarian!" "Yes," I replied. He came over and hugged me. "I am so happy to find a landsman, one of ours," he said, laughing. "I need your help. I am not a Jew. I do not know why I am here. I speak none of the languages spoken here by the guards. Can you explain to the SS that I am not a Jew?" I decided to try and help him. When not much was happening one evening, I walked over to the SS offices and spoke to an official. I explained to him that this Hungarian man had a grandfather who converted to Catholicism in order to marry a non-Jew. There was no way he could be Jewish. "I know all this," said the SS guard. "He told us everything when we picked him up. I'll say the same to you that we said to him. You have Jewish blood, so go to hell." A few days later, I was near the Hungarian man in the *appel*. He was selected for murder. He turned to me and, using my Hungarian nickname, he said in desperation, "Moshika, before I die I want to say the six words of the *Shema*," a central prayer to Jews, indeed their quintessential acknowledgement of the One God. It is said by Jews as part of *viddui*, the deathbed confession, which, incidentally, has nothing to do with the Christian concept of hoping to go to heaven. Rather, it is an admission by the dying person of not being perfect and it seeks to unite him or her with God. "I will say each word slowly and you repeat after me," I said to him. In his grief, he screamed the words loudly after I said each one.

"*Was ist Das?* What is this?" the camp commander, Josef Kramer, also known as the Butcher of Bergen Belsen, asked sarcastically, as he walked toward us. Kramer clearly knew fear when he saw it, and he absolutely knew the *Shema* well by now. "This is what a Jew says before death," I replied, feigning ignorance of Kramer's knowledge. Kramer drew his gun. With the butt, he hit my head, which started to bleed. Knocked out, I did not know what happened to the Hungarian. I learned from others that he had been shot in the head right after I was hit and that he died quickly. I was relieved for him. Whenever I think about this poor Hungarian non-Jew, I think about how, some twenty-seven years later when I was visiting the Bobover Rebbe Shlomo Halberstam in Manhattan, I recalled this incident. By the time I had finished the story, the *rebbe* was crying. Then he asked me if I ever knew any Jew who lost their *emuna*, their faith, while in the camps. I told him many did, and that I had lost my own faith before going to Bor. I explained to him how the Munkatcher Rebbe had helped me to see that it was crucial to keep up religious beliefs, and how he gave me ḥizuk, strength, to come back to Jewish observance.

Getting back to the war: As I was leaving my barrack one day, I bumped into a *kapo*, a prisoner functionary assigned to supervise fellow inmates. He told me that the Beast of Bergen Belsen had been listening to me and liked my singing voice. This did not make me feel good. Kramer loved the game of shooting prisoners as if he were hunting. He would wait until one came into his gun sight, aim right at the middle of the person's forehead, and then shoot to kill. He used to smile when he hit perfectly, and to curse in German if he missed the shot. The following Sunday, a guard screamed my number during the *appel* and I came forward. I was standing before a nineteen- or twenty-year-old Nazi who yelled, "You come with me to see Joseph Kramer." I was terrified, but I followed. Kramer – who was known as the Beast of Belsen – sat, ate, and drank while I stood waiting. Finally, he asked me if I could sing in German, and I said yes. He threw me a piece of fresh bread. I knew how to sing in German, I explained, "because when I was young, I used to pass a neighbor's window from which I would hear a record playing Yosef Schmidt." He was the great German singer who died so young, in fact the previous year. Kramer did not believe Schmidt was Jewish. I told Kramer he was. I said: "I heard the Schmidt songs over and over, and liked them very much. I got to know his music quite well, because I ended up visiting that neighbor's home on several occasions when I was back from my yeshiva in Munkacs. I also had Schmidt's teacher at the conservatory." Kramer asked me if I thought I was better than Yosef Schmidt. Knowing Kramer would look for any little mistake in my performance and use that as an excuse to kill me, I told him no, of course I was not that good. I sang a Schmidt piece, and Kramer looked shocked. He asked if I knew another specific German Schmidt song, and I said yes. I was very nervous as I sang it. I was thinking Kramer was trying to find any error so he could kill me. When I finished the song, he exclaimed, *"Lugner!* Liar! You are singing exactly like Schmidt and I love it. Now sing that song again." I sang it about eight times. From that day on he called me *lugner.*

To my eternal good fortune, I became important to Kramer, and this saved my life more than once. I even went home with him, leaving on Fridays and remaining at his place until Monday. I had to sing for him every Sunday. He made special requests. He was very fond of Italian songs, for example *Tiri tomba tiri tomba*. He loved my lyrical tenor voice, which he frequently praised. Because of my voice – and all the Nazis in the camp knew about it – I was the only inmate who got to go out into the camp's streets during lockdowns or after curfew. Nor did I have to scream *latrina! latrina!* during lockdown, though everyone else who had to use the toilet did. Other than those benefits, I was treated pretty much the same as the others, and of course I did not flaunt my good fortune. I still hated the Nazis from the very depths of my soul.

Because he liked my singing, the *Obergruppenführer* – just below the rank of high commander or *SS-Oberst-Obergruppenführer* – never chose me to make up the thousand to be killed. *Davka*, wouldn't you know it, one day there was a new Nazi on patrol who did not know who I was. He went around picking people to fill in the quota and he saw me and he pointed to me. I thought, "Okay, let them finish with me, kill me and be done with it." I walked with my head down. All of a sudden, I hear "*Lugner! Vas machtu dant?* What are you doing there?" It was the *Obergruppenführer*. So, I left the line and walked back to my barrack. All the people there were so happy, they said: "Moshele, they sent you back, you are alive!" And they were dancing and crying. I began to cry, and I was asked, "Moshe, why are you crying?" I said, "You know the Germans are very *pinklish,* exact. There must be a thousand victims, not one less and not one more. Someone else took my place. I cry for him." Until today, I mark his *yahrzeit*, the anniversary of his death. I know the day and the place, but I do not know the name.

***

One day, when I was lying down in my barrack trying not to think about food, I was summoned by a prisoner, who told me, "Godel

Chapter Three: Bergen-Belsen

wants to see you." I had no idea who Godel was, so I said "forget it." Then a friend of mine who had been in the camp for two years said to me, "If Godel calls, you must go." He explained that Godel was the leader of a group of Jews who had been in Bergen-Belsen for a long time. They were all strong and forceful, and they got special treatment. They were the so-called elite of the camp, if any Jew could be elite there. Nobody dared fight them or refuse what they asked. I went to Godel's barrack, and I could see right away how much better it was than the rest. My barrack had about five hundred people who had to be stacked in three-tier bunk beds. Godel's barrack had about eighty-five people who each had their own bed. Godel said, "You are Moshele *der Zinger*. Sing for me." I did as I was told. He liked my voice. He told me not to return to my barrack but to stay with him at his. I was happy to join Godel and his group. Their place was cleaner and they got better food. On my way back to my barrack to say goodbye to my old bunkmates, I changed my mind. I told the man who accompanied me that I would be staying in my old place. "I can't tell you exactly why, but I have this belief that this is the barrack I came into, and I will get killed here or I will be freed from here. I believe in how God leads me. But any time Godel wants me to, I will sing for him." About a week later, the guards were up early, which always meant trouble. As normal, we had to go out and stand for the *appel*. As we stood, we could see a large gallows, but we had no idea who it was for. Then they brought out the prisoner, Godel. We discovered later that his entire group had tried to escape, but were caught. Every single one was killed, except Godel. The Nazis kept him alive to make an example of him to the rest of us.

All of a sudden, the guard yelled my number, A855. I ran – I didn't walk – to the gallows, because we had to answer fast. The guard said I could sing Godel's prayer for the dead. That was apparently Godel's last request. By now, he was on a box with the rope around his neck. I went and stood close to him. "Moshele, sing

El maalei raḥamim. Sing it beautifully, so I can take it with me." I questioned myself: "Should I say it quickly so he will suffer less, or should I take a long time so he will stay alive longer and, who knows, maybe the Nazi guard will change his mind or maybe even *Moshiaḥ,* the Messiah, will come." I decided slowly was better to give *Moshiaḥ* time to get here. I sang. When I got to the part that needed his name, I asked him "Godel, son of who?" He began to scream: "Godel ben David from Sosnovska! Godel ben David from Sosnovska! Godel ben David from Sosnovska!" It was ear-piercing. It made the Nazi guard nervous, and he quickly kicked the box away. Godel died. I never finished the prayer.

***

Amidst the horrors of the camp, there was the odd event to celebrate. For example, one morning, a small group of us were secretly summoned by other prisoners, including Yosele Rosensaft, the father of a new baby, to go to one of the women's barracks. There, we saw an eight-day-old baby boy cuddling with his mother. It was time for the baby's *brit mila.* The boy was to receive the name Menachem at the *brit* ceremony. I officiated at this *simḥa,* though sadly we all had to force ourselves to be happy. I am pretty sure Menachem was the only child born in the camp, at least while I was there. You have to admit, a baby in such a place of death was truly a miracle. The other miracle is that all three in that family survived the war. But Yosele making it through was the biggest miracle of all. He narrowly escaped execution when he was recaptured after an escape attempt. We hid him carefully in the barracks for two months until the Nazi guards forgot about the incident. The next miracle with this family was that after the war, Yosele went on to make millions of dollars. When Menachem was thirteen years old, his father flew me from South Africa to Israel so I could sing at his bar mitzva. Then when Menachem – who eventually became

Chapter Three: Bergen-Belsen

a powerful New York City lawyer, was to be married – Yosele flew me to Herzliya, Israel, so I could sing there too. The wedding was a glittering three-week affair.

On Erev Rosh HaShana, the day before Rosh HaShana, in the Holland barracks, I spoke to Rabbi Davidi. He came to me and told me, "Moshele, you must help me. Last night, they brought in 1,400 Hungarian boys, aged nine to thirteen. They are all very religious. Many are Hasidim. Tomorrow, they will be sent to their deaths. They will be gassed at Auschwitz. Their last request is to hear *tekiat shofar*." They wanted to hear the sound of the shofar, a religious instrument made of a ram's horn that is blown every year on Rosh HaShana. Among the sounds it makes is *tekia* – a long single blast.

The rabbi continued: "A Nazi guard told me that I can go and blow shofar for the boys, but I am afraid to walk alone. I want you to come with me and be with me when I do this mitzva. Sometimes where I go I encounter problems, but with you I will likely not have any." A few hours later, he hid a shofar behind his shirt, and we started out. We soon arrived at their barrack. It had no beds. The boys were sitting on the floor. They surrounded us when we came in. The rabbi gave a quiet but very moving speech. I sang for them *Unetaneh tokef*, which means, "Let us speak of the awesomeness [of God]," a song which has been sung during Rosh HaShana and Yom Kippur services for hundreds of years. I also sang *Kol Nidrei* and the rabbi blew the shofar. Then we left. But when we were about two hundred yards away, we heard "*tzavei tzavei yeshuot Yaakov*," a song about the miracles of biblical times. All 1,400 children started singing together, and then they got louder and started to sing with a tempo. We were drawn back to their barrack. They started to dance in a huge circle, with the rabbi and me dancing in the middle.

Suddenly, the door flew open. By instinct, the rabbi and I dropped to the floor so no one at the door could see us. It was

Kramer. He was screaming and insulting the boys, saying things like *uerfluchte Kinder!* You cursed children! "Why are you singing and dancing?" he yelled. "Tomorrow you are going to be burned." A young boy, maybe twelve years old, who happened to be tall, approached Kramer and said in perfect German, "Tomorrow we will meet our Father, and you will no longer be able to enjoy yourself by troubling us and hitting us and screaming at us and cursing at us." The *Obergruppenführer* glared at the boy, turned around, punched the door hard with his fist and left.

The next day, Rosh HaShana, we heard those 1,400 children walking to the train singing at the top of their lungs. Rabbi Davidi later spoke about these children to the tormented adults: "We believe what the Gemara says, that *Moshiaḥ* will arrive when there is much *tzoras*, amid great pain." He also reminded us that it was important for every Jew to believe that, even one second before death, *Moshiaḥ* will come and save all of us. Many Jews did believe this, and it is why so many went to the gas chambers singing the song *"Ani maamin be'emuna shelema,"* which means "I believe with perfect faith." They would sing it over and over again. Because of the painful experience with the 1,400 children, ever since I left Bergen-Belsen, whenever I say *Kaddish*, a holy prayer for the dead, I always end it with *Ani maamin*.

While I was in Bergen-Belsen, I witnessed *Sonderkommandos* – who were, like *kapos*, prisoners who were forced to help Nazis by doing horrible chores, for example, throwing Jews, alive or dead, into fires. I was not the only prisoner who saw these workers rip little children away from their mothers' arms at the trains, while the mothers were screaming, then throw the children into the flames. But I did soon learn that having her child taken away gave the mother a better chance to survive, especially if she was strong or pretty. I used to curse the *Sonderkommandos*, but eventually I asked God's forgiveness for them when I realized they were themselves victims, who usually didn't live for more than three months.

Chapter Three: Bergen-Belsen

After that time, they were murdered, too. Like many pious Jews in the camps, the *Sonderkommandos* hoped and prayed that *Moshiaḥ* would come before it was their turn to die.

***

In the last two months before liberation, I did not sing for Kramer, because he knew the war was lost and he did not want to share his food with me. In fact, many of the Germans were running away, so instead of having forty or fifty guards at the camp we were left with only three or four. There was no longer any order in the camp. Everybody did what they wanted. The problem was, we were so weak we couldn't do anything. We didn't know what was happening, that the liberators were coming. We knew something was going on, but we had no clue what. I became so feeble I needed help just to get out of bed. Liberation came on April 15, 1945, but I was too weak to cheer. I didn't feel anything.

On Liberation Day, an English soldier picked me up; I weighed only 35 kilos. I was later told by a doctor that if this rescue had taken just one more day I would have died of starvation. Thank God we will never know. The soldier held up his two fingers and he kept repeating, "Victory! Victory!" in English. I had no idea what he was saying or signaling. How could I know he was implementing the idea of a shortwave radio broadcaster and Belgian refugee named Victor de Laveleye? According to the late American author William Manchester, in his humungous tome *The Glory and the Dream*, Laveleye suggested that the Allies "chalk the letter 'V' (for victory) in public places to show their confidence in an ultimate Allied triumph, and create a nuisance for the Nazis. It became the most popular symbol since the introduction of the crucifix." I eventually caught on to what the English soldier meant, but then I fell into a coma. When I awoke, I was lying in a bed in a big roundhouse full of beds. I remember thinking, "I have one plan, to get healthy. The way to do that is to eat." But like many others in my predicament, I did not know that eating would kill me. Praise God, I was prevented from gobbling lots of food at once by the devoted health care workers who looked after me.

As I lay in the bed naked, two nurses, sitting on both sides of me, were digging into my body and taking out the millions of lice that had died there. The ugly bugs were deep in my skin where they had presumably asphyxiated. I understood what the nurses were saying in German, though they were unaware I knew. They said, "This is unbelievable. He has not got a drop of blood." It took them eight hours to dig out every microbe. Each hour they changed to two new nurses. Soon, some soldiers brought me some sugar water. I complained loudly that I wanted to eat. A kindly English doctor came to my bedside and explained through a translator that it was for my own good not to eat yet. Only on the third day did they give me real food, porridge with water and sugar, for breakfast, lunch and supper. After six days they kicked me out, telling me I was weak but not sick.

Once I was out of bed and able to function normally, I thought I was in heaven. It was unbelievable. The two big relief organizations – the United Nations Relief and Rehabilitation Administration (UNRRA) and the Joint – gave us everything imaginable to eat, and everything was kosher. Two weeks went by and a whole huge new package arrived with more food. It was like getting a million dollars; better, actually.

When I was well enough, I officiated at a number of mass funerals. I did this till there were no more to do. I also continued to officiate at all kinds of occasions, a most memorable one being the first Rosh HaShana after the liberation. To fully describe that event that was held in September 1945, I must recall how Rosh HaShana was celebrated in the years before I was sent to the camps. Rosh HaShana is a very special two-day celebration for several reasons, one of them being that children and women fully participate in the first day service. During the rest of the year, on holidays and Shabbat, men are obliged to go to *shul* to pray, but the mothers stay at home to take care of young children. On Rosh HaShana, women with children of all ages attend the service, which is long. For the children, especially, this day was a huge event; they were very happy to have the privilege to go to *shul*. They very much looked forward to the feast. So, you must imagine the level of noise on Rosh HaShana with children of all ages present! Babies crying, toddlers crawling around, children screaming to each other, or asking mothers to bring them to the washroom or give them food!

From the point of view of the rabbi and the cantor, however, Rosh HaShana was a very challenging day, to say the least. Delivering a sermon or singing the prayers in a voice loud enough to be heard over this noise was almost impossible. Of course, both rabbi and cantor understood the importance of the participation of children, but still I remember those special days as quite difficult!

The first Rosh HaShana after the liberation saw several thousand survivors gathered together. We celebrated the 1945 Rosh HaShana outside, on the grounds where the barracks had previously stood, since there was no hall big enough to accommodate the multitudes. At the beginning of the service, I was sitting next to Rabbi Israel Zalmanowitz, who later became Chief Rabbi of Acre in Israel. Suddenly, the rabbi turned to me, overcome with emotion, and whispered, "I am overwhelmed. My mind is blank. I can't find anything to tell them. I have no books. Help me." I answered, "I don't know either. I also have no books." But then I quickly added, "Do you hear something? Can you hear anything?" Rabbi Zalmanowitz answered, "No, I hear nothing. People are just standing, quietly praying." I said, "You remember Rosh HaShana, the years before the Nazis, before the killings, before the horrible events. You remember the children making so much noise. Today, speak about the stillness, the quiet." Rabbi Zalmanowitz gathered his thoughts, looked at the immense crowd in front of him, and delivered a most moving sermon, filled with powerful emotions. His strong voice carried over to reach the thousands of people. At the end of his sermon, he started shouting, "Where is the noise? Where are the children? Where are Yaakov, Sarah, Rivka, Esther!?" He himself was crying at that time, but he managed to conclude by adding: "God bless the world!" Everyone present burst out crying, and cried and cried as if they could never stop, repeating the names of their own children and of all the other children they had known and loved and who had been murdered by the Nazis. In all of my life, I can't remember hearing so much crying. I still cry today every time I recall this event, every time I relive it.

***

During those months, I desperately wanted to get involved with the Joint, which I ultimately and successfully did. An immense Jewish relief agency based in New York City, it went into high gear after liberation. Thanks to the Joint, more than 227 million pounds of food, medicine, and other resources were shipped from the United States to DP – displaced persons – camps.

By late 1945, seventy thousand Jewish survivors had crammed into speedily established DP camps throughout Germany, Austria, and Italy. Dr. Joseph Schwartz, an innovative leader and the Joint's European director, was in a sense the savior. He quickly helped prepare a major report after an official tour of the camps. This report proposed that UNRRA participate in administering separate Jewish camps, with the Joint's help. Schwartz's plan, in effect, proposed rebuilding the Joint's predecessor into a streamlined organization. He put together a field plan that covered Europe and later North Africa, and he designed a highly proactive operational strategy.

Right after the war, part of Bergen-Belsen was turned into a hospital and a rehabilitation facility. As each barrack was emptied, it was burned to the ground to halt the spread of typhus. Any freed prisoners from elsewhere had to be deloused before being allowed entry. Evacuation was finished by May 19. Two months later, six thousand freed prisoners were taken to Sweden by the Red Cross to recover. The remaining survivors from Bergen-Belsen stayed and waited for repatriation, or to be sent to a new country to call home.

Together with other international organizations, the Joint distributed much-needed emergency medical assistance, but it also nourished the educational and cultural requirements of the Jewish refugees. The agency brought in Torah scrolls, books, paper, typewriters, ritual items, and holiday supplies. Money from the Joint went a long way to restoring a sense of community in the camps, helping to establish new medical clinics, schools, synagogues, and cultural institutes.

Because Bergen-Belsen was the first major concentration camp to be liberated, the international press gave it a lot of coverage. For the first time, the world saw the evidence of what had gone on behind enemy lines. After some sixty thousand people were liberated from the camp, five hundred of them per day began to drop dead from starvation and disease, mostly typhus. About fifteen thousand starving Jews died after eating too much too fast. At least 1,400 bodies at a time had to be buried in mass graves, an abhorrent task that had to be repeated over and over again. At first, the British made the Nazi SS guards find and bury the dead, but ultimately the British had to use bulldozers to move the multitudes of corpses into the overcrowded burial grounds. By the end of April 1945, countless thousands of nameless bodies had been shoveled underground. To this day, individuals lie unidentified in marked resting places. As late as 2015, a new mass grave was found in Bergen-Belsen, though the director of the site's memorial, Jens-Christian Wagner, said the grave would remain undisturbed: "We have consulted the Jewish community of Lower Saxony and according to religious laws, no digging is allowed," he was quoted as saying on the website of International Business Times. "That's why there's a decision not to start a dig. In any case, the whole camp has been declared a cemetery."

Also in 2015, Queen Elizabeth II and Prince Philip paid a somber visit to the former concentration camp.

By 1946, Belsen – as the facility came to be called by many – was the largest DP camp in Europe. It helped more than twelve thousand Jews, and in fact was the only exclusively Jewish camp in the British section of captured Germany. The freed Jews formed a committee to help with political, cultural, and religious activities, including finding lost relatives and spiritual healing. During the first few months alone, more than twenty marriages a day were performed. Over two thousand children were born to survivors. Schools – including a yeshiva, a high school, and a kindergarten – were soon established. Even a newspaper called *Unzer Shtimme*, Our Voice, was started. It wasn't until 1951 that the camp was completely empty. Most refugees had moved to Israel, the United States, and Canada. Josef Kramer was put on trial and found guilty by a low-level judge of the British military court. He was subsequently hanged.

To finish my discussion of Belsen, I want to mention here that, from the end of its existence as a DP camp until very recently – when I decided to no longer travel by plane – I was invited to return, with all other Belsen camp survivors, to the former concentration camp for memorial services. At first these well-attended events were held every ten years. Then about twenty-five years ago, they started being held every five years. Each time I went back to Belsen, I would lead services in saying *Kaddish*. I assume this practice of bringing back survivors to Belsen will continue until there are no survivors left, or with God's help, it will continue indefinitely. Here is how a newspaper article described the 1970 service. Beside one photograph of me looking somber, and under the headline "Cantor Kraus sings at Belsen, World Gathering at Memorial Service," the piece read, "Belsen survivors of many

Chapter Three: Bergen-Belsen

countries last week assembled to pay homage to the martyrs who did not survive and to recall the day of liberation, twenty-five years ago. They were joined by the counsellor at the Israeli Embassy in Bonn, Michael Peled; Brigadier-General H.L. Glyn Hughes, and other notable personalities. At the monument Rabbi Dr. Zvi Azaria, the Landers rabbi from Lower Saxony, recited a chapter of Psalms. Cantor Moshe Kraus, formerly of Johannesburg, sang *El maalei rahamim*." The article continued: "There were moving scenes as the gathering listened and then joined in reciting the collective *Kaddish*. Wreaths were then laid. Rabbi Dr. Azaria said in his speech, which he delivered in Hebrew and German: 'Here in Lower Saxony we have 233 Jewish cemeteries and only four hundred Jews alive. These figures speak for themselves. We bear witness to the degradation that befell Germany, and indeed humanity as a whole, in the years of the Nazis.' B.G. Hughes, who was the medical officer of the second British Army and [who] took charge of the rehabilitation of Belsen after the liberation, saving countless lives by his dedication and superhuman efforts on behalf of survivors, was given a standing ovation lasting several minutes. He said in his speech that he found it overwhelming and difficult to express his feelings. He could only say that his most treasured memory of those days was the courage and fortitude of the survivors."

***

Thankfully, I did get an important job with the Joint. I was hired as Chief Secretary of the Rabbinate for the organization in Germany. Dr. Schwartz, the Joint's General Secretary, was not too thrilled about giving me the job because there were many, many older and better qualified candidates, but I spoke German, which was essential. Moreover, I promoted myself shamelessly. I don't believe in acting overly modest, because if you appear like you think you are nothing, why should others think you are something? For this job, which paid the equivalent of six thousand dollars a year, I had to fly to London every month to help the British capital's *beit din*. I would advise the people involved and also bring them materials they needed for their jobs. I brought all kinds of formal documents, such as a *get*, Jewish divorce papers; *ketuba*, Jewish marriage contract; tefillin; and even ritual items, such as *lulavim* and *etrogim*, special plants used during the holiday of Sukkot.

Even after months doing this fulfilling job, and despite eating the best food I'd ever had, I still felt broken. Also, I had a great urge to travel to Bucharest – the capital of and biggest city in Romania – to possibly find members of my family. I was the oldest child, and I felt it was my responsibility to locate whoever I could in my family. I requested a leave of absence from Dr. Schwartz, who kindly gave it, but not happily. He begged me to hurry back: "As soon as you find your relatives, return." I told him I would stay there no longer than four or five months. I ended up staying seven.

I took the next train to Bucharest, but it was not easy. First, I had to wait a full two days at the train station until my German papers arrived. Also, it was overly crowded. There were many, many people wanting to travel to the same place. The reason thousands and thousands of Jews were going to Bucharest was because officials there were giving away large sums of Romanian money – 130,000 leu – to each refugee from a DP camp. Some three hundred thousand Jews came for the money, and many of them stayed, permanently. I thought perhaps my parents and siblings would try to go there to get some of the money. My idea was correct, as I found two of my beloved sisters, Rivka and Gittel, who had been in Auschwitz. They accepted the money. I did not. I asked how much 130,000 leu represented in US dollars. "In dollars it is two hundred," the official said. "Keep it," I replied. "I don't need it." I had about two thousand dollars with me that I had earned from my job in Belsen.

Chapter Three: Bergen-Belsen

I might as well mention this here: At some point not too long after the war, the German government offered me – as well as thousands of other Jewish survivors – fifty thousand dollars each – I believe only as a beginning – for the losses suffered. I did not accept the money, because I did not want to feel obligated to forgive them.

In Bucharest, I was hoping and praying to find my father and mother, who were only forty- and thirty-eight-years-old respectively when the war broke out. It was not long before I learned their fate, and that of my five youngest siblings. Despite knowing they likely would not have survived, I was still angered, shocked, and pained by the news. I couldn't accept that I no longer had a father, that I no longer had a mother. I couldn't believe that I did not have my other siblings, my uncles and aunts. They were all murdered. I am fortunate that I have the date my father was killed so I can commemorate him on his *yahrzeit*. A rabbi who worked at one of the crematoria at Auschwitz knew and recognized my father's dead body before he burned it. His body had just come from the gas chamber. Amazingly, and so thoughtfully, the rabbi wrote down the date and gave it to me later. His *yahrzeit* is the second day of the month of Kislev.

***

A short time after I found my sisters, I met Rabbi Alexandru-Yehuda Shafran, a philosopher of Judaism, a member of the Romanian Senate and the Chief Rabbi of Romania. He came to my hotel with Mishe Laiba, the president and treasurer of the enormous Malbim Synagogue, who became a close friend. For some reason, I remember that only Rabbi Shafran had a beard that day at my hotel. "Can we enter your room?" he asked politely. I ushered them upstairs and into my room. We all sat down. "Yesterday our *ḥazan* quit and went to Belsen," the rabbi explained. "We need a new *ḥazan* and we heard you were the last chief ḥazan of Budapest. We would like to give you a try on Shabbat in two weeks from now." I had ḥutzpa, so I asked, "Do you really think you have to try out the last chief ḥazan of Budapest before signing a contract?" They hesitated, so I said I wasn't interested. "I do not think I want to do that right now," I explained. "Who would want to start a new job as a ḥazan after what I just learned about my family? I do not have peace. I can't swallow that I have no father, no mother, nothing. I just can't swallow it. I am unbelievably depressed."

Before they left my hotel room, Rabbi Shafran asked me to see him in his office the next day. I agreed, and was there at 11 a.m. sharp. "Sit down," he offered. Then he started schmoozing with me about *yahadut*, Judaism. He was a clever man indeed. He somehow got me to relax. In the end, he persuaded me to try the position with his *shul*. "If you don't like it, you can always leave," he said in a quiet tone. "Nobody will force you to stay." I gave in and agreed to try it. To my surprise, I liked it right away. Malbim was a gorgeous synagogue with five thousand seats, fantastic acoustics, and a professional choir. Friday nights and Saturdays, it was packed, with men and women, unbelievable. On Friday night, the women kindled the Shabbat candles at home then raced to the *shul* to hear my *davening*. Unlike today, there was no *derasha* by the rabbi. Just my singing and *davening*. In fact, in those times, the rabbi had virtually nothing to do in *shul*. The ḥazan conducted services. The rabbi waited until near the end when he would do a couple of small rituals, but even the announcements at the conclusion were done by the ḥazan.

One day while I was *davening* at Malbim, a well-dressed man approached and introduced himself. It was Rabbi Moses Rosen. A week later, he was eating Shabbat lunch at the same home where I was eating. He mentioned that he was in Bucharest to look for a rabbinical position. Later that day, I was enjoying *shaleshudis* at the home of my great friend Mishe Laiba, and I mentioned Rabbi Rosen

Chapter Three: Bergen-Belsen

had impressed me. "Maybe he would be good for the Malbim *shul*," I suggested, "whenever Rabbi Shafran cannot attend. It is, after all, a huge synagogue." Rabbi Shafran interviewed Rabbi Rosen and hired him. Years later, Rabbi Rosen became Chief Rabbi of Romania, and whenever he talked about this job he loved, he gave me credit.

After *davening* one day in Bucharest, a man by the name of Peretz – I forget his first name – approached me. The richest Jew in Bucharest and a righteous Jew as well, he told me that every week in his home twelve men from the synagogue, plus the chief rabbi as leader, came and learned Ḥumash. "You give me so much naḥat," he gushed. "Please come on Wednesday nights." I heard from others that it was a huge *yiḥus,* or privilege, to go to his home for these classes. They focused on the commentaries of Rabbi Meir Leibush ben Yehiel Michel Wisser, a nineteenth-century chief rabbi of Bucharest, who was known as Malbim. I attended the classes and loved them. I couldn't wait for Wednesday nights.

There were supposed to be twelve guests and the rabbi, making thirteen people for the Wednesday class. But for three classes in a row, an uninvited man attended, making it fourteen in total. He was tall, well-dressed, spoke Yiddish, and he was always punctual. Peretz did not like this unknown guest, but what could he do? He did not want to be rude by asking him to leave. Usually when the rabbi finished his *shiur*, Peretz would walk the rabbi to the front door, where a chauffeur was waiting. (As a Member of Parliament, the rabbi was driven everywhere.) One night, before the rabbi could leave, the tall man stood up and spoke. He said, "I am a Jew from Russia. I was once in Tashkent, in Uzbekistan. I was hungry so I entered a restaurant, ordered food, and ate it. Suddenly, a few KGB officers came in and arrested me and some other men in the restaurant. They brought us into a room, and slapped us around. Then they separated us. They asked me, 'Who are these people in the restaurant?' I said, 'I don't know them. I just went to the restaurant to eat.' Then they said, 'How can you not know these people? You were with them.

You were dealing drugs with them.' For four hours, they repeated themselves: 'How can you not know these people? You were with them. How can you not know these people? You were with them. You are part of them. They are your people.'

"Then the KGB put me in a jail cell. Every day, they brought me upstairs and did the same thing, asked me the same questions. 'How can you not know these people? You were with them. They are your people.' Sometimes they only cursed me, but often they hit me. After four years, they let me go. Even without papers, I somehow made my way here, to Bucharest. One day, I was passing the Malbim synagogue, and on the spur of the moment I decided to go in. Since then, I have never missed a Shabbat. I like the *ḥazan* a great deal. Once, I was speaking with some congregants, and they informed me that the *ḥazan* is invited each Wednesday night to the *shiur* at the home of Peretz. I do not know anything about *Yiddishkeit*, nor about the great commentator Malbim, but I decided to go to Peretz's anyway. I'm sitting here and I am clueless about what is being said, but there is one thing I do know. One day, when I am dead and my soul enters heaven, I'll be able to tell the angels where I belonged. If, as the KGB says, you belong to the people you are with, then I am with my people right now. I will say in heaven, 'I was right there with Rabbi Shafran, Ḥazan Kraus, and their people, so I belong to them.' And this is why I am coming to you. Please allow me to stay. Do not be cross with me, and have a good night."

We were all sitting, listening. When the Russian finished, the chief rabbi rose and said, "You are here, and you belong here. I bid everyone a goodnight."

***

My beloved sisters moved in with me, and together we formed a small family. I continued to *daven* in the fine city of Bucharest. But

Chapter Three: Bergen-Belsen

things were getting tense. One Shabbat, a highly placed Russian officer, who came to our synagogue every week, finished *davening* and took a seat to wait for me near my small room at the *shul* where I kept some clothes and a few things. I liked this man. He was honest, pleasant, and kind. I asked him what I could do for him. He said, "Nothing. I came because I want to do something for you. I love your singing, but I do not want you to be trapped." First, he told me that he was the son of the Chief Rabbi of Poltava, a major city in Ukraine, at that time part of the Soviet Union. "Of course, I know of the place," I said. "It is a fantastic city with a fantastic chief rabbi." Then he told me to take the next train and run away. "Go anywhere you want," he urged, "just run away from Bucharest. The Russians are going to close the border and not even a fly will be able to get out."

Near the end of Shabbat, I went to talk to the *shul* president, Mishe Laiba, who was by then a great friend. I said to him, excitedly, nervously: "I'm going to tell you something, but you can't tell anybody because it will put the Soviet officer in jeopardy and he will get into trouble. But this is what I need to tell you. It is Shabbat now, and I don't travel on Shabbat. But right after, I am going to the train and I am taking it to Germany. Come with me. Leave everything. Come with your wife. I will share my food. I can't give you more because I don't have more, but my food is your food." He looked at me, and whispered, "Moshele, you will be sorry. Don't do it. What are you going to miss? So much. Do you need another thousand dollars? I will give you that. Don't leave. You have such a great position here. We love you. We want you." I responded: "I'm leaving straight away. I am not even going home to get the *shmatas*, the rags that I have there. I am getting my sisters, going right to the train, and we are going to Germany. If you want to come with me, I will be responsible for you. What I have, you will have." He said no again, and added, "You will be sorry." I said, "It may be you who is sorry. But I hope not." Sometime years later, the Israeli government – as part of a broad plan to in effect buy Jews from the Romanian government – paid a hundred thousand dollars to get Mishe Laiba out of prison.

The trip back to Germany wasn't easy. I had to look after my two sisters. And the borders were starting to be difficult. I had no passport, no real papers, only the temporary ones the Germans had given me. But I made it. In fact, the moment I told border authorities I was from the concentration camp, they usually let me go immediately. We had to cross the Romanian border, the Hungarian border, the Czech border, the Austrian border, and finally we arrived in Germany.

I returned to Belsen, now with my sisters. Within a very brief time, the two beautiful ladies met and married two perfect gentlemen. After their weddings in Belsen, one couple went to live in New York City, where they had nine children and lived long and deeply religious lives, while my other sister and her husband moved to Israel, where they had two children and also lived long happy lives as hasidic Jews.

Back in Belsen, I returned to my position as Germany's chief secretary of the rabbinate for the Joint. I was so grateful that the organization held my job for me. My main responsibility became to go every week to Bonn – which was the provisional capital of the recently formed Federal Republic of Germany – and take people out of jail. It wasn't easy. These were former prisoners of Nazi concentration camps who committed petty crimes after liberation, crimes such as trying to sell smuggled items from Poland, and perhaps theft. I appeared in court with them and argued for them like a lawyer. I almost always won because I told the judge these people had been in concentration camps and had suffered enough. "They've already been punished," I would say, and the judge would agree with me and set them free.

We were just in time for Rosh HaShana in Belsen in 1946. For those holidays there were five rabbis, and they all *davened* together with me as *ḥazan*. The funny thing is, every one of the rabbis claimed to have previously been a *rav*, a title given only to rabbis who had earned great respect. And each wanted to speak during Rosh HaShana. We decided to accept each rabbi's claim, which we learned months later were truthful. But at that time, since their *kehillot*, along with their documents, were no longer in existence, we could not get proper confirmation. It only seemed right to believe them. I took a hat and put in it five *tsetls*, notes, with all the main prayers of the *yamim noraim*, the High Holy Days. Every rabbi took a *tsetl*. They all *davened* and spoke in front of ten thousand people, and they all did excellently. The prayers for the *yamim noraim* were held in a huge sports arena. During Yom Kippur, one of the five rabbis, Rabbi Israel Zelmanowitz – who became an employee of Belsen's Yeshiva She'erit Israel that opened in 1945 – led a special part. His speaking and *davening* were incredibly moving. There was no microphone, but we had *maḥzorim* that had been sent from America. Many in the audience were standing and crying. He said *tefila zaka*, the prayer which says you forgive anyone who may have wronged you in any way. I was sitting on the *bima*, so I could see Rabbi Zelmanowitz up close. He was crying real tears. After Yom Kippur, many people thanked me for my *davening,* and said when *Moshiaḥ* comes, Moshe Kraus will be the *ḥazan*.

After the holidays, I received a letter from Rabbi Eliezer Silver, President of the Union of Orthodox Rabbis of the US and Canada, who was responsible for bringing many Torah scholars from Nazi-occupied Europe to the US and for raising millions of dollars for rescue efforts. The letter said I could not accept new *pesakim*, decisions about Jewish law, from the five rabbis until I got a signature from Rabbi Yehezkel Abramsky, the head of the London Beit Din. In other words, Rabbi Abramsky's word was final with respect to the five rabbis. These men of God had no end of problems for about eight months, after which Rabbi Silver wrote to me again and confirmed their legitimacy. There was no longer any need to get signatures from London for the five.

I gave some concerts after liberation, and I also enjoyed imbibing a little with my friend and teacher Rabbi Zelmanowitz. Sometimes I admit we would get a little drunk. Once, I gave a concert the night after getting intoxicated with Rabbi Zelmanowitz. In the middle of the concert, I had a serious a mental block. My mind just shut down while I was singing in Hebrew. The audience didn't know Hebrew, so I made up words from the *Midrash Shir HaShirim*, a part of the Talmud that explains halakha. Later, someone from the audience came up to me, pointed a finger at me, and said: "I understood exactly what you did. You can't fool me." I was embarrassed, but the suffering was so light compared to what I'd been through, I quickly got over it.

While I was living back in Belsen, Schwartz sent me away some thirty times to give concerts in many European cities, including Stockholm, Sweden; Copenhagen, Denmark; and even Bamberg, Germany. In Bamberg, a Bavarian town where Jews had lived for more than a thousand years, a quickly assembled DP camp had been set up, and for almost twelve months everything was a *balagan*, chaotic. Freed Jews were trying to get fed and settled. A rabbi by the name of Halberstam – not of the Bobover Hasidim, which reestablished itself in the United States after the war – tried to help a Jewish woman who came to him to get married. She had with her two witnesses who swore they had seen her husband in Russia, dead. After asking her a series of important questions, the rabbi happily married her to husband number two. Lo and behold, husband number one reappeared. Rabbi Halberstam was incredulous. He could not forgive himself for officiating at a bigamist wedding. He threw himself at a wall, and then banged his head against it until he was bleeding and unconscious. He was rushed to hospital, where he recovered physically. His spiritual recovery took a much longer time. This apparently was not uncommon. I am not

Chapter Three: Bergen-Belsen

referring to the rabbi's self-harm, but rather to spouses marrying when they were still married. People felt so bad emotionally right after the war that – on top of having trouble finding their families – they wanted to rush headlong into new marriages before they were a hundred percent sure their prewar spouses were dead.

At some point not too long after the war, I found myself giving a concert in Cologne, Germany, where Konrad Adenauer – eventually to become the highly successful first post-World War II Chancellor of Germany from 1949 to 1963 – had been installed as mayor by the American occupying forces. He extended his hand to me when he was mayor of Cologne but, being young and still bitter, I withheld my hand and stated to him clearly, "I do not shake hands with Germans." He said, politely, "Okay," and moved on. When I later learned that he had been involved in trying to assassinate Hitler and that he had spent time in prison during Nazi rule, I tried to find him to apologize. I got the chance at Belsen during a dinner with the committee to erect a monument to Bergen-Belsen victims. During the speeches at that dinner I announced my apology publicly, explaining I had lost much of my family in the Holocaust. Konrad Adenauer came up to the podium and embraced me. We both cried.

I stayed in my job with the Joint for three years. In 1948, still feeling lonely and dejected after the loss of my family and so many of Europe's Jews, I decided to move to Mandatory Palestine and help with what everyone knew was coming, the newly formed State of Israel.

The Life of Moshele Der Zinger

Yearly visit to Bergen-Belsen

Chapter Three: Bergen-Belsen

Memorial service in Bergen-Belsen

Chapter Four

Israel

When I arrived in Israel at the beginning of 1948 – just before massive waves of Jews from Europe and Arab countries had the same idea – Israel was not quite yet a nation state, at least not in the formal way countries are defined nowadays. In fact, Israel was still Mandatory Palestine. Why did I go? Jews, religious Jews with long *payot* and *kapotes* – sideburns and caftans – came from Mandatory Palestine to DP camps in Europe to urge their fellow Jews to make the move to the Land of Israel. They were all saying, "*Moshiah* is waiting to come into the world, but He needs more Jews in the Holy Land." Mandatory Palestine already had more than six hundred thousand Jews, many of whom were begging from afar: "Please come here. We need people. We need soldiers."

One religious Jew, I remember, was especially emphatic. With tears in his eyes, he begged a group of us: "Come to Israel. Don't go to America. Don't go to England. Don't go to Australia. Come to Israel." I had to think very hard. I had received a contract to be a *hazan* at a *shul* in New York. I had liked the terms, signed the document, and I had even gotten my plane ticket to go there. Then I heard this man's pitch for Israel. After a few days of serious thought, I decided to tear up my American ticket and contract. I was going to the Middle East.

On November 29, 1947, the United Nations General Assembly, endorsed – through passage of UN Resolution 181, with a few minor changes – the report of the United Nations Special Committee on Palestine. This meant there was to be "substantial" Jewish migration from the British territories, beginning February 1, 1948. It wasn't until May 14, 1948 – the day the last of the British forces left Haifa – that the Jewish People's Council declared the new Jewish State of Israel into existence.

What an exciting moment for the world's Jewish community, especially after the genocide in Europe! Though eternally and religiously a Jewish homeland, not since the Second Temple period, which ended in 70 CE, had the Jews had a defined place in *Eretz Israel* – the Land of Israel – that specifically belonged to them. But even then, in those early Julian calendar years, *Eretz Israel* was under Roman occupation. Indeed, the creation of the State of Israel was an incomparable moment in Jewish history.

***

When I arrived in Israel, to my pleasant astonishment, I was already popular. As the former chief cantor of Bucharest, the former chief cantor of Budapest, and a broken-down but appreciated *ḥazan* in two concentration camps, I couldn't walk the streets of Israel without being recognized and praised. It was incredible. Everybody wanted blessings from me! They believed a blessing from a former camp *ḥazan* was good for their lives and futures.

Despite this bittersweet situation, it was no secret when I arrived in Israel that I was feeling gloomy and alone. I was depressed and grieving for at least a few hours every day. What

Chapter Four: Israel

does such a dejected person do? I did the only honorable thing I could think of: I joined the army. Being a quick study, within a short time I was assembling tanks and, as needed, disassembling them. I got so good at the job I became a teacher, and I began showing other soldiers how to do the same tasks.

Once I was in the Israel Defense Forces, I was able to find my only living brother, Yoel Hershel, who was also in the IDF. Seeing each other and spending time together was comforting for both of us. He lived in Netanya with his wife. They eventually had eight children. To this day, I am still in contact with his children, my beloved nieces and nephews.

One day, I attended a wedding for a friend's son or daughter, I forget which. The friend was Moshe Glickson, and he had been the editor of *Haaretz* – Israel's oldest daily newspaper, established in 1918 – for fifteen years, from 1923. By 1948, it was the largest Hebrew newspaper in the world. Originally published only in Hebrew, today it can be read online in both Hebrew and English. Glickson was an important man, and also a very wealthy man, so all the government ministers, ambassadors, and consuls-general were at the wedding.

Moshe Glickson knew I was a *ḥazan*, so he asked me to do the *sheva brachot*, the seven blessings said under the *ḥuppa* at every Jewish wedding. I was happy to oblige. It had been months since I had sung solo for Jewish services, and even longer since I had been a *ḥazan* in a regular job. So, I was happy with myself that I sang very beautifully for the *sheva brachot*. Another military man at the wedding came up to me after, and said he wanted to talk. He introduced himself as Yigael Yadin, the army's chief of staff. In that, the first conversation we ever had, he offered me the job of chief cantor for the IDF. It was a brand-new position, the first time the IDF had ever had a spot for chief cantor. By accepting it I made history. Of course, it was still 1948, the first year of Israel's existence. Nevertheless, I made history.

Yes, it was 1948, and the ten-month War of Independence – which included several failed truces – was in full force. Because of the debacle of the 1947 United Nations Partition Plan for Palestine, war had become inevitable. The Plan would have seen the region divided into three areas, a Jewish state, an Arab state, and a separate international administration for the cities of Bethlehem and Jerusalem. The UNPPP was endorsed by Israel, but roundly rejected by the Arab states. The very day after Israel made its Declaration of Independence on May 14, 1948, it was attacked by the joint forces of three countries, Egypt, Jordan, and Syria, with help from Iraq. What had been civil war between Jews and non-Jews had instantly become interstate war. The Arab invaders, tightly in control of their Arab lands, quickly charged at Israeli forces as well as a few Jewish settlements. The international Jewish community held its collective breath. In the end, Israel not only trounced her enemies, but also gained territory.

Perhaps the most significant result of this war – besides the unnecessary deaths of Israelis and innocent Arabs – was the colossal transfer of people. Some estimates say seven hundred thousand Arabs fled or were sent away from Israeli lands, and – since every single one of the multiple Arab states in existence refused to absorb them – the vast majority of them became the infamous and abandoned Palestinian refugees. By the same measure, some seven hundred thousand Jews came out of or were expelled from Arab countries and were quickly and comprehensively resettled in Israel.

One of the most comforting holidays in 1948 was Pesaḥ, the first official one in Israel in two thousand years. I was honored to conduct the *seder* with Rabbi Shmuel Avidor Hacohen, who became controversial decades later for officiating at services without a *meḥitza*, a divider, between men and women. The *seder* included about five thousand soldiers, including Moshe Dayan – a military leader in 1948 and later the defense minister – as well as Yadin. Reportedly, the experience was so exhilarating that for the

Chapter Four: Israel

next week soldiers walked around humming and singing my rendition of the delightful Pesaḥ song, "Ḥad Gadya."

***

Being the Israeli army's chief *ḥazan* kept me busier than I had ever been, and too frequently sad. There were so many funerals and memorial services, it seemed like for my first two years of mandatory service I was constantly crying. I am not implying that funerals and crying were bad for a young man who had lost much of his family and had survived Bergen-Belsen, but they took a tremendous toll on me emotionally. I cried many tears for the young soldiers who died defending Israel, and at the same time I shed many tears for my own immense losses.

As mentioned earlier, as a hasidic Jew, I have always sought comfort in hasidic tales. Everywhere I traveled as a young man, and even as a boy, I always sought out older people to get their stories, to hear about challenging experiences they had in their lives. Being in Israel made this easier in some ways. In Jerusalem, I sometimes went from one *shtiebel* (a small synagogue) to another tiny *shul* searching out old Jews and old stories. One day, I arrived at the Chortkover *shtiebel*. Inside was sitting an old Hasid who had a face like a prophet's. He was giving a class from *Siddur Hayom*, the Order of the Day. Very quietly I moved to his table, sat down, and listened to him speak. When he finished, he turned to me and said, "*Shalom aleikhem*," which means peace be upon you. I told him who I was, and he gave me permission to attend his *shiurim* any time. I came as much as possible over the next three years. He never talked about himself, only about Torah and ethics.

One day I found him excited. "Moshele, Moshele!" he said when the other students had left. "Come here, I want to tell you a story. I was born in Chortkov ninety-six years ago to a hasidic family. I was the youngest of five brothers. My whole family were devout Chortkover Hasidim. In Chortkov, as in lots of cities during those days, there were Hasidim yes, but also lots of *maskilim*, those modern 'enlightened' Jews who were not fond of, and maybe hated, hasidic Jews, and who actively tried to change them. Since I was the number one pupil in the yeshiva, I was noticed by one of those *maskilim*. He decided to lead me away from Ḥasidut. The way the *maskilim* did that was very insidious. First, this man invited me to his home. Then he quickly introduced me to modern and secular German literature. That was all he had to do. I am sorry to say he succeeded so well that I became an atheist. I cut off all ties with my family. With his financial help, I ran away to Berlin, went to university, and became a medical doctor. While in university, I met and married a non-Jewish student.

"During World War I, I was enlisted in the German army as a medical officer, stationed in Vienna. One day, while I was walking down the street, I saw hundreds of Jews praying and crying. I asked what was going on. They told me that the Chortkover Rebbe, who had fled to Vienna because of the war, was gravely ill. 'We are praying for a *refua sheleima*, for a speedy recovery,' they said. At that moment, all of my emotions that I had suppressed for so long overtook me. I had a strong desire to see the *rebbe* once more. Being in my officer's uniform I had no trouble entering the room where the *rebbe* was lying, surrounded by his followers. At first, I could not see the *rebbe's* face, as he was on his side facing the wall. After a short time, he turned and asked for a bowl and a pitcher of water. When he got what he asked for he washed his hands and moved his wet hands over his face. He straightened out his beard. He started to say the longest prayer in the siddur, a prayer only recited on Shabbat. He used the Chortkover *nigun*. When he reached the words, *borkhi nafshi et Hashem*, my soul blesses God, the *rebbe* closed his eyes and his soul departed this world.

"Walking back to my hotel room, my mind could not grasp how a human being could be in such control until the last minute of his life. Right at that moment, I realized two things: one, there must be a God, which I had tried to deny for so many years; and two, that I had left Chortkov, but Chortkov had never left me. At that very moment, I went to the bank, withdrew all my money, changed into civilian clothes, and then took the first available boat to Palestine. When I landed, I changed my name, went to Jerusalem to the Chortkover *shtiebel*, and here I am until tomorrow. Please be here."

I was thoroughly engaged by that beautiful story, but I was stumped by the ending, "until tomorrow." I couldn't ask him, because I didn't want to interrupt him while he kept saying, "Until tomorrow. Please be here. Until tomorrow. Please be here." The next day I went to the *shtiebel*. The *rebbe* had died. I had the *zekhut*, the honor, to participate in his funeral, and to finally understand his words, "Until tomorrow."

***

During my first two years in the Israeli military, I met and married Rivka. We had met at a wedding, where there happened to be thousands of people attending. It was the wedding of a child of the Modzitzer Rebbe, leader of Modzitz Hasidim, a group that started in Deblin, Poland, and ended up after the war in Bnei Brak, Israel. Many cabinet ministers and government officials were celebrating with the *rebbe* and his family. In fact, everyone who was anyone in Israel wanted to attend. I was required to be there with Shlomo Goren, the Chief Rabbi of the IDF. Goren and I were among those at the wedding representing the government.

The *simḥa* was entertaining, relaxing, and a little unusual. Because there were so many people, the hosts decided not to use regular waiters and waitresses. Rather, friends of the *kalla* and *ḥatan* – the bride and groom – were waiting tables for other friends and guests. That was how I met Rivka. She had gone to school with the *kalla*, so she was waiting tables. She came up to me with a plate and offered me some food. I looked at her and I thought, "Okay, she is beautiful." I turned to Rabbi Goren and told him, "I am going to marry her." He laughed uproariously, but in the end, I got the last laugh.

About half an hour later, I invited her to take a walk with me. Then, when we were alone, I popped the question, as they say. She declined immediately. "I am only sixteen years old!" she shrieked. She called me a *meshugener*, Yiddish for crazy person. Later, she told me that she told her friend, "Tonight I met a madman." But we continued to socialize and get to know each other. I learned that her Polish parents had come to Palestine in 1933, where she was born. She lost many extended family members in the Holocaust. After she turned seventeen, we got engaged. After Rivka agreed to marry me, I went to see my future father-in-law, Rabbi Chaim Yitzchak Deutsch, a Gerrer Hasid, to ask for her hand in marriage. My father-in-law had never before heard this expression. He looked at me for a few seconds and said, "This is what you want – her hand?" I said "Yes," and he replied, "Just her hand?" I said "Yes," again, and he said, "So tell me – what will I do with the rest of her?" Six months later, in April 1951, we were married.

Our wedding was truly unforgettable. It was a difficult time of rationing in Israel, so having extra food was illegal, and virtually impossible to get for even a medium-sized wedding, which is what we wanted. The situation was so serious that police would climb aboard buses unannounced and check people's bags for illegal food. As a member of the IDF, I was entitled to certain privileges, certain illicit privileges, or so I believed, in order to have a decent wedding. Thank goodness my IDF friends agreed with me. A plan – one every bit as detailed and as ultra-secret as an IDF military attack – was hatched. First, some of my pals borrowed a *ḥevra Kaddisha* truck, used to transport dead bodies before funerals. By doing this, they were assured that no police would stop them. Who wants to stop vehicles carrying corpses? Also, I'm quite certain there was a government policy not to stop such trucks, even during rationing. Second, they drove for two hours northeast to Lake Kinneret – Israel's biggest fresh water lagoon – also known as the Sea of Galilee or Lake Tiberias. Next, my friends fished, and fished, and fished. Finally, they came back late at night, to my home, where they poured the fish into my bathtub. I spent the rest of the night cleaning and gutting the catch. The next day, the same truck picked up the uncooked wedding food and drove it to my favorite Hungarian restaurant, where the most delicious meals in the country were prepared. Rivka and I were married in an army mess hall in a quaint ceremony officiated by Rabbi Goren, with many IDF officers, local rabbis and ḥazanim in attendance. We ate the meal in the same mess hall, and everyone was unreservedly thrilled with the food. They were also quite happy for me and Rivka. Following the simḥa, she and I set up a cozy home in Tel Aviv.

Now that I was married, I very much wanted to leave the army after the mandatory two years, and possibly leave Israel, too. I was overwhelmed and frankly dispirited with all the death and sadness. I was anxious to join the private sector and to spend more private time with my wife. I wanted to see the world from a different perspective. Rivka was in total agreement. When the time came, I went to the proper army office to get my release papers, but when I arrived, there was a personal note there for me from Yigael Yadin, the army chief of staff. He wanted to talk to me. A military jeep was waiting outside to drive me to his office. When I arrived, Yadin was sitting behind his desk. He pointed to two forms in front of him. "One is your release, and I will sign it right now if you want to leave the IDF," he said. "The other paper is a renewal for two more years, which I hope you will sign. I want to tell you how much your ḥazanut has meant to the families of our lost soldiers. So many sad mothers and fathers have commented to me how they were unable to deal with the deaths of their children, but how your captivating and soothing voice brought them *niḥumim*, comfort." Blinking back tears, I signed up for two more years. Once more, Rivka was in total agreement.

***

When there was no military emergency the reservists were allowed to go home for the weekend, including Shabbat. But if they were needed by the IDF, they stayed in the army barracks over Shabbat. In these latter situations, when they were required to stay, we often had an *Oneg Shabbat*, a special Shabbat party. During these little celebrations, one rabbi spoke and I sang. One weekend, it was planned that the reservists would go home, but at the last minute they were told they had to stay. The young men were terribly disappointed, and they could not hide their feelings. They all grumbled loudly. The chief rabbi felt their pain, and wanted badly to help them. He looked over at me, and shrugged his shoulders with a look of helplessness. I saw that as my cue to sing to try and lighten the mood. I sang, but no-one even smiled. I tried another song; no-one was interested. By the third song and no positive response, I was about to give up. Then I had an idea. I started to sing *Hayom yom Shabbat kodesh*, which translates, "Today is the Holy Shabbat." Only four Hebrew words. I started very softly, and one by one the soldiers joined in, all across the large room. They slowly got louder and louder, until they were roaring. They sang *Hayom yom Shabbat kodesh* over and over, louder and louder. It ended up that we sang these four words all through the entire Shabbat, except when we slept. A few weeks later, the army officers told me they will never forget that Shabbat. One officer was commander Rabbi Eliyahu Yosef She'ar Yashuv Cohen, the former chief rabbi of Haifa. He visited Rivka and me in Ottawa about fifteen years ago, and honored us by speaking at a local event for Emunah, a

Chapter Four: Israel

charity that raises money for disadvantaged children in Israel and a group that Rivka has been involved with for forty years. Rabbi Cohen told the gathering the story of the singing soldiers who sang *Hayom yom Shabbat kodesh* for hours and hours and hours. It was Rivka's first time hearing about it.

***

It was while I was living in Israel that I started to become famous for my unique way of performing the Sukkot mitzva of *na'anuim*. *Na'anuim* refers to "shaking the lulav and etrog," which really involves holding four specific plant species – a *lulav, etrog, hadas* and *arava* (date palm, yellow citron, myrtle, and willow) – in a special way and shaking them in every direction. I alone, maybe on planet Earth, am able to make the four plants vibrate without moving my hands, at all. For proof, you can see me demonstrating this personal accomplishment on a YouTube video. While doing *na'anuim*, I always sing a particular prayer using a Leningrad *nigun*. Shlomo Nakdimon, one of the most well-known journalists in Israel, used to enjoy watching me perform *na'anuim*. When he was a boy, his father would make sure to wake him up on time for him to get to *shul* to watch me do it. In the meantime, other *shuls* would empty when their congregants would leave to come and see me perform *na'anuim* in my unique way.

***

When I lived in Uzhhorod, we had a non-Jewish neighbor whose name was Petrov. Petrov was a good man, a strong man, a Russian. But he was poor. He had a small ground-floor apartment with a sitting room and a kitchen, some *shmatas*, and a tiny yard. He also had a wife and two children. He was extremely good to his family, and to mine. My parents used to hire him. He did various tasks for us like cut wood and clean the yard. It was not like today, with electricity to make things easy. He always worked hard and did a great job.

But he could not do things for us on Shabbat because he was a *Szabbotnik*. *Szabbotnikkers* – as they are called in Russia – are Christians, but they do not observe Sundays as the Sabbath, but rather, like Jews, they keep the Sabbath on Saturdays. Petrov used to hire a young gentile girl who came to his house on Saturday to perform all the jobs he could not do, including warming food in the oven. Jews are not allowed to hire non-Jews to do cooking or other forbidden chores on Shabbat, but, based on Petrov's habits, I could see that *Szabbotnikkers* had different rules.

Twenty-five years later when I lived in Israel, I ran into Petrov. It happened one day during a weekend when Rivka and I were in Haifa to visit my cousin. On Saturday morning as I walked to *shul*, I heard a loud screech behind me, the brakes of a bus obviously. I kept my face turned away so as to avoid watching Shabbat laws being breached. I am always disheartened to see fellow Jews being *meḥalel Shabbat*, breaking Shabbat. Haifa is still the only city in Israel where public buses, in fact all means of public transportation, operate on the Jewish Sabbath. Why did Haifa start to do this? Because, in the beginning, the city was run by communists, who had the same philosophy as many early Israelis. Communists do not care about religious observance, but in Haifa, unlike every other city in Israel, the communists adamantly refused to succumb to pressure by religious citizens to ban public transportation on Saturdays.

So here I was on Shabbat in Haifa where city officials belligerently were running the buses.

But on this particular Saturday, a big man jumped off the bus, ran up behind me, and embraced me. He screamed, "Moshele, you are alive, Moshele!" He must have recognized me from my unique style of walking, I do not know. I had no idea who had me

Chapter Four: Israel

in a bear hug and who was talking to me like we were long lost friends. He finally freed me from his arms and I could see who it was. "Petrov!" I yelled, "What are you doing here?" He told me he had had a lot of trouble with the communists being a *Szabbotnik*. "*Szabbotnikkers* are considered religious," he explained. "So, I saved all the money I could and I came with my children and my wife to Israel." Because he could drive, Petrov explained, he got a job as a Haifa bus driver. I said, "Listen I want to talk to you, because I want to hear about the last days with my father and other family members. Come over to my cousin's on Saturday night. I can't do anything now, because it is Shabbat. Bring your wife and kids. I really want to see them too." He said okay, took my address, and walked back to the bus he was driving. I yelled after him: "Petrov, today is Shabbat, why are you driving?" He shouted back, "Moshe, two years ago I converted to Judaism, so now, like many secular Israeli Jews, I drive my car and bus on Shabbat!" I decided not to say another word. I nodded to feign understanding, and walked away shaking my head.

Telling the story of Petrov and his bus, and mentioning food rationing earlier, reminds me of something I witnessed on a bus one day. I was sitting, looking out the window, minding my own business, waiting for the bus to arrive at my stop, when I heard, "squawk, squawk, squawk!" I saw a man at the front fussing with a moving package. I realized immediately he was hiding a chicken that he was of course taking home to kill and cook, illegally. As fate would have it, a police officer jumped on the bus and started to check bags for extra food. The chicken started to squawk again. The food policeman stopped what he was doing. With a serious look on his face, he lifted his head, turned his ear slightly upward, and listened intently. He could definitely hear it, the illegal chicken. Then the squawking stopped. But the officer was not fooled. He took three long strides to the front of the bus. He stopped and looked around at the seated bus riders. As the cop looked directly at him, the man with the chicken cupped one hand beside his mouth and blurted out: "Squawk. Squawk. Squawk. Squawk!" making it seem that the silly noise had come from his mouth all along. The bus stopped. The embarrassed policeman got off and all the riders burst out laughing.

***

After four years, I absolutely could not take it anymore. Everything was too difficult for me. The endless soldiers' funerals were too sad, filled with the tears of their families and mine. These ceremonies kept bringing my mind back to the long months in the concentration camps. I'd had enough. The IDF still did not want to let me go, but too bad. I had received an offer from Basel, Switzerland, to be a cantor there for one year. The contract was to begin after the High Holy Days. I had another contract to sing during the High Holy Days in Antwerp, Belgium. So, Rivka and I flew to Europe in 1952. But things did not turn out the way we planned.

Chapter Four: Israel

At a military hospital in Israel

The Life of Moshele Der Zinger

Memorial for the IDF air force

Chapter Four: Israel

Moshe and Rivka's wedding

The Life of Moshele Der Zinger

Portrait from South Africa

Chapter Four: Israel

An officer and chief cantor of the Israeli army

Chapter Five
Antwerp

Rivka and I arrived in Antwerp, Belgium, excited about the next adventure in our lives. It was 1952. Though we originally did not intend to stay in Belgium, I ended up being hired as the city's chief *ḥazan*, a position I was honored to hold for the next six years. I came to this magnificent, ancient, and bustling city – perhaps my favorite in the entire world – about one year before the arrival of Rabbi Chaim Kreiswirth, usually referred to as Rav Kreiswirth, due to his enormous contributions to rejuvenating Orthodox Judaism in Antwerp, and also due to his other significant accomplishments elsewhere in the Jewish world. I was blessed to know and work with this distinguished *rav* for the next three years.

The Chief Rabbi of Antwerp's Congregation Machzikei Hadas, and a much esteemed *talmid ḥakham* from a very young age, Rav Kreiswirth helped found the now famous post-secondary yeshiva in Jerusalem, Mercaz HaTorah, a school that caters to English-speaking students of the Diaspora. Born only a few years before me in 1918, in Wojnicz, Poland, he fled to Lithuania after the German invasion in 1939. After surviving the Holocaust, he went back to his home country, where he tried to help Jewish children who had been protected by Catholics during World War II. From 1947 to 1953 he lived in the United States, where he served as *rosh yeshiva* at the heavyweight Hebrew Theological College in Skokie, Illinois. Against the advice of internationally prominent Jewish leaders at the time, he moved to Antwerp in 1953, where his main focus until his death in 2001 was to rebuild the Belgian Jewish community in that city.

I am certainty humbled and proud that Rav Kreiswirth once gave a whole *derasha* about my work. He discussed how I sang particular words, why I sang them a certain way, and what each different emphasis meant. He pointed out that *ḥazanut* is not just songs. When a *ḥazan* is singing, he is translating and explaining words and meanings as he goes. I felt privileged to have my singing spoken about in such a meaningful sermon.

***

Antwerp has a world-class diamond industry, but it also has a fascinating history, which Rivka and I were eager to learn when we arrived, especially the role of the Jews.

The Jews first appeared in Antwerp in the thirteenth century, around the time of Henry III, the Duke of Brabant. The Jews felt his wrath in the year 1261, when he made it known that he wanted them exiled and killed. Seeking refuge in the early 1500s, Spanish "crypto Jews" – those who professed another religion – began settling in Antwerp. Through the centuries, they were often refused citizenship and experienced other forms of discrimination. But they survived and grew to form a community of thirty-five thousand before World War II, a community greatly contributing to the diamond industry.

Chapter Five: Antwerp

On April 14, 1941, the city's Jewish community suffered through the so-called "Antwerp pogrom," wherein a number of pro-Nazi groups burned down two synagogues, broke the windows of Jewish businesses, destroyed religious icons, and badgered Jewish residents. The following year, in September, about 1,500 Jewish men were coerced into labor in northern France. With assistance from local police, three separate deportations from Antwerp occurred before November 1942. By 1945, only fifteen thousand of the city's Jews had survived. In other words, the Holocaust claimed about 57 percent of the city's Jews.

Following the war, Antwerp again became a large center for ultra-Orthodox Judaism, partly due to the efforts of Rav Kreiswirth. Hasidic Jews were attracted by him and to the rebuilt modern city, to the point that about fifteen thousand Hasidim live there today. Some of the many types of hasidic groups in Antwerp include Pshevorsk, Satmar, Belz, Bobov, Ger, Skver, and Klausenburg. Antwerp has an impressive network of *shuls*, Jewish stores, *ḥederim*, and associations.

***

Rivka and I were originally invited to Antwerp in 1952 just for the *yamim noraim*. We agreed to come for the High Holy Days on one condition: that we be able to leave quickly after they ended so we could be in Basel, Switzerland, in order to start my one-year contract, which I had already signed. The permanent *ḥazan* in Basel had left, and I was to take his place for at least twelve months.

I performed a beautiful series of *ḥazanut* in Antwerp to finish off the High Holy Days, after which Rivka and I ran to our hotel to retrieve our things and take the next train out. But when we got there, our suitcases were gone. We were surprised, to say the least, but not upset as we knew that the *shul* officials who had hired me had a key to our hotel room. We were sure they must have taken our packed bags, though for what reason we had no idea.

We rushed to the front desk to ask if the clerks there knew anything, if they saw what had happened to our bags. We were told a message was left for us to go to the Jewish Community Center. We ran to the JCC and, out of breath, I asked the *shul* officials, "Where are our bags? Why did you take them?" A member of the ḥazan High Holy Days Recruitment Committee directed us to another room. We did as we were told. In that room, we found the rest of the dozen or so committee members, sitting patiently. One of them, Mr. Nyfeld, the *shul* president, explained to us that the congregation had never heard me sing before the holidays, and that now everyone was in love with the way I *davened*, the way I made prayers sound, my voice. "Unfortunately," he continued, "the congregation threatened to lynch us, all the committee members, if we let you leave Antwerp." I paused as I took in the enormity of this threat, and then I reminded them: "But I have a contract with Basel." Nyfeld answered, "No problem. We will handle everything." He rose out of his chair, leaned toward me, and again spoke: "Moshele, please, you have a wonderful city here. You will be our chief cantor. You cannot turn that down." Not wanting to have any lynch-style murders on my conscience, I agreed. The committee paid a total of five thousand dollars to break my contract with Basel. In 1952, five thousand dollars was a lot of money.

When I started working in Antwerp, everyone *davened* in a temporary *shul*, as the Nazis had destroyed the city's biggest synagogue. After the war, the municipal government decided that this important house of worship should be completely renovated. The rebuilding was completed in 1953, to a dazzling finish. It was called the Great Synagogue of Antwerp, not to be confused with the Great Synagogue of Belgium, which is also called the Great Synagogue of Europe. That year, there was a great opening ceremony for the Great Synagogue of Antwerp. It had a great choir, a great rabbi, and, of course, a great *ḥazan*. I led the service. The great grand opening was everything we hoped it would be.

As we got to know Antwerp, we happily discovered the large number of *shtiebels* dotting the local streets. I thought this was terrific, but as it became known that I was the chief *ḥazan* of the city, many of those *shtiebels* emptied, as their members came to my *shul* – the Great Synagogue of Antwerp – to hear me sing. This was, of course, flattering, but it also caused some problems. For example, one Shabbat, a tiny *shul gabbai* marched rather stiffly into our sanctuary and right up to the *bima*. He cleared his throat to interrupt the service. In a kind and gracious tone, our rabbi asked him what he could do for him. "There is no minyan at our *shul* because everyone is here," he stated angrily. "Please come!" A few people giggled, but a couple of dozen rose and went out the door with him to help his cause.

In 1953, our choirmaster sadly passed away. This meant our great *shul* needed a new person to take his place. Some of us had heard about a famous choirmaster and conductor who had left his position in Jerusalem and was looking for a new job. His name was Shlomo Goldhor, he was twenty-two years old, and we felt right away he would be a good fit for us. We brought him to Antwerp. His plane arrived in Brussels, which is only thirty minutes away by car from where I lived. I drove to the airport to welcome him and pick him up. This was 1953, remember, when Jerusalem was not much more than a village. In Brussels, Shlomo was not ready for what he saw for the first time in his life. Escalators! Moving stairs! He traveled up and down them about ten times. We brought him home to live with Rivka and me for a few weeks until he found an apartment.

While he was staying with us, he wanted to mail a letter to his family. We did not have any stamps, so I took him to the dispensing machine close to the train station. I gave him some money and told him to go to the big box, put his coin in the slot, press the button, and then wait for the stamps to come out. He had never seen such a device and, again, he was thrilled. I still had inside me that big brother trickster that had worked so well with my younger siblings. I noticed a large, fat man with his belly button sticking out leaning against a wall next door to the station. I said, "Shlomo, to use the stamp you must do this. Go over and push that man's belly button, which will cause his tongue to stick out. Then you can wet your stamp on his tongue and put it on the letter." Before I could tell him I was joking, he raced over and pushed the poor man's belly button. Thank God the man had a sense of humor, though I still wonder why. I thought for sure he would hit Shlomo, which would probably have been more legal than what Shlomo did to him. At that moment, Shlomo yelled, "Moshe, something is wrong. The tongue did not stick out."

***

Living in Europe again, Rivka and I were privileged to travel almost constantly all over the continent. I gave concerts in just about every country, including England, the Netherlands, and France. We visited so many major cities: Amsterdam, Strasbourg, Vienna, London, Manchester, Glasgow, Liverpool, Paris, and on and on. I went to some of these places many times. It was like a fantastic dream. The way I gave concerts was like this: tell a story, sing a related song, tell another story, sing another related song, and so on until the end of the concert. People seemed to love the stories almost as much as the songs. Like every good Hasid, I always told stories with a moral, or an uplifting message. There is no other kind of hasidic tale.

I cannot possibly tell you about every concert or tour, but one or two stand out. The European road trip we took still makes us laugh to this day. In 1956, I was invited to Zurich, where I was to give a big performance. Because we lived in Europe, we took

Chapter Five: Antwerp

the train almost everywhere. It was so convenient. But friends of ours, the Boyoviches, made an offer we could not turn down. Mr. Boyovich said, "My wife and I are going by car to Basel the same week because I have a sister there. We'll be driving right through Zurich, so we can take you." We thought this was perfect as it would give us time with our good friends. We were also excited to see places we'd never seen, including small cities in France and the countryside of Luxembourg, the latter being just about the smallest country in the entire world.

An important part of this story is that, until we came to Canada in 1976, we traveled on Israeli passports. We set out with the Boyoviches and arrived at the Luxembourg customs and immigration office, which comprised five officials sitting in a little hut. Two came out to our car and through the window asked for our passports. We gave the documents and watched as the Luxembourg officials did their job and checked the passports carefully. About five minutes later they brought the Boyoviches' passports back, but not ours. So, we sat and we sat and we waited and we waited. It felt like a very long thirty minutes. We thought, "What are they doing? Maybe they think we are smuggling diamonds or something. Why don't they come back with our passports?" Eventually, another official came. He walked all around the car, looked inside it, stood back, looked inside again. Then another customs agent came out of the hut and did the same thing. Then yet another worker. We were getting nervous. We didn't have a clue what was going on. Finally, they gave us back our passports, saying, "Thank you, you can go." Our friend said, "Wait a second. What happened here? Why did you take so long with the Kraus' passports?" They explained.

To understand the end of this anecdote, you must remember this was 1956, the time of the Suez War, when Egypt nationalized the Suez Canal. This act of aggression prompted Israel, Britain, and France to invade the Egyptian Sinai. The three allies won a few military objectives, but withdrew quickly after being threatened with serious economic consequences by US President Dwight Eisenhower and the Soviet Union, thereby terminating once and for all whatever international power the British Empire fantasized it had left. At the same time, the Suez crisis launched Israel – which won back some crucial navigation rights – onto the world stage.

Getting back to our car trip, the Luxembourg officials told us they had never in their lives seen Israeli passports. They were intrigued, they said, and they wanted to show ours to all their colleagues. They had never seen Israelis in the flesh either, so they were also curious to see what we looked like.

We continued on our way feeling relieved. Eventually, we arrived at the French border and some very small town of which to this day I cannot remember the name. I do remember clearly though that it was late at night, and it was raining so hard we could not see clearly in front of us. We decided to stop and stay the night, and continue driving the next day. We went to a small hotel where, as usual, we had to turn in our passports at the front desk. They were to be returned when we checked out. Each couple took a room. I said to Rivka I would take a shower first. As I was showering, there was a knock on the door. Rivka answered it and she saw three men, all dressed in perfectly pressed suits, looking dreadfully serious. Now you have to understand that in those days, passports listed all kinds of characteristics, including height, weight, eye color, and profession. As the chief cantor of Antwerp, my passport said chief minister. In French, this translates to premier minister, or prime minister.

To help explain how this happened, it is a fact that since the days of Napoleon, clergy of all religions in some European countries, including Belgium, were paid by the government. I am not sure if this is still so. Thus, as I was essentially an employee of the Belgian government, my passport said "minister." Baffling, I know.

Chapter Five: Antwerp

Are you starting to imagine the confusion? After we had gone upstairs, the front desk clerks had studied my Israeli passport. They concluded I was the prime minister of Israel! I think they all shouted at once: "The prime minister of Israel is here!" They immediately called the hotel manager, who called the mayor, who called the local newspaper editor. All three were now dressed up in their finest clothes and standing at our hotel room door.

By now I was at the door too, wrapped in a towel, looking quite perturbed. The mayor said, "We apologize, Mr. Prime Minister. If we'd known you were coming, the local government would have made a big welcome party for you. We would have invited the press. We would have put out the Israeli flag." As soon as I heard the word flag, I understood the misunderstanding. Rivka on the other hand was almost fainting. She thought maybe she had married some kind of important political spy. What entered my mind at this point had been happening to me since I was boy, whenever I realized I was in a situation where I could pull a harmless prank. My hair still dripping wet, I went up close to the hotel manager, I held my finger to my lips and said, "Shhh... Please keep this a secret. I am *incognito* on a clandestine mission. Only the highest of high officials know."

Because I did not speak French, and just to make absolutely sure they understood the importance of my assignment, I said, "Wait. I will get my private associates. They speak better French." I got dressed quickly and went next door. I called out to my friends, hoping they had not yet gone to bed, and mostly that they would play along. They came out and asked what all the commotion was about. I told the story again about our surreptitious work. They nodded their heads aggressively, and explained everything in French. The three men promised to keep the top-secret information to themselves, shook everybody's hands, and left down the elevator. When they had gone we laughed for a solid fifteen minutes, then went to sleep, completely comfortable in the knowledge that we were safe and the Israeli prime minister's classified endeavor would probably never be revealed.

We left early the next day, about 5 a.m. As we talked and laughed some more in the car about the incident, my friend commented, "You should have told those guys the truth, no?" "No," I answered, "it was too funny." But for weeks afterward, we kept looking over our shoulders. And we checked every French and Israeli newspaper to make sure the Shin Bet, the Israeli security agency, was not looking for an imposter of the Israeli prime minister.

One more memorable incident happened on our legendary trip with the Boyoviches. We arrived in Switzerland and went right to Basel to see some sights and visit Mr. Boyovich's sister. While there, we learned that the Boyoviches had spent the entire war in Basel. This meant, according to Mr. Boyovich, that he knew many, many people in the city. "Everybody here knows me," he bragged. "Why, you ask? During the war years I didn't have a work permit, so I couldn't get a job. I had a lot of time on my hands. I used to walk the streets, stop in all the cafes, drink ersatz coffee, and talk to people. I had nothing else to do. So, now, everybody knows me here." As he was busy telling us about his tremendous popularity in Basel, a young man came over and stood beside us. Boyovich stopped talking, looked at the curious onlooker, and asked him, "Do you know me?" He answered, "I do not know you, but I know Cantor Kraus." We, including an embarrassed Mr. Boyovich, could not help but laugh. It turned out the young man lived in Basel, but he was learning in a yeshiva in Antwerp, where of course everybody knew Ḥazan Kraus.

***

While in Europe, I was invited to give concerts and *daven* in many cities. One of my most memorable experiences began in Glasgow, Scotland. I say "began" because it was a long, intricate occurrence,

Chapter Five: Antwerp

involving police in two countries, a colorful gift for Rivka, and a bloody nose for an unsuspecting pedestrian.

A synagogue in Glasgow had invited me to *daven* for a Shabbat, and then give a performance on the following Sunday. Scheduled to leave for Antwerp on Monday afternoon, I was left alone that Monday morning in the Mendelsohn home, where I'd been a guest for the entire weekend. The Mendelsohn family had left for work and school. It was a beautiful day, so I decided to take a walk in the city. My eye caught sight of an absolutely breathtaking outfit in a store window. A mannequin was wearing a plaid skirt, a plaid blouse, a plaid vest, plaid gloves, and a plaid hat, and was holding both a plaid umbrella and a plaid purse. I thought I was in love all over again. I just had to buy the entire getup for Rivka, who, for a reason I do not remember, had stayed behind in Antwerp. I went into the store and explained to the manager – as best I could since I did not speak English – that I wanted to buy the mannequin's clothes and accessories for my wife. He asked what size my wife was, using hand movements. Since this was the first time I had ever bought her clothes, I did not know. I began to search the store for a woman my wife's size to use as an example, but to no avail. So, I stepped outside and looked up and down the sidewalk. I saw a woman just the right height and weight. I marched up to her confidently and began signaling her to follow me into the store. I said in broken English, "You come. My wife." Meanwhile, my hands were making flailing gestures, going back and forth pointing at the two of us and then the store.

She ran. I chased her. She ran faster. I ran faster, too. Finally, we arrived at the police station. Unable to understand me, the police officer took me to a phone where I called Mr. Mendelsohn. He came to the station right away. "You brought us so much joy and pleasure," he scolded me in Yiddish. "Now you go and get arrested and shame us." He finally gave me a chance to explain and everyone laughed, a little nervously. The policeman accompanied me and the lovely lady back to the store, just to make sure I wasn't lying. The store clerks backed up my story, and the forgiving woman even tried on the outfit to help me before I bought it.

When I got home I laid all the clothes and accessories out on our bed to surprise Rivka when she came into the bedroom. Upon seeing the gifts, she screamed, "What did you do? How did you know my size? There is no way this is going to fit me." But it did, perfectly, and she loved it. Being the naive young girl that she was, she put on the entire ensemble, including the hat and gloves, and went out for a walk. Only one minor car accident occurred when several drivers screeched to a halt; they stopped watching the road to watch Rivka. Then a pedestrian turned to look at her and he walked into a street sign, banging his nose but not injuring himself badly. Police were called about the car accidents. They could not be legally blamed on me or Rivka. Thankfully, no one was hurt. Rivka continued to wear the high-quality plaid clothes and accessories, except that she was careful to show off each piece individually, and use it with other garments. I can happily report that she wore the outfit safely for the next thirty years, until she could no longer stand to look at any of the parts, at which time she sent them all to Israel for our nieces to enjoy wearing.

***

It was not unheard of for Jewish children who had been sheltered to come out of hiding after the war as converted Christians. It was always upsetting, and – despite the best efforts of certain Israelis and other determined Jews to reclaim these children – not all of them came back to Judaism. Virtually all of them were orphans, having lost their parents in the death camps. While living in Antwerp, Rivka and I were invited to a Shabbat bar mitzva where I was to perform in Grenoble, a beautiful town with a 650-year-old university in southeastern France, and which happened to be the center of the first major scandal dealing with conversions of Jewish children. It was to a Catholic school in this town in 1944 that the parents of two Jewish boys, Robert and Gerald Finaly, sent them for their safety. After the war, after both the mother and father were murdered in Auschwitz, the boys' aunt and uncle, who lived in Israel, wanted to retrieve them and raise them. But in 1948, the boys were baptized without the family's knowledge or permission. The situation became an international scandal when a police investigation uncovered that some Catholic nuns and priests had secretly kidnapped and smuggled the children into Spain in 1953. Due to the endless hard work of their many individual and institutional advocates, including one lawyer – whose name was Mr. Kaner – the boys were ultimately reunited with their family after an eight-year-long fight in the courts.

Kaner, a Grenoble resident, was Jewish but also a committed atheist. He came to the bar mitzva we attended to honor his friend, the father of the boy celebrating. He told me, adamantly, that he did not believe in anything. He said he never *davened*, never observed Shabbat, and, *davka* – despite expectations to the contrary – on purpose, he never ate kosher. He did not care about being a Jew at all. I sang at the bar mitzva the way I usually sing, making all the beautiful Shabbat songs sound heavenly. I sang Musaf, an extra prayer said on certain days, like Shabbat, in a particularly heart-rending and inspiring way. Not being able to control his feelings, Kaner got excited. "Yeah, yeah, now there's a prayer!" he noted loudly, disturbing a few people sitting near him. As time passed, he became even more energized, particularly when I sang the mourners' *Kaddish*. Near the end of the service, he couldn't restrain himself at all. He bounded up onto the *bima* and burst out crying. He clapped his hands together, obviously very emotional, and yelped: "From now on I want to be a religious Jew!" He faced the rabbi, sobbing: "I want to be a good Jew." This unbelievable incident was covered in all the French newspapers and beyond, because Kaner was a well-known lawyer. It really was incredible. He eventually went to America, changed his name, and, if I am correct, continued to practice Judaism.

***

Two truly wonderful Antwerp experiences have occurred since I have been living in Ottawa. When the rebuilt Great Synagogue of Antwerp was fifty years old, in 2003, I was invited back to celebrate with the Jewish community. I had led the special service fifty years earlier, and the community remembered me and wanted me to come back and conduct the special service again. Many others were also invited, such as members of the old choir, including the choirmaster Shlomo Goldhor, originally from Jerusalem. After the service, there was a big *kiddush* – a repast before the noon meal. Then, on *motzei Shabbat*, the Saturday night after Shabbat ends, the community gave a party for us. At the party, I told a group of people some of the cute stories about Shlomo, including the belly button incident. Shlomo laughed along with everyone else. I was pleased, because not everyone is such a good sport when tricks are played on them. Present for the Sunday celebration were representatives of the king and top officials of the government. People came from all over Europe for this Sunday gathering, which was covered by all the press, including newspapers, radio, and television. I was deeply honored. It was a huge compliment that they remembered me. I was humbled also because they published a brochure about me that said: "The public in our city who love ḥazanut are invited to a special Shabbat service with our distinguished cantor, the greatest cantor in our generation. He's known all over the world. He performs such beautiful *tefillot*. He was in our city fifty years ago with a choir and with the conductor of the choir, Dr. Andre Deutsch. *Kiddush* following." Imagine that. They called me "the greatest cantor in our generation." No other Jewish community in the world has ever said that about me. This was a tremendous honor.

In 2014, the Great Synagogue of Antwerp invited Rivka and me again for a Shabbat service and a huge *kiddush* afterward. I was already 91 years old, but we had to go for one last trip back to the city I loved more than any other. By that time, many of our friends had passed away, but we were excited to meet their children and grandchildren. For example, we were happy to meet the president of the Jewish community, Willy Khan, whose parents had been our close friends. Every person has two sides to his life: the public side and a private side. I prefer my public side; why? It is very simple. In public, I am loved, honored, respected, admired; I'm referred to as the man who speaks to God. In private, it is slightly different. In private, I take out the garbage.

***

If life had been different, I would have stayed forever in Antwerp. I loved the city and the Jewish community. My position required a lot of hard work. I had to work all week. It was not easy. Often, I had to work on changing something in my singing. People get tired of the same tunes, week after week. They like to hear new melodies. I had to spend time writing music and composing songs. No, it wasn't easy at all, but that was no problem for me. I loved Antwerp. I would never have moved from there, if it were not for my wife. I would be in Antwerp to this day. That was my best position ever.

But my Rivka – after living in sunny Israel – could not stand Antwerp's weather. In that almost perfect city, there are only two types of dry conditions: just before the rain and just after the rain. It was a wet climate. Rivka became an insomniac due to the weather, after she'd grown up so accustomed to the sun. The doctor told us weather can wreak havoc with some people's minds.

The Life of Moshele Der Zinger

He recommended that we move to a sunnier climate. So, in 1958 we moved to Johannesburg, South Africa, where we stayed for twelve years.

Opening of the rebuilt synagogue in Antwerp

Chapter Six

Johannesburg

I f it was a comfortable climate she wanted, Rivka could not have picked a better place than South Africa, where about seventy-five thousand Jews live today and where I happened to get hired at the prestigious Johannesburg Oxford Synagogue. The official tourist description is telling. "South Africa is a subtropical region, moderated by oceans on two sides of the triangle-shaped country and [by] the altitude of the interior plateau," says directasia.com, in the advice section. "These account for the warm, temperate conditions so typical of South Africa – and so popular with its foreign visitors." According to the website, the coastline is almost 2,800 kilometers long, and goes from a northwest desert border with Namibia, "down the icy Skeleton Coast to Cape Agulhas," then north along the extensive beaches and emerald hills on the shores of the Indian Ocean, to the perimeter with Mozambique in the northeast. Rivka wanted to escape the rain, and she succeeded. Sunshine is practically another name for South Africa. Its annual average rainfall is 464 millimeters, versus the average rainfall for planet Earth, which is about 860 millimeters.

Jews in South Africa have been part of the country's long and controversial development since the birth of that country. Interestingly, Jewish cartologists and scientists from Portugal were part of explorer Vasco da Gama's team when in 1497 he landed on the Cape of Good Hope on his way to India. Over the centuries, they were present through South Africa's tumultuous development into the country it is today, including travels into South Africa's interior and Rhodesia, the Boer War, apartheid, and the birth of the African National Congress.

Despite the fact that some of its leaders spoke out against apartheid, Israel maintained its diplomatic status with South Africa throughout the apartheid period, though relations became strained at certain times. Increased South African violence in the 1970s caused a major exodus of white citizens, and Jews were no exception. Between 1970 and 1992, more than thirty-nine thousand Jews left South Africa. They were understandably afraid about the future. Children increasingly were sent to live and study in European and North American countries, where they ended up remaining permanently.

Today, the part of the Jewish community that has survived and thrived is the ultra-Orthodox, which now represents about 20 percent of the Jewish community in Johannesburg and under 10 percent in other cities. Levels of antisemitism are consistently low compared with those of other major Diaspora countries and the intermarriage rate is a mere 5 percent. Many of the Jews who have stayed believe that post-apartheid South Africa needs their backing, and that it will soon pay social and economic dividends.

When Rivka and I settled in Johannesburg – which today is home to South Africa's largest Jewish community of about fifty thousand people – we were following in the footsteps of thousands of Jewish immigrants. Many came to earn their wealth in gold.

Chapter Six: Johannesburg

The Great Synagogue – modeled after a mosque in Istanbul – was opened in 1914. Johannesburg's other major *shul*, the Poswohl Synagogue in Mooi Street – started by Lithuanian immigrants – was recently declared a national landmark. Over the years, Johannesburg saw the development of numerous Jewish organizations: the ḥevra Kaddisha; a soup kitchen; an ambulance service: a bikkur ḥolim group for visiting the sick; and a Jewish hospital, which was erected in 1896 to cater to Orthodox Jews who demanded kosher food and who were more comfortable with Jewish doctors and nurses. Though today it is part of the Johannesburg General Hospital, it still offers kosher meals for those who want them. There is also a Jewish museum containing, among other artifacts, two Torah scrolls found in Mozambique, as well as ancient, African-sculpted, precious, stone mezuza covers. For centuries, it has been a widely held mitzva to encase in individual covers – often made of wood or ceramic – a piece of parchment with specific Torah verses written on it. Mezuzot, with the carefully written holy words inside, are nailed to the doorposts of almost all the rooms of Orthodox Jewish households, as well as the front door.

There was a period of exodus from central Johannesburg in the 1960s and 1970s. During this time, many of the city's historic synagogues were forced to close or move. The Great Synagogue itself moved four miles away before it shut down completely in 1994. It is now a church, but the Star of David and the sign saying Hebrew High School still remain.

***

Our decision to live in South Africa really began after I was invited in 1957 to give a performance there. I had been asked to give a solo benefit concert for a new yeshiva that the Jewish community was anxious to open. I was happy to do this for free. It was held in the elegant Empire Theatre, which sadly no longer exists as a show hall. Accompanied by a marvelous pianist, I sang ten songs that were enjoyed by some 1,500 people. The event was a huge success. Yeshiva College, also known as Bnei Akiva Yeshiva, opened soon after the concert, and fortunately is still open to this day.

For some reason that I now forget, Rivka remained in Antwerp when I gave the benefit concert for the new yeshiva. When I came back to Belgium, she asked me what the weather was like. I told her I had been offered two full-time positions. "But what is the weather like?" she asked again. I told her I was not considering either job at the moment. "The weather," she stated loudly. "What is it like?" I mentioned both jobs had some promise. "You are driving me crazy, forget it," she exclaimed, throwing her hands in the air and turning to leave the room. "Oh, by the way," I called after her, "the weather is gorgeous all the time. It's spring all year." That was it. The decision had been made. "We are going there to live," she announced, not even thinking to ask in which cities were my job offers, what salary proposals I had, or what the working conditions would be like. Nothing. It was a sunny place, so we were going to live there. That was it.

We arrived in Johannesburg in 1958, home at the time to some sixty thousand Jews, about half of South Africa's total number. Rivka's English was quite good, but I did not speak a word of it. I spoke five other languages, but not English. Language aside, one of the first things we both noticed was how well-dressed people were in the cities. We thought this was fantastic, as both of us always tried to wear stylish and tasteful clothes. In fact, when a newspaper rated the best-dressed men in Johannesburg, I was number six. I couldn't believe it. Why was I not number one, or maybe number two?

There was a ladies' guild at the Oxford Synagogue where I worked. Every Shabbat morning after services – which started at about 8 a.m. and ended before lunch at 11 a.m. – the guild prepared a *kiddush*. Because the women knew that I did not comprehend

Chapter Six: Johannesburg

English, they prepared a little Yiddish welcome party during the *kiddush*. For this they invited a lady, Alushka Freeman, to speak in Yiddish in my honor. Alushka was very distinguished, and she took the time to tell the story of her life. Like me, she was a survivor of Bergen-Belsen. "In Bergen-Belsen, almost no one had a name," she said, pronouncing the words in perfect Yiddish. "The Nazis gave us numbers. Each prisoner was a number. But there were a few outstanding individuals who were each given a name. One young man we called 'Moshele *der Zinger*.' Why did we call him that? Because almost every day, after we were finished with whatever labor or boredom we were forced to endure, when we were hungry and thirsty and physically hurting and tired, when we used to practically crawl back to our barracks – where about two hundred women lived on top of each other – this man named Moshele *der Zinger* used to go from one barrack to the next and sing to us in Yiddish. Usually, he sang cheerful songs just to encourage us and to give us a tiny bit of happiness. We did not know who he was, but we called him Moshele *der Zinger*." When she finished speaking I went to her, and said in Yiddish, "Alushka, I am Moshele *der Zinger*." She burst out crying. I burst out crying, all the ladies burst out crying. There was so much crying, even though on Shabbat you are not supposed to be sad and cry. But no one could help it. Everyone was moved by this story.

Soon afterward, the Johannesburg Oxford Synagogue offered me a contract for life.

***

Rivka and I had an elderly neighbor, a Jewish woman living on her own except for her two servants, a maid and a chauffeur. The two servants each came from a different tribe with completely different dialects, so they could not communicate with each other in their native languages. But each servant had worked for two different Jewish employers for many years before they were hired by our neighbor, and from their former separate employers, they both learned both English and Yiddish. Our neighbor, their new employer, could only speak English. When the servants needed or wanted to speak with her, they spoke English, and they talked to each other in English. However, when they wanted to talk about their employer without her knowing what they said, they spoke to each other in Yiddish! It was hilarious to listen to these two black South Africans speaking perfect Yiddish. Rivka and I enjoyed listening to them gossip in Yiddish about their unsuspecting boss. The Jewish neighbor asked us what the Yiddish words meant, and why we were laughing. We got good at thinking on our feet and never telling her anything negative about what was being said concerning her.

Yet another story: One day in the late 1950s, I was recording some music in my office and the phone rang. When I answered the call, I did not realize I had forgotten to turn off the tape recorder. The person on the phone asked to speak to our maid. So, I called her and she answered the phone and spoke in her own tribal language, whatever it was. When she finished and was about to leave the room, I realized that the tape machine had recorded her side of the entire conversation.

For fun, I played her whole conversation as she stood there totally amazed. She had never before seen anything like this. She stood in total silence and slowly walked backward until she reached the door. She backed out and disappeared for the rest of the day, not saying a word during the entire episode.

The next morning, there was a knock on the door and there was our maid, along with several other maids from other apartments. They did not believe her when she told them a machine was able to speak her language in her voice, and they all wanted to see this for themselves. I invited them to come inside and played

Chapter Six: Johannesburg

the tape. Each one of them reacted the same way as our maid had the day before. They backed out and left without saying a word.

Eventually, our maid came back and resumed her duties. From that moment on, she never went near the tape machine. In fact, she dusted all around it but never touched the machine.

***

During our years in South Africa, either in Johannesburg or through our travels in that vast country, our lives were enriched by meeting so many people from different walks of life. We constantly would feel the legacy of the many European countries involved in the making of Africa. One practice that held steadfast was the British tea tradition. Tea was offered and served many times a day. Rivka, who does not drink tea, always made sure to inform hotel clerks that no maid was to knock at our door at 6 a.m. to bring us tea. She did just that as we stopped at a hotel on a trip to Cape Town, and yet, there was a knock at our door the following morning, at six. Rivka opened the door to find a hotel maid carrying a pot of steaming liquid. "I asked *not* to be awakened with tea in the morning," she said to the maid. The maid replied "Yes, Madam, so I didn't bring you tea. I brought you coffee."

***

At one point, I was invited back to give another concert at the Empire Theatre. For all the hundreds and hundreds of performances I have given throughout my life, none has given me a review quite like the one I received after my second show at the Empire. Until today, this review remains my favorite, mainly because it is both intellectual and positive. "Kraus gave a rich and varied display of the cantor's art," the review began. "Mr. Kraus' voice is that of a lyric tenor, warmed with emotion and dramatic color. In a program consisting mostly of liturgical airs, exacting in their range and florid figuration, his voice never lost quality or sweetness. Mr. Kraus, in fact, has easy command of all the ornaments of the cantor's art, but uses them with discretion and without ever losing significance. He sustains his top notes with grandeur and amplitude, slips into a silken mezzo-voce, and floats his divisions (which are every cantor's or oratorio singer's pride) with precision and grace. His style is intimately of the synagogue, but the operatic touch is there, too, and with it, the catch in the throat that could be either. A cantor, in short, that every congregation must warm to, and last night's audience responded readily and enthusiastically. The final comic song (with a refrain for the audience) had everyone in a good mood, even though the cantor was complaining of the Rand's arid atmosphere. Ray Smith was a faithful accompanist at the piano. – L.S." When I cut this tiny article out, I forgot to write the date, the name of the newspaper or the author's name. But I treasure it for obvious reasons.

***

We traveled around in South Africa, including to game reserves and resorts. One of the latter we especially enjoyed was Muizenberg, a beachside suburb of Cape Town. Located where the water line of the Cape Peninsula bends around to the coast of False Bay, it is believed to be the original site of South African surfing. To get there by car took nine hours, at least half of them through part of the 350,000 square mile Kalahari Desert. On the way back, we took a longer route, the Garden Route. This went through Port Elizabeth – one of the largest cities in South Africa and one of the country's major seaports – and through East London, in the Eastern Cape Province and on the Indian Ocean coast. In the latter place

Chapter Six: Johannesburg

we stopped for Shabbat. We also traveled through North Rhodesia and South Rhodesia, now Zambia and Zimbabwe respectively.

After we *davened* in North Rhodesia, we stopped to see the Kariba Dam. This fascinating hydroelectric dam – said to be one of the biggest in the world – is situated between what is now Zambia and Zimbabwe and is 128 meters high and 579 meters wide. The first stage of building the dam between 1955 and 1959 cost $135 million. The second stage, finished in 1977, cost $480 million. The two stages together cost a total 86 lives, from both accidents and animal attacks.

From this mammoth and completely man-made dam, we went to the completely God-made Victoria Falls. We had to see the falls, also located on the border of what is now Zambia and Zimbabwe. Though neither the highest nor the widest waterfall in the world, says Wikipedia, "it is classified as the largest based on its width of 1,708 meters and its height of 108 meters, resulting in the world's largest sheet of falling water." Before we went too close, we were given raincoats, rain boots, and rain hats – to protect us from the constant spray – and a stick to walk with to prevent slipping on the soaking-wet walkway. We were totally overwhelmed. There was even a permanent rainbow. All of this from God. It made me sing *Kol Hashem bekoaḥ, kol Hashem behadar*, about God's power and God's beauty. Years later, when we lived in Canada, we heard constantly about the amazing Niagara Falls. So, we were quite excited when we finally got a chance to see them. When we got there, Rivka and I looked at the falls, then at each other. We shrugged and said with our eyes, so no-one would hear: "That's it?"

We traveled north as well, to Laurenco Marques, Mozambique, which changed its name to Maputo after independence in 1975, and was declared the country's capital. The very reason we went was to stay at the world famous Polana Serena Hotel, advertised as both having "tradition" and being "modern." That's because it was built in 1922, and, according to the Internet, "belongs to an elite class of world-famous luxury hotels, which includes such timeless legends as Singapore's Raffles Hotel, London's The Dorchester, and Paris' The Ritz." The Shabbat we spent there was unforgettable. For one thing, the *shul* had been completely closed for years, but it opened especially when the former members heard I would be there. I did not charge them any money for my work that Shabbat, since they had a total of only five *shul* members, three men – a president and two *gabbaim* – and two women. But many of the hotel's guests were Jewish, and they were thrilled to attend Shabbat services. It turned out to be a lot of fun. Thirty of us walked to and from the *shul* for thirty minutes each way, singing Hebrew songs the entire time. When we got back to the hotel, Rivka had a surprise for everyone. She had brought about ten long tins of *cholent*, a kind of stew eaten on Shabbat, which was served hot as she had told the hotel kitchen how to prepare it, by placing the tins in boiling water. Everyone loved the food.

***

One of the most exciting parts of living in South Africa was having guests come and visit with us. We so enjoyed showing them around, the beautiful landscapes, the animals, everything. One treasured guest was the widely known Yosef Shlomo Kahaneman, the Lithuanian rabbi known as the Ponevezher Rav, who became head of the reestablished Ponevezh Yeshiva, located in Bnei Brak, Israel. This world-renowned school was founded in Panevezys, Lithuania, where Rabbi Kahaneman had proudly been an elected parliamentarian before World War II. The yeshiva currently has over a thousand students, and is ostensibly the leading Lithuanian-style yeshiva in Israel. Rabbi Kahaneman was more the school's promoter and fundraiser than he was its *rosh yeshiva*. He was sometimes called the greatest money collector in the world. Once, when he came to stay with us in South Africa in 1968, we

Chapter Six: Johannesburg

had a special piece of property to return to him, something I'd held onto for sixteen years. Here is the story of how I came to have it in my possession.

In 1952 we bumped into the Ponevezher Rav in the airport in Paris. At that time, there was no direct flight from Israel to Brussels, as there is today. On our very first trip from Israel to Belgium, Rivka and I had to change planes more than once, including after one fairly long stopover in Paris. We wanted to send a telegram to Israel to let Rivka's family know that we were safe. To our astonishment and pleasure, at the telegram office, we bumped into Rabbi Kahaneman. After a quick hello and brief conversation, he asked me what I was searching for as I began to look around distractedly while worried about getting to the departure gate. "A pen," I answered. "Here, take mine," he said. Right at that moment he had to run off to catch his flight, so I had no chance to return his pen. Sixteen years later, while Rabbi Kahaneman was visiting us in Johannesburg, I finally gave it back. He was completely stunned to say the least, but he pretended that he'd been wondering all along where it was and that he was so relieved to finally find it.

Of course, he planned to make some appointments while in South Africa to raise money for his yeshiva in Israel. He had been given some names of people to see. One man was a very rich Jew in Port Elizabeth, a place well known for its luxurious beaches and wildlife reserves. Because the man he was to see had a brother who was a cantor, Rabbi Kahaneman wanted me to go with him. I declined, because I considered myself bad luck for fundraising. "With me there you'll collect maybe one dollar," I said. "I do not care if I collect one dollar or one thousand rand (about three hundred dollars)," he replied. "I care only to be received with honor with the famous Moshe Kraus in Port Elizabeth." So, I agreed to accompany him, and we flew there the next day. We attended *shul* in the morning, and he began to ask the congregants after prayers if they would like to donate to his yeshiva. He jokingly told people

The Life of Moshele Der Zinger

the minimum was one thousand rand. He did collect some money, but not the minimum he was seeking.

The next day at 9 a.m., we went to the prearranged appointment. It happened to be with the *shul* president, a very important man in the community, a very rich man. I do not remember his name, but he invited us into his kitchen. We ate breakfast with him. He told us that he never used to give money to charity. Then he had a massive heart attack. God helped him and saved him; he was even able to work again. Since then, he had changed. He gave away lots of money to many Jewish organizations. Rabbi Kahaneman then began to talk and tell the man about his yeshiva in Israel. No one had to help this rabbi sell his school. He could talk; yes, he could. He explained how his yeshiva had a thousand pupils and depended very much on generous donations from Jews all over the world. When he was finished, the host said, "Rabbi, I would like to honor you. You are obviously a great rabbi. Like me, you have Lithuanian roots. But yeshivot don't say anything to me; they don't do anything for me. I do not believe in them. You can come to me about anything, but not yeshivot. I'm sorry."

Despite the rebuff, Rabbi Kahaneman didn't get upset at all. He was used to the occasional rejection. He began to talk for another five minutes, but the man cut him off. "I'm sorry, rabbi," he said. "You tried your best and you are an excellent speaker, but I don't give to yeshivot." We got up, said our goodbyes, and we each gave the man a blessing. Just as we were about to walk out the door, Rabbi Kahaneman turned to the man once more, and said, "I want you to know I am not insulted and I am not cross with you. I'm cross with myself. You didn't give me any donation because I did something wrong. It is my fault." The man looked surprised. "Rabbi, what is your fault?" he asked. The rabbi explained: "Every day when I pray, I always say an extra prayer that the children in my yeshiva will learn to study Torah, that they will love the Torah the way I do, that they will understand that the Bible is everything.

Chapter Six: Johannesburg

But if I cannot raise money for the yeshiva, these students will not even have enough to eat, so they will not be able to learn. 'Forgive me God,' I pray, 'and I beg You. Let the people I see receive me with honor. Make it that they shall be good to me, and nice to me, and generous to me.' Today I didn't say the prayer because people told me, 'This man, the *shul* president, will easily donate three thousand rand. You will have no problem. He is a safe one to ask. The money is in your pocket.' So, you see, it is not your fault, it is my fault because I didn't say the prayer. I wish you good health and all the best."

The man got excited. "Rabbi, please, come back," he said. "Sit down." We went back into his home. He took out his check book and he wrote Rabbi Kahaneman a check for ten thousand rand. "Was that reverse psychology?" I asked after we left. "I don't know," the rabbi responded. "It was the truth, though."

***

Another guest we were blessed to have was Mr. Gur-Ayre, a Lubavitcher Hasid from New York City. Lubavitch, which is also called Chabad, is both the largest and the most widely known hasidic sect in the world. The reason for this is that Chabad is dedicated to outreach like no other group. Chabad has outreach workers representing it in every corner of the earth, wherever Jews can be found. Gur-Ayre was sent to South Africa by the unrivaled Lubavitcher Rebbe Menachem Mendel Schneerson, of blessed memory, to meet one Sam Cohen and pick up some money. Rivka and I are not Lubavitchers, but we knew Gur-Ayre quite well, so he stayed with us in Johannesburg. I told him that I knew Sam Cohen. He lived nearby, and I'd been to his home a few times. Cohen was well known because he owned the OK Bazaars Department Stores, which were situated all over the country. "No, no," said Gur-Ayre. "That is the wrong Sam Cohen. This man lives in Kimberly," which at that time was in South West Africa and is now called Namibia. I knew exactly where he was talking about. Everyone in South Africa knew about Kimberly. It was the first site where diamonds had been found in the country by the De Beers brothers in 1871. The resulting rush for claims gave the place its first name, New Rush. From 1871 to 1914, a staggering fifty thousand miners excavated a massive hole with shovels and other tools, uncovering about 2,700 kilograms, or six thousand pounds, of diamonds. Today, the Big Hole has a surface of seventeen hectares, or forty-two acres, and is 463 meters wide.

Gur-Ayre and I flew to Kimberly the next day. We went to *shul* the following morning, and asked people if they knew a Sam Cohen. Kimberly had a small Jewish community, but still, no one had heard of him. We went back for Minḥa and Maariv, the late afternoon and evening prayers, but none of the new people who came to *shul* had heard of him either. I said to Gur-Ayre we might as well leave. "No!" he insisted. "The Rebbe sent me, and he knows." We were walking back to our hotel discussing what to do next when we bumped into a man as we rounded a corner. "The Rebbe sent you, didn't he," the man said. "I am Sam Cohen." We were surprised, but not overly. After all, the Lubavitcher Rebbe had sent Gur-Ayre, and the Rebbe rarely made mistakes. It turned out that Sam Cohen lived with his wife outside Kimberly at the top of a supermarket built into a mountain where black South Africans shopped. "I had a dream," Cohen continued, "that the Rebbe sent you and that I was to give you two bags of money." That sounded about right, Gur-Ayre informed him. Sam Cohen gave us two huge bags containing about three million rand. This caused Gur-Ayre another problem, as he could not legally leave the country with that much South African currency. We needed another miracle, and we got it. Gur-Ayre was introduced to a lawyer in Pretoria, one of South Africa's three capital cities – along with Cape Town and Bloemfontein – and the seat of the country's executive branch

Chapter Six: Johannesburg

of government. The lawyer assisted him in exchanging the money for dollars and taking all of it legally to the United States.

***

During another visit, we had a close call at a game reserve, the reserve that happens to be among the biggest in the world. It is called Kruger National Park, and it's located in northeastern South Africa. Set up in 1898 to protect the wildlife, it is home to all manner of African creature, including elephants, buffalos, lions, leopards, and rhinos, as well as hundreds of other mammals and birds, such as eagles, storks, and vultures. Rivka and I used to go there from time to time just to observe and be fascinated. One day, a few weeks after a friend of mine passed away in Israel, I spoke to the widow who told me that her only daughter was having a very hard time coming to terms with her father's death. This young girl happened to be spoiled, which made her mourning extra difficult. I suggested that the daughter come to stay with us for a while. Maybe time away from her normal life – in a new country, with new people, and new experiences – would help her heal. The widow thought this was an excellent idea, and the seventeen-year-old girl flew down to stay with us for a summer. We happened to know a South African couple who also had a seventeen-year-old daughter. Thinking it would be a nice treat for both girls, we invited her to come along on a trip to Kruger Park.

We left in the morning driving in our car, myself and Rivka in the front seat and the two girls in the back seat together so they could talk. We gave each of them a camera so they could take pictures. The first animal we saw was an elephant standing next to a tree. He had his trunk wrapped around the tree, and he pulled it out. The power of this elephant was unbelievable! We learned later that they love the roots, which are sweet. The girls were busy snapping photos from the car windows of the huge animal eating, and they kept saying, "Go nearer. Go nearer," so they could get some real close-ups. Of course, we knew the regulations, one being that we shouldn't go too close to the animals. But the girls were keen, so we inched the car up little by little. We ended up too close, dangerously close. When the elephant finished eating its root, he started to walk toward us. Naturally I put the car in reverse. But just then I realized two cars, one in front of the other, were behind us.

It is important to know that the roads in this reserve were just single-car-width beaten paths. So, if two cars met face to face, they both had to go up past the road's edges and squeeze to get by, very carefully. Backing up, I didn't know what to do. Shouting was useless, as there was no way the other drivers would hear me. The elephant was advancing toward us. The elephant literally touched our hood with his raised leg. Just in time the two cars behind us saw what was going on and they both reversed quickly. I managed to back up enough and just in time. We had seen death in front of us, but we narrowly escaped.

Rivka and I had read in the newspaper only one week earlier that three young boys who were at the reserve had foolishly teased a few elephants. They had gone too close in their car, and eventually one elephant rushed and crushed their car. The three boys had been killed. When we saw the elephant coming toward us, all we could think of was that story about the boys. Of course, we did not say anything to the girls, but it was terrifying for Rivka and me.

***

In 1963, Rivka and I had a once-in-a-lifetime opportunity to see the Shah of Iran. We were flying El Al home from Tel Aviv to Johannesburg. Being the early 1960s, stopovers could be extra-long. For this trip, we had to wait for our next flight from a Thursday to a Sunday, in Teheran. It was to be a restful weekend as I had no performances. Since this was an unofficial holiday, in most places I

Chapter Six: Johannesburg

went to, in an effort to remain anonymous, I did not give my real name. I called myself Moshe Sapir and told people I was a diamond merchant. On Shabbat, we were guests in an Ashkenazi *shul* where many Israeli *shliḥim*, representatives of Jewish organizations, *davened*. I was given the honor of being the *maftir aliya*, the last person on Shabbat to read and chant from the Torah. Although I was not trying to be entertaining, my voice was quite distinctive, and someone recognized it. After services, I was told someone overheard two congregants talking. One said to the other, "Are you sure this is Moshe Sapir? I could swear it sounds just like Moshe Kraus. I remember him from the Israeli Army."

But the most exciting part of the stop in Teheran happened after everyone had left the synagogue. As we were walking to our hotel, we noticed hundreds and hundreds of people standing on both sides of a main road. We asked what was happening, only to learn that the Shah himself was to drive by in a motorcade after picking up Soviet leader Leonid Brezhnev at the airport. We decided this was worth seeing. We were not disappointed.

In short order, two golden horse-drawn carriages drove by. The first one carried the Shah, who cut an imposing figure, all decked out in his decorated military uniform, full of shiny medals. Representing the mood of his country, Brezhnev sat beside him in a drab grey suit and tie. The second carriage held the two women. The shah's third wife Farah Diba looked like she just stepped out of the House of Christian Dior. Mrs. Brezhnev on the other hand, well, let's just say frumpish would have been too much of a compliment.

***

In late 1963, Rivka and I traveled to Turkey so I could give a concert in Istanbul. I am pretty sure this is the only time in my life that my talent almost started a riot. There were so many people crowding to get into the hall that the organizers had to shut the door on hundreds of people. No problem; they simply broke down the door. It was crazy. Before I left the concert hall that night, I was presented with a beautiful solid-silver engraved tray to commemorate the occasion. As it turned out, the Israeli ambassador had come from Ankara to hear me, and he was among those unable to get in. He did not consider this a problem. He simply waited for the concert to finish, went to meet me as I was leaving, and brought me to the consulate office. There he asked me to give him a private performance, which I was more than happy to do. The Jewish community of Istanbul was gracious in that it provided me with a chauffeur-driven car and guide. The guide was a Turkish Israeli yeshiva student, Ishak Haleva, now the chief rabbi of Turkey.

I was very proud of the review given in Istanbul's *Roving Reporter Jewish Times*, which said: "Ḥazan Moshe Kraus of the Johannesburg Oxford Synagogue is on a special European holiday tour with his wife. This is Moshe Kraus' first time in the Turkish capital, where there is to be found a substantial Jewish community. The reception for him here was little short of ecstatic. He sang to a packed audience twice." One of the regular daily papers in the city, *Le Journal d'Orient*, published an eight hundred-word rave review of my concert, ending it with, "We would like to thank Moshe Kraus for his spiritual words in addition to his music, and we wish him great success on his concert tour in Europe." One other paper's headline said: "Cantor Kraus is a Turkish Delight."

One synagogue invited me to sing on Shabbat. I was happy to oblige because *shuls* in Turkey are known to be unique, and I wanted to have the experience of *davening* in one. When I arrived, the *shul* leaders asked me to sing specifically in the way of their *ḥazanim*, who happened to number three for one service. Also unusual was the way they sang their melodies, using multiple pitches for just one word. A single word in a prayer or poem in the liturgy had ten or more different notes. I listened for a while

Chapter Six: Johannesburg

to learn the method, and when I repeated exactly what I heard back to them, everyone laughed uproariously. Not too hurt or embarrassed, I asked what was so funny. I was told they could not believe how funny they sounded. They had never really listened to themselves until I echoed their voices.

I was fortunate in Istanbul to perform the mitzva of *bikkur ḥolim* on an institution-wide level. The city has a Jewish hospital, where I went from room to room to room singing songs in Hebrew to cheer up the patients.

Also, while in Istanbul, I was approached by the head of the Red Crescent Society, the Muslim equivalent of the Red Cross, to ask if I would give a concert, for no pay, to raise money for the organization. He wanted me to sing at the Topkapi Palace, a museum that once served as the home of the Ottoman sultans for about four hundred years, and is now a major tourist draw. I agreed, but on the condition that the concert be done together with the Jewish community, which in Istanbul is quite depressed. He said he would ask his committee and get back to me. I gave him the name of the hotel I would be occupying in Istanbul when he had the answer. A week later, I received his telegram: "The answer is no because my Muslim colleagues did not agree."

Dr. Nahum Goldman, founder and president of the World Jewish Congress and an outstanding speaker, came for a tour when I was the chief cantor in Johannesburg. He *davened* at my *shul*, as well as at *Beit Knesset Hagadol* – the Great Synagogue. Dr. Goldman stayed at one of the local millionaires' homes so as not to drive on Shabbat. When he came to my *shul* for the first time, he was very impressed with my singing. In those days, a speaker on his own, even an exceptional Yiddish speaker like Goldman, could not make a full *parnasa*. So, speakers would take almost any kind of singer – an opera singer, a Yiddish singer, a *ḥazan* – along with them. This kept *ḥazanim* like myself busy. Dr. Goldman, considered one of the best speakers in the world, could entertain in three languages, German, English, and Yiddish, but even he had to have a singer with him on stage. After he heard me sing, he frequently arranged for me to join him on his speaking tours. He paid me a lot of money.

One day, at the height of the international Cold War, Goldman phoned me and stated, without emotion: "You are engaged by the Jewish World Congress. We have a letter from Soviet General Secretary Leonid Brezhnev. Brezhnev wants a Jewish artist to tour all over behind the Iron Curtain, probably to show he is not antisemitic." Before me, one candidate Goldman had thought of was Jan Peerce, one of the world's greatest operatic tenors at the time. "I also thought about Moshe Koussevitzky," Goldman said, referring to a cantor who found fame all over Europe around the same time I did, and who was one of four brothers who were all excellent cantors. "But I decided you are the best," he concluded. "What took you so long?" I replied. We both laughed, but I was nervous, for obvious reasons.

"I proposed, and the committee agreed, that you will go for three months," he said. I told him my congregation would never let me go for that long. He replied, "No problem. I already spoke with your *shul* president before I spoke with you, and he thinks this is great." Then it must be great, I thought, anxiously.

Jan Peerce, I'd like to point out here, who was considered for this tour before me, became a good friend of mine and Rivka's. I met him when he came on tour in South Africa. Later, he came to our *shul* in Johannesburg to hear me sing, after which he gave me many compliments. We invited him to our home to eat, but before he came, he mentioned to Rivka that he does not eat fried food. Rivka replied, without a hint of sarcasm, "I never fry." After that we enjoyed many meals together, including at his home in the New York State town of New Rochelle. I heard from him again years later when he wrote me a letter in 1981, praising a tape of mine that he'd heard. "I enjoyed the tape immensely," he wrote.

Chapter Six: Johannesburg

"You are a great artist, and I hope that when you are in New York you will please call me." He gave his phone number and signed off, "with great affection." I was tickled pink.

Getting back to Dr. Goldman, he explained I was to give a series of concerts in, among other places, Budapest, Prague, Belgrade, Warsaw, Leningrad, and Moscow, which are in, respectively, Hungary, Czechoslovakia, Yugoslavia, Poland, and, regarding the last two cities, Russia. I also sang in Serbia, Lithuania, and Ukraine. Brezhnev was eager to show the world that the communists were accessible and not antisemitic. He especially wanted to show the Jewish world that the Soviet Union was an open society. To do this, the organizers arranged for me to give sizable concerts. Since I was a guest of the Soviet government, the Soviets paid for everything, and I stayed only in five-star hotels.

Secretly, I was also recruited by powerful, knowledgeable, and trusting leaders of the South African Jewish community to help as much as possible to free some Jewish *refuseniks*. These were Jews who desired to leave the USSR, but were forbidden to do so and were often imprisoned for even applying for exit visas. The connected South Africans trusted me implicitly, or so they told me. They said they knew I would be discreet, and could do the secret jobs; that all I needed were nerves of steel. I met with them surreptitiously a few times before my trip so they could inform me about the Jews who would contact me when I was in certain communist cities. I was not to do anything proactively to meet them. I could not write anything down on paper.

We started the tour in Belgrade. While there, Rivka and I had lunch with the Israeli Consul. It was very pleasant, but he put a fear in us that we had not felt since the Holocaust. I explained to him that I wanted to take Rivka to Uzhhorod – now part of the Soviet Union – to show her where I grew up. The Consul said, "Sure, go. But do it at your own risk. If for some reason someone does not like the color of your eyes, or your teeth, they can throw you in prison. No one will ever hear from you again." The hair now firmly erect on the backs of our necks, Rivka and I made the decision simultaneously and immediately not to go to Uzhhorod; indeed, to not take any unnecessary risks on the tour.

But the trip was not all serious or scary. Sometimes, it was actually dreadfully boring. One particularly mind-numbing experience occurred in an airport, of all places. It was at the very start of the communist state tour. We were supposed to leave Belgrade, our first stop, to fly to Budapest for Shabbat. The flight was a short one, leaving at nine in the morning, so we assumed we'd be in Budapest in plenty of time to relax before Shabbat started and before I had to be at the *shul* to lead *davening*. We assumed, but we were wrong. We arrived at the airport just as probably the worst snow storm in a decade, if not a century, hit the city. Our flight was delayed, and delayed, and delayed. We realized pretty quickly that we would not be in Budapest that day. We decided that if we went to a hotel we could leave the next day after Shabbat and arrive in time for a scheduled concert. Only problem with that idea was the storm was so bad there was no way to drive into the city to a hotel. These were, unfortunately, the days before airport hotels. So, we did the only thing we could do. We sat in the airport, on a bench, overnight, and all day on Saturday, with no food, no bed, no comfort. We caught the flight to Budapest right after Shabbat, and I had just enough time to change into my tuxedo during the taxi ride to the hall. We did not even have five minutes to freshen up. I made it to the concert hall in time for the opening, but I had had no time to rehearse even for one second with the pianist. But what a professional he was! The concert was well attended and widely praised. Ironically, when the show was over, many in the audience were crying because they had never seen such a well-dressed artist. Most of their local artists, I was told, were always dressed in *shmatas*.

When I later sang in Bucharest, it was in the most beautiful hall in the city, and it was completely packed with Jews. Chief

Chapter Six: Johannesburg

Rabbi Rosen, who credited me with getting him his job, was thrilled to see me. We still had a special connection from 1948. I felt very happy because many in the Jewish community remembered me.

In Leningrad, I met a Jewish communist who was more committed to communism I think than Russia's Lenin and China's Mao Zedong combined. He was Leningrad's censor. He asked to see my music before the show. He thumbed through the pianist's sheets, saying, "*Nyet, nyet, nyet*" about every third page. I realized I was not to sing anything that would give Jews hope. No Zionist songs. No *Moshiaḥ* songs. No songs with the word "Jerusalem." The censor told me if I defied him and sang any of these words, I would rot in Siberia. But I knew the whole concert was propaganda for the communist regime. This meant the international press was there, which meant I was safe. The journalists gave me courage. So, even though the pianist would not play the music, I sang the songs anyway. Rivka was trembling with fear.

Our most dramatic experiences occurred in Prague. It must be told that, while we were in the communist cities, Rivka and I were followed twenty-four hours a day. This security was not hidden. When agents were at our hotel, they were sitting in chairs on both sides of our room's hall-side door. Whenever we left the hotel, they followed us, openly. That was okay. We did not mind too much. In Prague, the Jewish Community Center luckily served kosher food; it was the only place we could eat. The meals were very plain, not tasty, but at least kosher. And when we went to the JCC to eat, no one would ever even come to talk to us. They believed we were spies. In those days, everyone was spying on everyone. No-one trusted strangers, so no-one would talk to us. They were afraid of the authorities. They were afraid of each other. If we greeted them, they wouldn't even nod. When the weather was pleasant, though, we would walk to the hotel instead of taking a taxi. When we did this, some Jews would follow us and start talking quietly to us. They would only talk to us in the street to make sure no-one was listening.

We heard horror stories, unbelievable horror stories of what the government did to people. I do not want to repeat what I heard they did, even to children, killing and torturing them. One day, two men followed us. When they caught up they told us that they were brothers, one a doctor in a hospital, the other working for the police, though we never found out which force. These men told us all kinds of stories. To my utter surprise, the doctor told us that he knew me from *ḥeder,* in Uzhhorod. I did not remember him.

They both told us the same story about after the war. They survived, and they both came out communists. They believed communism sounded fair and wonderful. Rivka and I already knew that in theory communism sounded great, but in reality, it was the opposite. The brothers now agreed with us. They told us that the communist leaders were rich and everyone else was poor. But for themselves it was too late, they could not do anything. They explained that if they said anything, they would either be killed or sent to Siberia. Everybody spied, they said, all their neighbors, friends, and colleagues. We never saw the policeman brother again, but the doctor came the next day to the JCC. He knew when we would be there to have a meal, at lunchtime. We again walked back to the hotel, and he told us the following story.

"In the 1940s I was a very dedicated communist, and I met a woman who felt the same. She was from South Africa, but had been expelled for communist sentiment and activity. I met her here in Prague. We fell in love, got married, and had three children. This was many years ago. After some time, I saw that communism was all a lie, and my dream was shattered completely. I was deeply disappointed. But I could not do anything about it. I could not even tell my wife how I felt, because I was afraid she would report me. I am still afraid she will. So, I cannot tell her even now how I feel. But I can tell you, because you are an outsider. Here in the street it is safe to talk to you. I hope you don't have a recorder." In those days, recorders were very rare, but I assured him I didn't anyway.

"I am telling you all this," the doctor continued, "because I have to tell someone." We left him, but I was so upset I could not sleep the whole night. The next morning, I called the man's wife. I told her I wanted to come and see her, alone. She said her husband was at the hospital working, so now was a good time to come to her home. When I arrived, I told her to come into the kitchen. I was afraid to talk in the living room. "I want to tell you something," I said. "I am taking my life in my hands, and your husband's life in my hands, but I have to tell you this. I heard that you tried to return to South Africa. I know that the government would not let you in. But how do you feel today?" She answered, eagerly: "I left my home, my country, my family, because I believed so strongly in communism. It was the ideal, the utopia. But that was then. I have completely changed. I am very disenchanted. But I am afraid for my life. I am afraid to talk to my husband, because I am terrified he will report me to the government."

When I heard this, I was excited. I then told her the story about her husband, and she started to cry. I told her I would come again that night with my wife. When Rivka and I arrived, after the three kids had been put to bed, we all had a long conversation. The doctor was grateful that I had taken the risk and discovered his wife's attitude. It was a huge relief for both of them to know how the other felt. They then asked us if we would help them. "We want to leave this country, we want to run away, but we can't," said the doctor. "We are afraid for the children." I told him I could not promise anything, but I would try to help.

When I was finished with the concert series – after Rivka and I finally had got back together in London, England – I called London's Chief Rabbi Israel Brodie. I told him the whole story of the doctor and his family. "I want to get them out," I said. The rabbi asked, "How can we do that?" Then we worked out a plan together. The reason I had gone to London was because England was the only country in the world at that time that had, for their diplomats, a special school system for students from almost any country. For example, Hungarian diplomats could have their children learn in the Hungarian language. Czechoslovakian diplomats' children could learn in their language. When I got back to South Africa I called the doctor. I asked him when was the next medical convention in the free world, in Europe. He told me there was a convention in Switzerland in about seven weeks. I told him to apply to go, to tell the Prague authorities it was a very good conference and that he should attend. It would not be a problem because he was the chief medical officer of the hospital. I told him to leave everything behind, but take his family for a ten-day holiday at the same time. He did exactly what I said, and in fact he made sure his wife left for Switzerland a few days earlier with the children.

From Switzerland, after the conference, they went to London, where the chief rabbi had made arrangements, procured them an apartment, some money – everything they needed. Eventually, they moved to Sussex, where he became head of the main hospital. I am pretty sure they remain there to this day.

After I returned to South Africa, I went to a wedding. This was not unusual. At my synagogue there were sometimes ten weddings a week, and not just among our congregants, who numbered about 2,100 members. Many people who belonged to other *shuls* had their weddings at the Oxford synagogue because it was huge. There were 1,500 seats in the big *shul* and room for six hundred more in the hall for the *yamim noraim* or major *smaḥot*. At this wedding, as was normal, the officiating rabbis and the *ḥazan* who sang during the ceremony were announced. Right after my name was proclaimed, there was a loud noise in the crowd, after which someone yelled, "Is there a doctor in the house? Is there a doctor in the house?" I thought to myself, humorously, "Why do we need a doctor? Did someone faint when they heard my name?" I learned that that was in fact exactly what happened. When the woman heard the name "Moshe Kraus," she screamed, "Do you know who this man is? He saved my daughter and her family. He took them out of Prague and helped them move to Sussex, England. He saved their lives!" Then she fainted.

Back to the tour behind the Iron Curtain. While I was performing in Prague I also met Shmuel Singer, someone else with whom I went to *ḥeder*. When Rivka and I were in our hotel one day, we heard that a local citizen wanted to visit us, but was not allowed in the hotel, which was only for tourists, foreigners, and diplomats. If a local resident wanted to come into the hotel, he or she had to explain the reason and leave their passport at the front desk so the hotel employees could check the identity. The document was returned on the visitor's way out. Shmuel told the desk that he wanted to see "Moshe Kraus. I remember him from childhood, from my home city." Finally allowed into our hotel room, he told us this story: "I am a religious Jew. I have four children, three girls and a fifteen-year-old son. Many of the Jews here are assimilated because it is practically impossible to live as an observant Jew in the Soviet Union. We cannot easily get kosher food. We cannot easily observe Shabbat. But I am still a Jew, and I want to save my family. The communists won't let me out of the country. I want to save my children." I asked him what he was doing for *parnasa*. He told me he was an opera singer. "I can sing extremely well," he said. "And I can learn new songs." I thought that was perfect, as he could be employed as a *ḥazan* in South Africa. It turned out that he was able to get a visa to come to Johannesburg for three seasons of *yamim noraim* to *daven* in my *shul*. When he came the first time, I told him to come three weeks early, so I could teach him to sing like a *ḥazan*. It was not hard as he could read music and he knew the *nusakhim* of the High Holy Day prayers.

When he first came, Shmuel stayed with us for the three weeks, and he learned everything he needed to from me. He was ready to sing during the holiday services. When he arrived for the third year, he told me he had a terrible problem. "My son is now eighteen, and he is enthusiastic to be a young communist. He is dedicated to the communist cause. He does not care anything for *yiddishkeit*. He does not want to be a Jew anymore. He wants to be like his friends. I need you to help me. I will give you all my four kids. Please take them. Just promise me you will help them stay Jews." I responded, "Let me see what I can do." I again got in touch with London's chief rabbi, but this time also with the city's chief ḥazan. Remember, it was important that it be London because of its special education system that allowed children's schooling in different languages.

I told Shmuel, "Go apply with the government to leave for London, where you are needed as a cantor for one year. The children will go to the Czech school there. Buy all the books needed for the entire school year. Close your apartment in Prague as if you will be gone for one year. Take only a few suitcases, clothes for the children, what you would need for a year. The main thing is the books for the school, so that the government will believe you are serious. They will see you are going as a cantor, the children will be in school, and you will come back after the school year." Of course, they never went back to Prague. The whole family, six people, eventually moved to South Africa.

The boy came also, but not without some harsh deceit. When Shmuel told me he had trouble with his communist-loving son, I gave him one piece of advice. "It is ugly," I told him, "but it is effective. Tell your son, 'If you come willingly, great. If you decide to not come, I am going to call the police and tell them you stole money from me, that you have done many terrible things to me. And I'll make sure they put you in jail.'" Shmuel did as I suggested, and his son sobbed and sobbed. Shmuel said again and again that he was going to the police. Finally, the young man agreed to accompany the family.

Chapter Six: Johannesburg

When the concert tour behind the Iron Curtain was over, Rivka and I were getting ready to leave Prague and fly back to our home in South Africa. We said to each other that this was the last trip we'd ever make to communist countries. Though we didn't really mind it at first, the twenty-four-hour-a-day surveillance did start to make us feel uncomfortable. In fact, Rivka was at the end of her rope with the guards. A week or so before we were scheduled to leave, I received an urgent message that I had to return to Bucharest immediately for maybe ten days to help someone. Rivka was disappointed, and said she was going to go ahead and leave without me. We said we'd meet in Brussels, but if I did not turn up there in three days, she was to fly ahead to London and wait for me. While in Prague by herself, Rivka was taken every night to the opera by Shmuel Singer and his wife. And when it was time for her to fly to Brussels, Singer even drove her to the airport. He left right away, though, not even imagining what problems Rivka would have.

Every time a traveler wants to cross a communist border, they must show a passport and all their jewels and money. Every single item must be written down on a proper record sheet for the authorities, with a copy given to the traveler. The problem was, I had gone back to Bucharest forgetting to give the needed papers to Rivka. The official at the airport asked her for the papers. Shaking from fear, she told him. "My husband left on another flight and forgot to leave me the documents." The border patrol looked at her with contempt, and chortled: "Oh, right. That's a new one, a creative twist on the ol' my-dog-ate-my-homework excuse. Now I've heard them all." He must have pushed a hidden button because, as Rivka told me, two big burly police officers came up to either side of her. All she could think about were the words of the consul in Belgrade: "If for some reason someone does not like the color of your eyes, or your teeth, they can throw you in prison. No one will ever hear from you again." She went hysterical, screaming, "I will disappear forever. No one will ever find me! It is over for me!" The frazzled official relented. He sternly said, "I will let you go this time." In her head she said, decisively, "There will never be a next time." And there never was.

Rivka flew to Brussels, full of gratitude that she had been allowed to leave Prague. She waited a few days for me in Brussels, and when I didn't turn up, she went on ahead to London, where we finally reunited.

When I was ready to leave Bucharest, I sat on a plane for hours. I had no idea why I was waiting, and I asked the steward if I could please wait back in my hotel room. He said no, as it was hard to know when the plane would fill up. "What? I am confused," I said. He explained to me that the airline liked to fill up empty planes with *olim,* Jews who wanted to go to Israel. The *olim* in Bucharest at the time were taken from refugee camps, put on empty planes until they were full, and then taken to Israel. The *olim* who eventually came and filled up the plane I was waiting on didn't trust me, to put it mildly. I said, in my friendliest tone, "How are you?" Not one person answered, because they thought I was a non-Jew and would get them in trouble. Indeed, they thought I was a spy. So, I started to sing to pass the time. Food was served. "Do not eat this food because it is *treif,*" I said to a woman among the *olim* close to me. "Oh my God, he's a rabbi!" she shouted. "He's a rabbi!" No one ate any food for the entire flight, but everyone started liking me and talking to me.

My flight went to London; Rivka's flight went to London. We both took taxis to the same hotel, at the same time, without knowing what the other was doing. In those days, people with luggage went through a separate hotel door at the side of the building. Rivka had lots of luggage so she had her taxi drop her off at the side door. From there, she got into line to wait to see a clerk and get a key to her hotel room. Wondering if she'd ever see me again since we'd split up in Prague, she was nervous and sad. All of a sudden, she saw me out of the corner of her eye, at the exact same moment I saw

Chapter Six: Johannesburg

her. Even though we were a couple with a strict policy of showing absolutely zero public signs of affection toward each other, we threw that rule out the window. She ran over to me and grabbed me and hugged me so hard I thought I would explode. I hugged her back. Laughing and smiling like a couple of teenagers, we approached the hotel clerk at the desk. He gave us a stern look. We realized at the same time what was going on. First, we were traveling at a time when a top-class hotel like the one we were in would never allow an unmarried couple to rent a room together. Second, that hotel clerk believed from the core of his cerebellum that we were not married. "We are married!" we said together. "Why did you arrive separately?" he asked, simultaneously wondering why a married couple would look so happy. He even said he thought we made up the names we gave him. We were about to show our passports, when Rivka thought of something else. "Look at our clothes," she said. "They are made of the exact same material. What unmarried couple would bother getting clothes made of the same material?" He nodded in immediate agreement, and gave us the same room.

At some point, the Singer family was ready to leave London and move to South Africa. But they had a major problem. They had no visas. They had the additional problem that South Africa was insanely anti-communist, having recently passed into law "The Suppression of Communism Act of 1950." Surely, the government was going to be highly reluctant to allow two former citizens of Czechoslovakia to move into its southern paradise. I carefully explained to Percy Yutar – at the time a junior state prosecutor and later to become attorney general – how the Singers had turned against communism, fled their country, and were now essentially refugees. Percy held out his hand, palm up. "When little hairs grow right here," he said, indicating the middle of his bald metacarpus, "your friends will be welcomed to this country." I insisted on having a meeting with a Pretoria cabinet minister, someone who had the power to grant visas on compassionate grounds. I got the meeting and begged. I even cried. I got the visas.

Shmuel Singer's family was in South Africa, but with nothing, so Rivka and I worked hard to help them. First, we made sure their story was published in the local paper. Then we went from family to family in Johannesburg and asked for extra things. We collected furniture, food, money, and clothes. People in our community – not just the Jews – were helpful and generous. They even made sure the family got an apartment. And I got Shmuel a job. He was employed as a cantor in a *shul*. The Singer family remained in the city for many years. When we left in 1970, they were still there. We heard the son became a surgeon in Johannesburg, and then he moved to the United States, where he is a famous doctor. Shmuel and his wife moved to Australia to be with their married daughter. She ultimately had to put Shmuel in a nursing home, where he died.

***

The 1967 Six Day War erupted in the Middle East on June 5, and lasted until June 10. The Jews of Johannesburg were aware of the fierce fighting, but we had little news, and we were biting off our fingernails from worry. It turned out to be a decisive victory for Israel on three fronts. The small country, which launched a surprise pre-emptive strike against Egypt's mobilizing air force on her perimeter, gained crucial air power dominance in the region. Israel simultaneously invaded the Sinai and Gaza with ground forces. Lying, Egyptian President Gamal Nasser related to Syria and Jordon that he had conquered Israel's air force, provoking them to attack Israel. By the end, Israel had rightfully captured East Jerusalem, Jordon's West Bank, and Syria's Golan Heights. Most of the captured territory continues to cause international consternation to this day.

Chapter Six: Johannesburg

But at the time we did not know how the war was progressing. All we knew was that there was an emergency in the recently created Jewish homeland. Thus, we did what any red-blooded Jew would do: we raised money for Israel. The emergency appeal went out immediately, and caring people began donating quickly, gold, silver, jewelry, money – anything they could afford. Using the list of names and addresses provided to me by my synagogue, I approached a well-known and extremely wealthy Jew in our city. I knocked on his door, gave my speech, and waited for a response. He looked at me with cold eyes and blurted out: "Israel cannot win. It is a lost cause. Therefore, I will not waste my money trying to save Israelis." I tried a few more angles but nothing worked.

Finally, I asked him his Hebrew name and his mother's Hebrew name because I wanted to say *Kaddish*. "What!" he screamed. "Why would you do such a thing?" I answered, quietly, "Because a Jew, to say he is not interested in his fellow Jew, is dead." The rich man yelled and turned every color of red. Eventually, he calmed down and wrote me a check for the equivalent of three hundred thousand dollars. This incident quickly became well-known all over Johannesburg, as word about the large donation by the originally stingy man spread instantly. In fact, canvassers asking for money for war victims started telling people, "You better give, or we will send you Cantor Kraus."

In the late 1960s, the situation in South Africa was also tense. Nelson Mandela was still in prison, but there was every indication he would soon be released and that uncontrollable violence would erupt. I believed in my heart that angry, frustrated blacks – many of them living in poverty and denied a political voice for decades – would take out their revenge on the whites. Thankfully, and incredibly, the riotous violence never happened. By some miracle, Mandela managed a peaceful transition to black rule. All I can say is, God bless Nelson Mandela!

The Life of Moshele Der Zinger

It was around 1968 when – still working at the Oxford Synagogue in Johannesburg – I wanted to get out of my lifetime contract. The Six Day War had made me and Rivka think of returning to Israel. We were still quite young, and believed the move would not be too difficult for us. Moreover, we believed it was the right thing to do. However, it took me three years to convince the Oxford *shul* to let me go. Even though South African Jews have always been staunch Zionists, and though I kept telling them I wanted to do a positive Zionist act and move to Israel, they did not want to let me go. We ultimately left in 1970, and returned to Israel.

It was morning when we landed in Israel from Johannesburg. The first thing I did, even before checking into our hotel, was buy the local newspaper to see what was going on. The front-page news was about a death. It turned out be the death of a dear friend of mine. His funeral was at 11 a.m. I told Rivka I must go. She took a taxi to the hotel, and I took another taxi to the funeral. When I arrived, all the Romanian Jews were there, and many of them recognized me. They were yelling, "Moshele, Moshele!" They were so happy to see me. All of a sudden, a man came up to me, pushing a wagon, with a person in it. I didn't know the man being pushed, but he looked quite sick. Someone then whispered to me, "Do you know who that is? It is Mishe Laiba." I screamed, "Mishe Laiba! My good friend and the president of the Malbim synagogue in Bucharest!" We both began to cry. He said, "I am so sorry I did not listen to you. The communists took me and kept me in jail for six years. The Israeli government paid a hundred thousand dollars to free me. But after six years in prison, I could not walk anymore. Excuse me, please say hello to my son, who is pushing me in this wagon. He is a successful lawyer. I am so proud." After we talked for a few minutes, he said to me – reminding me of the exact last words we spoke to each other just before I fled Bucharest, when I was begging him to come with me: "You were totally right. I am the one who is sorry."

Chapter Six: Johannesburg

While we lived in Israel for eighteen months, Rivka and I informally adopted her brother's six children, all Ger Hasidim, after their mother died tragically at a young age. At the time, the children were ages six to fourteen, and very well behaved. The children continued to live with their father, but we provided significant help for many years so that they could enjoy all the *smaḥot* and milestones of life, including bar mitzvas and weddings, and so that they could have as much education as they wanted. Rivka and I never had our own children, so we were more than happy to give this large gift to Rivka's beloved brother and our adored nieces and nephews.

During our eighteen-month stay in Israel, we were fortunate to entertain the Mexican ambassador Rosario Castellanos in our home for a Shabbat dinner. She was not Jewish, but she was interested in Judaism, particularly Hasidim. Castellanos was extremely well known in Mexico as a writer and a poet. She died young and tragically in Tel Aviv, which I will explain later. One day in 1971, I was approached by the Foreign Minister of Israel, who told me that the Mexican ambassador wanted to experience a hasidic Shabbat. He asked if we could invite her, which we were happy to do. We invited her as well as two couples from Mexico who were traveling in Israel. At that time, not unlike today, electric rates were very high in Israel. Since Jewish law forbids the use of electric light-switches on Shabbat, rather than turn a light on for the entire twenty-five hours from Friday evening to Saturday night, we have always used timers on some of our switches so they will go off at a specific hour when the light is no longer needed. Normally, we set the dining room light to shut off at 10 p.m. But since the ambassador was coming, we set it for an hour later. As it turned out she was very curious about Hasidim, because, she explained, she was a writer. She asked hundreds of questions about different *rebbes* and hasidic dynasties. At 10 p.m. we heard a knock at the door. It was Castellanos' driver, wondering if she was coming out. She told him to wait longer. After more questions, the lights went out at 11 p.m. We sat in the dark asking and answering questions until midnight.

Several years later, in 1974, when we were already living in Mexico City, we were devastated to learn that she had been electrocuted by an antique lamp when she plugged it in. She left a ten-year-old son. Her body lay in state in the Mexican National Art Center, a place similar to our National Arts Center in Ottawa, Canada. We went and signed the special guest book. I wrote "Haval al de'avdin u'lo mishtakhin," gone and not forgotten. We attended her funeral and a later memorial event for her. Later, in order to honor her, a park was named after her in Mexico City.

Every Sunday in Mexico City, Jews go to the Jewish Community Center to socialize. We enjoyed these weekly gatherings. While there, a few people told us they really liked the news article. Confused, we asked, "What article?" "The one in the *Excelsior*, which is the Mexican counterpart to *The New York Times*. Castellanos wrote a regular and popular column in it. They were referring to her article about the Shabbat dinner with us in Israel. The piece was titled "*La Cena Con el Hassid*." She described the whole evening, the clothes, the food, the atmosphere, the lights on timers, and the discussion about hasidic dynasties. "I was ambassador in Israel for two years," she wrote. "For that entire period, I was invited to different Shabbat dinners, and for that entire two years, everyone served me Mexican food. Only the Krauses served real Jewish food, and I loved it." It is funny: At first, when she knew the ambassador was coming, Rivka had tried some practice cooking of Mexican food. But she soon realized she could never compete with the ambassador's chef. So, she decided to prepare her own food. And she thought, with total acceptance, "If the ambassador does not like my Jewish food, she won't come again. That's fine." It turned out the ambassador loved her food. It taught Rivka a life lesson: Be who you are and it will always turn out right.

Chapter Six: Johannesburg

Native dancing in South Africa

Cantor Kraus and his choir in Johannesburg, South Africa

The Life of Moshele Der Zinger

Memorial Service in Johannesburg, South Africa

Chapter Seven

Mexico City

After those eighteen wonderful months living in Israel again – until the High Holy Days and the terrifying Yom Kippur War in 1973 – Rivka and I decided to accept an invitation to move to Mexico City and take a permanent job at Mexico City's largest synagogue, Nidjei Israel. This stunning and prestigious house of worship could hold more than a thousand people, so I was pleased and honored to accept the position. Before this employment offer, we had been to Mexico City three years in a row for the *yamim noraim*, which meant we knew what we were getting into, and that we could live there contentedly. Of course, we were thrilled with the warm and gentle climate. In truth, the congregation had begged us to stay. "There is a war in Israel again," the *shul* president said. "Everything there, all the concerts and performances, have been canceled due to the emergencies." We stayed in Mexico City until 1976, enjoying virtually every single moment of our time.

Mexico, today, is home to around forty thousand Jews, most of them descendants of nineteenth- and twentieth-century immigrants. The majority, about 75 percent, are in Mexico City, which has more than two dozen *shuls*, though it is difficult to get exact numbers as the government census – which asks for religion – is puzzling, referring to some Protestant groups that practice Jewish rituals as Jewish.

Interestingly, despite their best efforts, Jews in Mexico are not as unified as other Jewish communities. A unique Jewish fact about Mexico is this: Some 90 percent of Mexican Jews do not intermarry, and just about as many attend Jewish day schools. Though it's true that all Mexican Jews identify as Mexican, and though it's also true that Jews tend to separate themselves from other Mexicans, for some reason, the descendants of Jewish immigrants retain social divisions based on where their ancestors came from. Still, Mexico has many social, scouting, and Zionist organizations for Jewish youth in an attempt to integrate them more. Mexican universities all have chapters of the Mexican Federation of Jewish Students, a highly popular organization. There are numerous outreach groups as well, for example, Moishe House in Mexico City's ultra-cool Condesa neighborhood. Its mandate is to be a social hub for young Jews, and make them feel less isolated from mainstream Mexican society. The Jewish radio program "El Alpha" has primarily non-Jewish listeners. Tribuna Israelita arranges programs at private post-secondary schools to raise public awareness about Israel and Judaism. And on and on.

***

Davening at my synagogue in Mexico was, at first, next to impossible. Why? Because of the chaos. First of all, you must realize that when I sing during services, I demand complete quiet. If someone sneezes, I stop and wait for the commotion to end. But Mexican synagogues, I learned, had zero decorum. They were not quiet at all. People walked around and chatted with each other, noisily.

Chapter Seven: Mexico City

So, on my first day, I just stood on the *bima*, doing nothing. The synagogue president asked me what I was waiting for. When I told him, he and the two *gabbaim* went all around the sanctuary, telling everyone to be quiet. When it was like a cemetery, I began. When I left to move to Ottawa several years later, Mexico City's Nidjei Israel president wrote to me to say he was very sorry I left, in part because the noise and chaos returned to the sanctuary every Shabbat.

After being in Mexico City for several months, Rivka and I were fortunate to meet the Brenners. They were a kind, dignified, gracious family, and they were also a non-religious, secular family. Mr. Brenner himself was a very well-known and respected figure in that part of Mexico City. A short time after we met the Brenners and their two sons, Mr. Brenner died of natural causes. It was extremely sad, in part because he was not that old. Mrs. Brenner asked me if I would be kind enough to teach her sons – who were recently married – to say *Kaddish*, the deeply moving prayer that children say every day for eleven months following a parent's death. She also asked me to teach them to say the daily Minḥa and Maariv prayers, too. With pleasure, I taught them everything she asked me to. They were attentive and willing students. I also made sure the congregation helped the family observe *shloshim*, the thirty days mourning period following the burial. After the *shloshim*, the *shul* arranged a special service honoring the Brenners, which I conducted.

About a month after the service, the two brothers came to my home for what I thought was a visit. They politely thanked me for teaching them to say *Kaddish*, for teaching them about *shloshim*, and for conducting the special service. Then they quietly put an envelope on the table and turned to leave. I realized immediately it had money in it. I caught them at the door and explained to them that I do not take payment for these types of occasions. I said perhaps they could give the money to a charity, maybe in my name, whatever they chose. They retrieved the envelope, said thanks again, and then left.

A few days later, I happened to bump into Mrs. Brenner. She embraced me, and started to cry. "You don't know what you did for me," she said, "and for my sons." I should mention that this family was extremely wealthy, and that Jewish organizations always pestered them for donations. "You are a man who did several jobs and deserved to be paid," she continued, "yet you refused payment. You are the only one who refused to get paid for helping with events surrounding my husband's death. I want to thank you. You put my sons' faith back in Judaism. I know that of course not everyone takes money, but many do. My sons know that all the Jewish groups want money. And here, this happened with you. You gave my sons *emuna, naḥat*." After all those compliments, we became even better friends. The Brenners, who owned a private island and even a private plane, often flew to the United States. Because I refused the money, whenever they went to the US they brought us back delicious kosher food, all kinds of kosher delicacies, special salamis, cheeses, you name it, things that we couldn't get in Mexico City. They showered us with gifts. King Solomon said, "Set sail your bread in the water, and some day it is going to come back." With respect to the Brenners, this couldn't have been truer.

Rivka and I often traveled to Cuernavaca, the capital of Mexico's state of Morelos. Established some 3,200 years ago, and a designated archaeological site, it is popular with both residents of Mexico City – seventy-five minutes by car – and tourists, probably because it is the "City of Eternal Spring," a nickname it earned for its idyllic climate. We went for both those reasons, and because of the perfectly situated Jewish retirement home, where I liked to give free concerts. One day on our way to the retirement home, we were bumped from behind by another car while stopped at a stop sign. We were not injured, but the other driver was. He was

Chapter Seven: Mexico City

covered in blood after hitting his forehead on the steering wheel. An uninvolved driver stopped and told me to "Go, go, go! You will go to jail!" I could not take his advice, primarily because a man had been injured, but also because I did not want to break the law. At that time in Mexico, all drivers had to stay at the scene of an accident until the police figured out what happened. There was no exchanging insurance numbers, and figuring everything out later. But the injured man, who was wearing a military uniform, had to be cared for. I was worried about him, even though he was insisting the accident was not his fault. Someone called an ambulance, and he was taken away to hospital. I was too upset to remember to get the other car's license plate number before the injured man's friend drove his car away. I sent Rivka home in a taxi and the police took me to the police station. "We cannot let you go until we understand the whole story," I was told over and over, even after repeating what had happened about twenty times. I was there for many hours, without food and without even being given bathroom breaks. The police tried to find the other driver by calling all the hospitals, but he seemed to be nowhere. Finally, I remembered his military uniform, so he was located at the military hospital. At least he finally admitted the accident was his fault.

Meanwhile, Rivka went to see the Brenners to explain what had happened. Mrs. Brenner jumped into action. She pulled out a huge suitcase and placed in it ten thousand dollars in cash, for the bribe. The truth was, in Mexico at that time, nothing ran smoothly except by greasing the hands of officials. We gave some men some money, and the police let me go.

***

In 1974, I almost went to jail again. Well, not really, but many people thought so. Remember, I worked at the Oxford Synagogue in Johannesburg between 1958 and 1970, until I was able to get out of my lifetime contract. Rivka and I then lived in Israel for eighteen months, but by 1974, we were already settled in Mexico City, when I got an urgent wire from the South African congregation. "Hello Ḥazan," it said. "We heard rumors you are in trouble. Stop. We want to help you. Stop." I was stunned. I ran to a phone to call the rabbi of the Oxford Synagogue. In those days, there was no direct dialing. I had to go through the operator, and it took four tries. "Where are you calling from?" he asked me. "Aren't you in prison? We heard you were caught selling drugs. It sounds preposterous, so we will help you any way we can. We will send any amount of money." I explained that everything was fine, and we both left the conversation wondering how this ridiculous and incredible story got legs. A few months later, Rivka and I traveled to Johannesburg for me to sing at our old congregation and to visit old friends. While there, I asked everyone I met from whom they had heard that awful rumor. It all came back to the same person: the current ḥazan of the *shul*. When I confronted him, he vehemently denied starting the rumor. But when I pressed him, he broke down and admitted he had made up the falsehood. "I am so sorry, Moshe," he said through tears. "I was so sick of everyone here comparing me to you: 'Moshe Kraus this, Moshe Kraus that.' The jealously ate me up, so I started the lie. I am so sorry. Please forgive me." Of course, I forgave him. After that, every time I saw him for the rest of his life, he apologized again.

***

During our four years in Mexico, Rivka and I traveled all over South America, so I could perform. We went to Brazil, Colombia, Argentina, Chile, and Peru. We also went to Costa Rica and Panama, both of which, believe it or not, are part of North America. Panama, which used to be part of the struggling and proud 185-year-old democracy of Colombia, became independent and thus part

Chapter Seven: Mexico City

of North America in 1903. The South American border begins at Panama's southern perimeter since, despite popular opinion, there really isn't a continent called Central America. Anyway, in short, we traveled anywhere in the region where there were Jews.

In Buenos Aires, the capital city of Argentina, Rivka and I met our devoted friends, the Geros. Henri Gero was a well-known violinist and a Yiddish humorist, and his wife – I cannot remember her first name, shame on me – was an enchanting opera singer, but not as famous as Henri. They frequently traveled together to perform concerts, duets, and storytelling. We thought they were delightful, and that their entertainment, like mine, was high-class. As couples, we did much together, including attending each other's performances. A word about Rivka. Whenever she was in the audience while I was singing, she never sat in the front row. Why? First of all, she knew she would be recognized there and she did not want to disrupt the show by saying hello to people behind her. Secondly, in the back rows, she could usually hear what people were saying about my singing, and she appreciated hearing those impromptu informal critiques. She always entered the concert hall when it was dark so she could take her seat at the back of the room, *incognito*. Then she listened carefully to hear what people in front of her were saying about me. This is how we in fact met the Geros. When Rivka overheard Mrs. Gero utter a gushing compliment about my voice during a Buenos Aires concert, she just had to meet her.

Once, when I was in Buenos Aires giving a concert, I told a story. It was a story I repeated often in South America, and my friend Henri applauded it. He said it did not matter if the story was true or not, it was wonderful and inspiring. I assured him, and I assure you, it happened. This is it: the Leningrad Story. If you recall, I was giving concerts behind the Iron Curtain in 1964. After conducting a Shabbat service at the Great Synagogue in Leningrad, I had lunch with the rabbi, and then went back to my hotel to rest. Thankfully I was dressed while I napped – I would not have wanted to answer the door in my sleepwear – as I was awoken abruptly by a hard knock at the door. In those days in the Soviet Union, whenever you heard a loud knock on the door, you got a concomitant hard knock in your heart. I opened up immediately. A uniformed Russian officer was standing before me. I admit I was scared. Remembering that this was the Soviet Union and no one could trust anyone, I thought for a moment maybe something bad had happened at the lunch.

Surprisingly, the officer began to talk in Yiddish. I calmed down. He told me a story. His father had been Jewish, his mother Christian, and his father often sang a beautiful Hebrew song. He continued: "My father told me that I, his son, was not Jewish because my mother was not Jewish, so I should not say *Kaddish* for him when he died. But he said I could sing this beautiful song for him." The officer began to sing, and he sang the same lovely song about eight times. I memorized it, and after that surprise meeting I sang the song at almost every concert I gave. I called it the Leningrad song, and I always sang it using his tune, which I called the Leningrad *nigun*.

The Leningrad Story continues. When I was in Israel in the early 1970s, I bumped into the Minister of the then Israeli Cultural Department, a man by the name of, I believe, Dr. Frimer, who liked to give speeches and do anything else that would raise money for his government ministry. He asked me to give a series of concerts for his department, and I said I'd be happy to, if I was paid. He offered me a contract to do ten concerts. One was in Binyamina, near a Chabad, or Lubavitcher, village. In the middle of this performance, I heard, "Doctor! We need a doctor!" Because the lights were in my face, I could not see what was going on. When everything calmed down, I went ahead with the concert. At the end, when I was in my private room close to the stage, I heard a knock at the door. It was the head of the nearby Chabad village. He told me that the man who fainted was the very man I had spoken about, the Russian officer with the Jewish father. The man had converted to Judaism and had joined the Lubavitcher hasidic sect. He fainted at the story because he was overwhelmed with emotion, but I was not to worry as he was recovering. Later, I went to see the man, and we embraced and cried. I met his family. The whole affair gave us both such *naḥat*.

One day, I traveled to Caracas, Venezuela, where I was scheduled to give a concert on the Sunday night after I had led the Shabbat *davening* in one of the city's synagogues. Before Shabbat began, I was told by Rabbi Rosenbaum, at whose home I was eating, that the *shul* we would be attending used a microphone on the *bima* during Shabbat. To me, this was completely against Jewish law, the law forbidding turning on electricity on the Sabbath. Some Orthodox Jews hold that as long as you don't turn the microphone on or off, it does not break the halakha. If you just speak and the microphone happens to be there, everything is fine. I do not hold that as acceptable, and I explained this opinion to Rabbi Brenner, the Chief Rabbi of Caracas and the *shul*'s spiritual leader. I told both Rabbis Brenner and Rosenbaum I was sorry, but I would not be *davening* at the *shul* on Shabbat. Rabbi Brenner was so insulted that he canceled the Sunday night concert that was also to be in his shul. I was sorry, but what could I do? It turned out that during *shaleshudis*, Rabbi Brenner and I were eating in the social hall of his *shul*. I sang *Yedid nefesh*, a Shabbat song, using my own melody. Rabbi Brenner loved it so much he uncanceled the concert. I was extra happy to sing in his *shul* Sunday night.

Another time, Rivka and I traveled to Panama for a short vacation. While walking down a main street together, I felt a hand in my pocket. It was a pick-pocket trying to find my wallet, which was not there. On the other side of my body I was holding a bag like a purse that had everything in it, including passports, other identification papers, and money. The pick-pocket maneuvered to my other side before I could say, "Hey! Get your hands off my.... pocket!" Holding the strap of my bag he jumped on the back of a waiting moped, where a driver was already revving the mini-motor. The two tore away on their little vehicle, which sounded much like a sewing machine. There was no way I was letting them take the bag with all those important documents, so I ran very fast after them until I could get my hand around the bag's strap. Before I knew it, I was being dragged along the ground on my stomach. Luckily, a car got in their way. They had to stop and when they did I was able to grab back the bag really fast and hard. With it safely in my arms, looking dirty and scuffed up, I returned to my hotel, where Rivka was in the lobby on the phone to the police. She hung up when she saw me and we had one more display of public affection, our second and last, so far.

***

After a few years in Mexico, Rivka and I decided it was time to find a quiet, clean city to retire in. We wanted to find a pleasant place in a first-world country. Though there is no question but that Mexico is a fantastic country and Mexico City a fantastic city, the grinding poverty there is omnipresent, insidious, and impossible to ignore. Of the eight million people in the city, fully half are dreadfully poor. We always carried money to give to the children who begged in the streets, but it was painful to constantly see them. The fact that the deficiencies of the country could not be rectified quickly affected us subtly all the time, ultimately making ordinary life difficult.

We were fortunate to have a maid in Mexico City, to whom we of course paid a proper wage. But it was still not enough to make her life and the lives of her children easy. In fact, she used to bring her son to work instead of getting a babysitter, which was fine with us because he was cute and very well-behaved. When she heard

Chapter Seven: Mexico City

we were leaving the country, she was upset, especially because she could not afford to give us a parting gift. Rivka explained that a gift was not necessary. "I know," the maid said triumphantly, "I will give you my son!" Rivka could not believe her ears. "No, no, sweetie," Rivka said gently. "Your son is six years old. He will miss you too much." "No problem," she replied, tears in her eyes. "I have a baby at home. You can have her." You can imagine the difficulty Rivka had explaining to the maid the problems we'd have trying to get through customs, trying to convince the border officials that the baby was nothing more than a simple going-away gift.

How did we choose Ottawa? Well, like most of my stories, the answer begins in a foreign country, this time the United States, Miami to be exact. Rivka and I were there while I was giving a concert in 1975. We happened to meet two gentlemen, pillars of the Ottawa Jewish community, and sadly both now of blessed memory. One was physician Dr. Edward Shapiro and the other was Alex Becherman. They told me that Ottawa's Congregation Beth Shalom was looking for a ḥazan and I should come for a trial run. "I don't do trials," I politely informed them, without a hint of arrogance. "But I love to do concerts." They laughed, and invited me to sing at a concert. That was all it took. One visit to Ottawa, and both Rivka and I were hooked.

The Life of Moshele Der Zinger

Unión Israelita de Caracas
קולטור־צענטער
שלום־עליכם
קאראקאס

INVITAN A SUS MIEMBROS Y A TODA LA
COLECTIVIDAD HEBREA DE CARACAS A UN

CONCIERTO

de

CANTOS JASIDICOS

DEL RENOMBRADO CANTANTE INTERNACIONAL

MOSHE KRAUS

QUIEN RETORNA DE SU EXITOSA GIRA POR EUROPA,
ESTADOS UNIDOS, CANADA Y SUR-AMERICA

Moshe Kraus

Lugar Sede de la Unión Israelita de Caracas
Av. Marqués del Toro, San Bernardino
Fecha: 12 DE SEPTIEMBRE DE 1973
HORA: 8:30 P. M.

מיר האבן דעם כבוד אייך איינצולאדן
צום איינציקן געזאנגס־אוונט פון דעם
וועלט בארימטן זינגער און חזן
מ ש ה   ק ר א ו ס
וועלכער וועט פארקומען:
מיטוואך, דעם 12־טן סעפטעמבער
8.30 אוונט
אין די זאלן פון דער
"אוניאן איזראעליסא"

Invitation to Cantor Kraus' concert in Caracas, Venezuela

Chapter Seven: Mexico City

Cantor Kraus and his choir in Mexico

Chapter Eight
Ottawa

Rivka and I are often asked, "Why did you choose Ottawa? Why not Toronto? Why not Montreal? Why not New York?" People from Ottawa know the answer right away, but for others, I will explain. New York and its diminutive kissing-cousin Toronto – two cities which we absolutely love to visit – are quite simply too big. When I visited Montreal for the first time, as I was walking down the street, a stranger shouted out to me, "*Juif*," pronounced "Jweef," which was a slur against me as a Jew. In Ottawa, in forty years, I have never once heard an antisemitic comment. By the way, we still love to visit Montreal – I sang for the *yamim noraim* there for two years in a row – but Ottawa is definitely, and permanently, home.

A most wonderful event took place on May 5, 2016, during the National Holocaust Remembrance Day Ceremony, an experience that will stay in my heart forever. The somber observance is held every spring at the imposing National War Museum in Ottawa, located on the majestic Ottawa River. In 2016, I am told, more people than ever turned out, about one thousand. The young, dynamic, new Prime Minister of Canada Justin Trudeau – son of the late Prime Minister Pierre Trudeau, who led Canada for some sixteen years in the 1960s, 1970s, and early 1980s – donned a *kippa* and presented me with the first-ever Cantor Kraus Catalyst for Change Award. The Canadian Society for Yad Vashem crafted this decoration in my name, in order to honor people who work diligently for the cause of Holocaust education. The words engraved on the award say: "Presented to Cantor Moshe Kraus, who lends his beautiful voice and works passionately and tirelessly to fulfill his life's mission to commemorate the Holocaust, while educating communities about the Shoah's universal lessons."

Just before he handed me the gift, the prime minister said: "I might point out that I have the extraordinary privilege of being the second Prime Minister Trudeau to have the honor to know Cantor Kraus and to have felt blessed, moved, and inspired by him, and by his incredible gift of song." I was practically speechless when I was presented with the beautiful thick glass plaque, but I managed to tell him thank-you. Of course, I cried.

***

Rivka and I settled into our apartment in downtown Ottawa, where we've lived for four decades. When I first arrived here, I noticed that it was hard to find men who wore *kippot*, on their heads, unlike today. Now, such sights are common. When I arrived, I was told by some in the community that no one would mind if I went outside without my *kippa*. I replied, "They'll get used to me wearing it. My father taught me how to be a proud Jew."

When we first arrived, I enjoyed my job at Beth Shalom synagogue very much. Unfortunately, I had to leave the job after only four years. I would have stayed longer before retirement, but I did not agree with the height of the *meḥitza,* the divider to separate men and women during *davening.* Using a *meḥitza* goes back to Talmudic times, and the reasoning is to essentially prevent flirting between the sexes during such a serious time. After discussions, the *shul* leaders at Beth Shalom did not want to raise the *meḥitza,* so I left my job. Within a number of years, the synagogue became Conservative, a stream of Judaism that philosophically allows for the *meḥitza* to be eliminated altogether.

Some of the congregants were unhappy to see me leave, and one person in particular – an accomplished chemist – put his feelings in a letter. "Dear Ḥazan," his letter of June 29, 1980 began. "When you informed me yesterday that this was your last Shabbat at Beth Shalom, I really had a sinking feeling in the pit of my stomach. The congregation's loss will be greater than yours. Beth Shalom never before had a cantor like you, and never will again. Each performance was a work of art, and truly a labor of love. Your heart and soul were in it. I can assure you that you made the Sabbath services more meaningful and enjoyable for many of the worshippers, and they will sorely miss you. I, for one, will miss greeting you and our occasional little chats. May you and your dear wife enjoy a bright and successful future in a less political and more congenial atmosphere. I feel fortunate to be able to count you amongst my friends." When I read this letter, not surprisingly, I cried.

After I stopped working full time, I became a freelancer. One of the wonderful gigs I got for thirty years was to travel to Miami, Florida for Pesaḥ. We always left before the first *seder,* and came home a day or so after the last day of the seven-day festival. This meant we did not have to clean our home for Pesaḥ, a grueling chore that every religious Jew grumbles about for at least a month before the holiday starts. As a freelancer, I also performed in Montreal and Toronto more times than I can possibly remember. Beautiful cities all.

The Life of Moshele Der Zinger

From 1983 and for the next fifteen years, I traveled to Budapest for the High Holy Days. It was a wonderful annual trek that both Rivka and I enjoyed to the fullest. The World Jewish Congress sponsored the longest parts of these trips, beginning right before *Seliḥot* – the special prayers and poems said on the days leading up to Rosh HaShana – and ending after Sukkot, the eight-day fall festival when Orthodox Jews build sukkot, temporary shelters for meals and sometimes sleeping, in their back yards to remember the forty years that the Children of Israel wandered in the desert after leaving slavery in Ancient Egypt. Also, for five years until I retired about ten years ago in 2010, the Budapest government invited me to come for Hanukka.

In Budapest, I sang in the Great Synagogue that had been rebuilt after the Nazis destroyed it. The careful and solid reconstruction was done by the world's best-known developer, Olympia and York, a company owned mostly by the Reichmann brothers. Hungarian Jews are eternally grateful to the Reichmanns, who happen to be Orthodox Jews originally from the tiny Hungarian *shtetl* of Beled and who eventually settled in Canada. But every time I went to Budapest, I could not help but envision the city like it was before the war. It made me nostalgic. The *yamim noraim* in Budapest constitute more than the most religious time of the Jewish year. Indeed, Jews come to the city from all over the world, and they come for the express reason to sit in the Great Synagogue in the very seats used by their fathers, their *zaides*, or even the seats used by their great-grandfathers. The *shul* is always tightly packed during these holy days. This annual incursion of thousands of people from all over always made the Budapest holidays even more spiritual.

Once, about twenty-five years ago, a man fainted in the crowded Budapest sanctuary. Many people gathered around him until he woke up. The man, who was about my age, eighty-five, began to breathe hard, and then he spoke. "I want to sit beside

Moshe Kraus," he panted. When I approached him he said to me, "Moshe, do you know why I fainted? When you came in and some people near me told me who you were, I was overwhelmed. I remembered the evening with you and the Stropkover Rebbe. I was there that night, too, when everyone gathered outside the window. I just saw him five months ago." I thought, wow, what a wonderful coincidence. Then I remembered that would have been impossible, since that *rebbe* died in 1954. The current *admor*, or spiritual leader, of Stropkov is Rabbi Avraham Shalom Halberstam. He runs some yeshivot and other religious organizations in Jerusalem, as well as a few other Israeli cities. The man who collapsed continued: "I will give you the name and phone number of this *rebbe*." The name he gave me was Chaim Yosef Gottlieb, who died in 1867! He was the original or second Rebbe of Stropkov, I am not sure which. Gottlieb had been a fascinating man, a devoted student of Rabbi Moshe Schreiber – a nineteenth-century scholar who strongly opposed Reform Judaism – and the author of *Tiv Gittin veKiddushin*, a book about the finer points of the laws of marriage and divorce. Gottlieb's sons published the work in 1868 in Uzhhorod.

    I realized this poor man was confused. To be kind, I listened anyway. I think he thought we were playing a bit of Jewish geography, seeing who knew who, when, and where. "As I was dining with friends just last night," the gasping man continued, "Gottlieb came into the restaurant. He was about my age. I told him I *davened* in Presov, a city in eastern Slovakia, with Rabbi Meir Lau, the chief rabbi of Tel Aviv. Rabbi Lau's father, Rabbi Moshe Chaim Lau, was the chief rabbi of Piotrkow Trybunalski, in central Poland, where I also *davened*. Just last night, Moshe Kraus, I remembered that when I was a boy there was a man from Miami who wanted to pay to dismantle the *shul* in Piotrkow Trybunalski brick by brick and ship the entire structure off to Israel. He offered the city a hundred thousand to move it to the main street in Jerusalem. This would have helped bring tourists. However, the city didn't agree." I said that was too bad, and then, being extremely tired, I bade him a good night and walked away.

I have so many stories to tell about Ottawa, that literally, I do not know where to begin. I will say this though, living in Canada's capital and so close to Parliament Hill, I ended up getting involved in political decision-making slightly more than I normally would. For instance, in 1985, I supported the Deschenes Commission of Inquiry on War Criminals in Canada. It recommended changes to Canadian laws to allow for either the criminal prosecution or, under civil law, the deportation of suspected war criminals. Though in the end only a small number of Nazi cases were subsequently and successfully acted upon, at the time I cheered on this commission. I wrote a long, detailed letter to Justice Minister Ray Hnatyshyn, telling him why I supported the work his ministry was doing. He wrote me back a personal letter in 1988. At least, I think it was personal. Written on gold-embossed, high-quality stock, ministerial paper, the letter included a long summary of how Bill C-71 came to be enacted, a paragraph on why he thought the legislation would be successful, and a closing that seemed quite intimate: "With kindest regards, I remain yours sincerely."

Several years later, the government announced it was no longer going to be prosecuting Nazi war criminals. I again wrote to Mr. Hnatyshyn, who was now Canada's Governor General, but he sent me what could only be described as a form letter. That just about ended my active involvement in government decision-making. The Canadian government was harshly criticized from many quarters for ending its Nazi hunt. Even the Simon Wiesenthal Center got in on the act and condemned the Canadian government. The Center is the international human rights organization which brought a number of suspected Nazi war criminals – who had been hiding all over the world – to trial. The Center published a paper claiming

Chapter Eight: Ottawa

an estimated two thousand Nazi war criminals were able to gain Canadian citizenship by lying on their immigration papers. This number has been challenged, but the Simon Wiesenthal Center nevertheless made excellent points.

Since retiring in Ottawa I have had more time to write, which I have done often with the help of local professional writer Kinneret Globerman. One piece we wrote together was published in the *Ottawa Citizen* on May 1, 2000. The headline was "The Man was a Saint," and it discussed the story of my uncle Leizer Schwartz, who everyone called Leizer Potiker because he was the Chief Rabbi of Saros Potok. He was known as one of the greatest scholars in all of Hungary during his time. But he was not the saint in the headline. Kinneret and I told the story like this. In 1943, when I was chief ḥazan of the Shomrei Shabbos Synagogue in Budapest, to my utter surprise, a priest came to my door, all decked out in his religious garb. "The Bishop of Saros Potok wants to see you immediately about a very important case. He is waiting for you in the Royal Hotel. Please accompany me." I thought this must be significant. I grabbed my coat and went with him. Curious neighbors were looking out their windows, wondering what I was doing walking with a priest. I was curious, too; I had never before spent extended time in the company of a priest or bishop. We arrived at the hotel eight minutes later, where I met the bishop, who asked me to ride with him in his car while he traveled to meet the government minister of the interior. "I will explain everything during the drive," he said. In the car he told me that two days earlier, the police in Saros Potok had arrested my uncle. "They took him to the Tolontz Haz, the most horrible jail in Hungary," he said. "I immediately contacted Budapest authorities and was told he is accused of being communist and a communist agitator. I asked a colleague in Budapest to arrange for a meeting with the minister of the interior, to ask him to release him. And we are heading there now to obtain your uncle's release." You have now met the saint, whose name I never asked for because at first, I was too apprehensive, then I was way too excited, during our time together. Asking completely slipped my mind.

Soon we arrived at the minister's office. "What can I do for you, Your Holiness?" he asked the bishop. "Your Excellency," said the bishop, "you have in the Tolontz Haz jail a man who goes by the name Leizer Schwartz. He is the Chief Rabbi of Soros Potok. I have known this man for almost twenty years. And I will give you an account of his activities for every day in those twenty years." For the next twenty minutes, the bishop, who lived close to my uncle, related my uncle's daily activities: "I see him rise every single day at five. You could set your alarm clock by him. Then I see him as he passes by my window on the way to the ritual bath, or *mikve*. He spends fifteen or twenty minutes there, after which he takes his prayer bag and goes to the synagogue. He has breakfast at eight. At nine he goes to the *beit din*, the religious court, where he sits as a judge. At 12.30 p.m., he goes home for lunch and has a brief nap. He is back at the religious court at 2 p.m. At five, he gives a lecture from the Talmud. At seven, he attends evening prayer. He has dinner at eight, and then he sits down to answer letters. He answers every single letter addressed to him. At midnight, he says a prayer by candlelight. What is that prayer, son?" he asked me. "It is to remember the destruction of the temples," I replied. "Then," the bishop continued, "he goes to sleep and everything starts all over again the next day. Now, Your Excellency, I would like to ask you: Number one, how can a religious man be a communist? Number two, when did this rabbi ever have the time to be a communist agitator? Therefore, I appeal to you, who I believe to be a good and loyal Christian and an honest Hungarian, please release Leizer Schwartz. He is innocent. As a bishop, I hope my characterization of this man is enough to convince you to give me a letter of release that I may take to the jail warden. Thank you for fulfilling my request." The minister responded promptly: "There is nothing I can do. It is not in my hands. I am very sorry you made this journey for nothing."

Dismayed, the bishop asked: "You will let me leave empty-handed?" No reply came. The bishop stood up, unbuttoned his frock, took it off and let it drop to the ground. He removed his religious head-covering and threw it on the desk of the minister. Then he said: "In a country where you can take an innocent, decent man and throw him in jail, in such a country I don't want to be a bishop. You be the bishop!" He walked to the door to exit the room when the horrified minister stopped him, told him to sit down, then he himself ran out the door. Within thirty minutes, he was back with a letter. "Here is your letter, Bishop," he said. "Now go and take your Leizer Schwartz back to Saros Potok." After many happy thank-yous and goodbyes, we left. Once outside, the bishop blessed me, and asked me to bless him. I said: "I thank you for what you did for my uncle, and God shall bless you, that whomever you will bless shall be blessed." He handed me the letter, jumped into his chauffeured car, and left.

I ran. I brought the letter to the prison, and the warden opened the prison gate for me to go in and find my uncle. I entered a dark, cavernous hole, and called over and over again: "Leizer Schwartz! Leizer Schwartz! Leizer Schwartz!" He did not answer me back, but I did hear beautiful, heavenly singing. I turned toward the music, and saw about seventy-five men standing on a mound, and all were harmonizing in Yiddish and making soothing symphonious sounds. Such grace and elegance in such a hellhole! I learned they were Jews who escaped Poland, came to Hungary, and were caught and imprisoned.

I finally found my uncle, teaching a group of Jewish prisoners Talmud without a single note or textbook, all from his memory. He was over the moon to see me. We embraced, and walked out of the prison. On our way to the train station, he said, "You know, Moshele, according to Jewish law, we are not allowed to commit suicide. Our lives don't belong to us, they belong to God. But if I ever come back to Tolontz Haz, I hope I will not be faced with the choice to live or take my life, because I don't know if I will be strong enough to resist the temptation to kill myself."

***

In 2004, after I'd been living in Ottawa for almost thirty years, I had an unexpected emotional reunion with a childhood friend, in front of 150 people. I was about to introduce the speaker, Maurice Katz, Ph.D., who was to discuss his experiences in the Holocaust, when I realized I was going to be introducing a school friend from Uzhhorod from more than 70 years ago. "When I saw who tonight's speaker was, I almost fainted," I said when I stood up and spoke to the audience. "I, too, was born in Uzhhorod, and I was a frequent guest in the home of Dr. Katz's parents." I remember his mother well because she was extra kind to me as a child; she always gave me sweets. She knew I loved candy, and she called me Moshe the *nasher*. Dr. Katz rose quickly, and said: "Don't tell me you are Moshele Kraus! We went to the same school!" We embraced. Many in the audience cried, before applauding with joy for us. Dr. Katz then told of his horrendous experiences during the Holocaust. I remember that his experience ended the way mine did, with a continuing love of God and a damaged but ultimately restored belief in the goodness of humankind.

It was while I lived in Ottawa, in 2003, that the federal government finally passed a law that required it to hold an annual commemoration of the Holocaust, thus ushering Canada into the twenty-first century to join the United Nations and dozens of other first world countries. The law itself is beautiful in its simplicity: "An Act to establish Holocaust Memorial Day. Preamble: Whereas the Holocaust refers to a specific event in history, namely, the deliberate and planned state-sponsored persecution and annihilation of European Jewry by the Nazis and their collaborators between 1933 and 1945; Whereas six million Jewish men, women, and children perished under this policy of hatred and genocide; Whereas millions of others were victims of that policy because of their physical or mental disabilities, race, religion, or sexual orientation; Whereas the terrible destruction and pain of the Holocaust must never be forgotten; Whereas systematic violence, genocide, persecution, racism, and hatred continue to occur throughout the world; Whereas the Parliament of Canada is committed to using legislation, education, and example to protect Canadians from violence, racism, and hatred, and to stopping those who foster or commit crimes of violence, racism, and hatred; and Whereas Yom HaShoah, or the Day of the Holocaust, as determined in each year by the Jewish lunar calendar, is an opportune day to reflect on and educate about the enduring lessons of the Holocaust and to reaffirm a commitment to uphold human rights; now, therefore, Her Majesty, by and with the advice and consent of the Senate and House of Commons of Canada, enacts as follows: This Act may be cited as the Holocaust Memorial Day Act, Yom HaShoah, or the Day of the Holocaust, as determined in each year by the Jewish lunar calendar, is proclaimed as Holocaust Memorial Day – Yom HaShoah."

Thank you, Canada. And thank you for presenting me with the first annual Cantor Kraus Catalyst for Change Award at the most recent Holocaust Memorial Day ceremonies in Ottawa. And thank you for inviting me to participate with Canadian officials in many previous such ceremonies, where I could emphasize the need for education and never forgetting. During the 2010 ceremony, I echoed Liberal Party Leader Michael Ignatieff, stating that genocide must never happen again, and calling "never again" a simple message that must remain in the hearts of future generations. That year, I talked about returning to Bergen-Belsen the following week, in order to reinforce this critical message. "It hurts me to go there, but I must go," I said. "This is the most important thing, not to forget what happened so it shall never happen again."

***

Most of my interactions with journalists have been very positive. I believe a free press is truly important in keeping citizens informed and governments honest. Throughout my life, I have spoken with dozens of different reporters about my experiences in the Holocaust, about my childhood, about my travels, and, of course, about my singing.

I have also been evaluated by my share of music critics, but none so illustrious as Ottawa's Jacob Siskind, who sadly died in 2010. Among other work, he was a music critic for the daily newspaper mentioned above, the *Ottawa Citizen*. He was also often heard on CBC, Canada's public radio station. His obituary described him like this: "He set an exemplary standard for journalistic criticism. He was highly esteemed by musicians, critics, and readers for the liveliness, insight, and erudite scholarship that distinguished his reviews." He never gave a compliment that wasn't deserved, and he was not afraid to say negative things even about the most popular music. For instance, in the same 1985 review in which he called "Requiem" by Andrew Lloyd Webber "eclectic" and "cheap," he referred to a cassette I released the same year as "some of the most glorious tenor singing I have had the pleasure to hear." He noted that since I was retired, I could give concerts for my own pleasure, and, spiritually, "the pleasure of God," who gave me my talent and my voice. The cassette, called "*Dash M'Anash*," is unfortunately no longer available. It was a collection of some of my favorite hasidic material, including *Malokhim, Shalom Aleikhem, Shir Hamaalot, Yehi Ratzon* and *Shabbos*. While Siskind castigated my piano accompaniment for a few good reasons, he called my voice: "the envy of many an operatic tenor," "a cantorial art at its more highly developed," and "an incredibly high caliber."

Five years later, in 1990, Siskind wrote about me again, this time focusing on my retirement activities. "Moshe Kraus is a man with a mission," he wrote on March 21. "He is a devotee of Hasidism, a Jewish sect that extols the virtues of both God and man. It is his purpose these days to explain the spirit of the movement to those unaware of its philosophy. He does so through a program, called *Dash M'Anash*, that he has been presenting in concert on several continents. Most recently, he presented his program in Frankfurt's Goethe University, where he kept his audience enthralled for several hours answering questions from the floor after the 45-minute concert." Siskind then kindly announced the upcoming Ottawa performance at the Orthodox Machzikei Hadas synagogue, a concert that was a huge success and in which my musical accompanist was the excellent and well-known local pianist Evelyn Greenberg.

Siskind then gave a simple explanation of the job of Orthodox cantors, as well as my opinion of the changes in the profession. "Cantors represent the congregation at prayers in the synagogue during services," he quoted me as saying. "Their recitation of familiar prayers and their embellishment of traditional melodies has long been considered one of the beauties of Orthodox religious services. As a traditionalist, Kraus despairs for the future of cantorial music, as it was known at the turn of the [previous] century." At the time, I was bemoaning the influence of recordings which, I told him, have influenced the discipline in the negative. "Before," I told Siskind, "one went to hear what each cantor could and would do in the expression of his personal view of traditional prayer. Each cantor had his own way of expressing himself, and it was this variety that made cantorial singing the art that it was. With the introduction of recorded music, it became possible for anyone to copy the best work of others, to imitate rather than to create and develop on the basis of an individual personality. It all

The Life of Moshele Der Zinger

became too easy. Cantors today are too often pale copies of the great art of the cantors of the past. The art of improvisation has been lost." If I had not actually said this – as quoted by Siskind in his column – I would have to say, "I could not have said this better myself."

Siskind noted that though I had released a few recordings and tapes, I had chosen not to record my best material and compositions. He did not give the reason, but it was because I did not want it memorized and copied by other cantors. Siskind then pointed out, correctly, how in my retirement I had left behind much of my cantorial sounds to concentrate on hasidic music and tales. He said, correctly again, that the general public sees hasidic Jews "as strange people who wear fur-trimmed hats, long suitcoats, beards, and curled hair at their temples. Kraus sees them as representing a way of life that is based on the Bible... [and whose name] Hasidim takes its roots from the Hebrew word *ḥesed*, which means loving-kindness." The journalist again quoted me: "When God created the world, one of the things he created was *ḥesed*. The Baal Shem Tov, when he founded [the hasidic] movement, added other attributes like *simḥa*, happiness. You must always be happy, no matter what. According to the Baal Shem Tov, one must do kindness for its own sake, without calculation, without expecting something in return." I meant every word he quoted me as saying.

In the year 2000, the *Ottawa Citizen* covered the move of Hillel Lodge, the city's only Jewish nursing home, from downtown to the city's west-end Jewish community campus. The move was extremely positive, but it meant I could no longer walk from my home to the lodge's tiny *shul* on Shabbat. The paper's religion writer Bob Harvey, who sadly died in 2014, wrote about how the transfer to a brand-new building miles away was stopping some Orthodox clergy from attending the lodge's Sabbath synagogue services. I thought Harvey wrote a very positive *Ottawa Citizen* piece about Orthodox Judaism. He noted how some non-residents of

Chapter Eight: Ottawa

the nursing home walked up to eight kilometers to attend services at the old residence. He was so right. I remember well how Rabbi Israel Rabinowitz used to walk that long, long way to read from the Torah, every single week, winter and summer, freezing cold or melting hot. He never let us down. But with the move – now right around the corner from Rabbi Rabinowitz's home – I would not be able to return the favor by walking eight kilometers in the opposite direction in order to sing for the residents. Harvey wrote: "During his time with the synagogue at Hillel Lodge, Mr. Kraus always refused payment for his services. He said he and other non-residents of the lodge saw their service at the lodge synagogue as simply a mitzva, a good deed." I told Harvey I hope that when I die, "my mitzvot will outweigh my sins and I will go to Paradise, where I can study Torah and listen to the great rabbis [already there], like Moses and Isaac." Well said, well quoted.

***

We were very fortunate to have a generous gentile friend in Ottawa, one Patrick Rooney, president of One World Forest and Biofuels, an environmental company that carries out, among other projects, forest planting in arid places, including China. He was once invited to China to see the conditions there. He saw firsthand how there is much desert. In fact, it is encroaching on the cities and the arable land. This man did two unforgettable things for me. He saved my life, and he had a forest planted in China named after me. As far as I know, I am the only person in the world to have a formally planted and personally named forest in China.

I owe this man my life. For two years every single morning, he came to my door at 6 a.m. and drove me out to Ottawa's west end Young Israel Synagogue so I could *daven* with a minyan. One Thursday morning, on our way, I mentioned to him that I had pain in my right chest. He had recently lost an uncle who had not dealt with strong pain on the right side of his chest, so he wanted to take me to the emergency department of the nearby hospital. I told him to ignore my situation and drop me off at the *shul*. After all, aren't heart conditions felt in the left arm? Apparently not only there. He ignored my pleading and drove me to the Civic Hospital. There I saw a doctor, who performed an angiogram. During this procedure, a catheter is advanced up an artery from the leg to the heart so dye can be inserted. The doctor said, "This is going to hurt." After it was over I asked, "You call that pain? I was in Bergen-Belsen, which should have been called 'Camp Pain.'" The doctor tried not to laugh. He reached over and gave me a hug. And they say physician bedside manner has gone the way of the Iron Lung. Not true.

After that I fell into a coma for two weeks. It turned out I had a 99 percent blockage. The doctor later said that if I had waited only thirty minutes longer before coming to the hospital, I probably would have died of a massive coronary attack. I was surprised to have a heart condition, because I have never been overweight. My diet, full of vegetables, is quite good. Yes, I still enjoy *noshing*, snacking, and I definitely did not ever shovel snow, a popular pastime in Ottawa! In truth, I have hardly been sick a day in my life. Even the Holocaust did not make me sick. It made me weak, yes, very weak, and spiritually sick, but not physically ill, even in the concentration camps when contagious diseases were rampant. Clearly, God is always on my side.

Chapter Eight: Ottawa

The Right Honourable Justin Trudeau, Prime Minister of Canada, and Cantor Kraus present the first Cantor Kraus Catalyst for Change Award at the Holocaust Remembrance Day ceremony in Ottawa (May 2016). The award was created by Yad Vashem and recognizes Canadians who have shown their dedication to Holocaust education

The Life of Moshele Der Zinger

Presenting The Cantor Moshe Kraus Forest in China to Cantor Kraus

Chapter Eight: Ottawa

Cantor Kraus composing music on his piano in Ottawa, Canada

Elie Wiesel visiting Cantor Kraus at his apartment in Ottawa

The Life of Moshele Der Zinger

Cantor Kraus with Canadian Prime Minister Stephen Harper (left)

Receiving a gift from the Torah Academy of Ottawa

Chapter Eight: Ottawa

Yom HaShoah Ceremony on Parliament Hill in Ottawa, Canada. From left to right:
Alan Baker, Israel's Ambassador to Canada;
The Honourable Peter Milliken, Speaker of the House of Commons of Canada;
The Honourable Noël Kinsella, Speaker of the Senate of Canada;
The Right Honourable Stephen Harper, Prime Minister of Canada;
Cantor Moshe Kraus;
The Right Honourable Herb Gray, former Deputy Prime Minister of Canada

Conclusion

In 2006, I was honored by Ottawa's Jewish Youth Library (JYL), a Chabad organization that puts on special events for adults and families in the community, and runs children's camps and nursery schools. Founded and operated by Dr. Josef and Devorah Caytak, the JYL, is known for its elegant and classy fund-raising events, and the night I was honored was no exception. Right before the big event – in which three famous *ḥazanim* and world-renowned accompanist Daniel Gildar of Philadelphia came to sing and entertain in my honor – about a hundred people gathered at the mansion of Jozef Strauss and his wife, pillars of the Ottawa Jewish community and the kindest people you'd ever have the pleasure of meeting. Then, immediately following the concert, the Strausses hosted a dinner at 11 p.m. for some thirty guests. The reason for the late dinner is this: *ḥazanim* generally sing on empty stomachs, so by the time the event was over, the three famous cantors were quite hungry.

The Life of Moshele Der Zinger

In a promotional letter to the community months before the event – written by my friend and author Kinneret Globerman – Devorah Caytak was quoted as saying this: "We want to honor Cantor Kraus' contribution to Jewish life before World War II, during the war, and after the war. That contribution is enormous. Never in cantorial history, apparently, has there been a cantor with a career spanning seventy years. Or has there been a cantor who has sung the *Kol Nidrei* an astonishing 210 times. And never has there been one who was invited to places no other cantor had ever ventured." Quoting me, Globerman continued: "There wasn't a wedding, a *ḥevra kaddisha seuda*, a Talmud Torah or yeshiva fundraiser, nor a city in Europe... that didn't invite me to grace their meals."

As a gift and part of the event, local artist and friend Rabbi Elie Benzaquen painted a gorgeous picture from the photograph of my tatty and me at my bar mitzva. He did this onto a large 16-by-20-inch canvas, with colors added to brighten the picture. It now hangs proudly in my den, where I can see it every day and remember what a wonderful father I had, and what a fantastic family I came from.

That amazing night in 2006 – held at Ottawa's relatively new and very impressive Jewish Community Center – involved the three world renowned cantors putting on a unforgettable evening. They were: Ḥazan Pinchas Cohen, who works at Manhattan Beach Jewish Center, situated in – where else? – the middle of Brooklyn; Ḥazan Shimon Kugel, of blessed memory, a guitar-playing delight, originally from South Africa, who spent years in New York trying to spread *yiddishkeit*; and the great Ḥazan Benjamin Muller, the Chief Cantor of Antwerp. Five months before the three-cantor event, Kinneret wrote a complimentary and captivating article announcing the event being planned. In her excellent prose, she managed to condense my life into twenty-five paragraphs for the *Ottawa Jewish Bulletin*. She began the piece by describing that

Conclusion

treasured photograph of myself and my tatty taken at my bar mitzva. She noted that extreme show of affection, for the times, that my tatty and I shared: "[The photograph] shows a solemn-eyed boy and his father, the father's hand resting solidly on the young lad's shoulder as they both stare squarely at the camera." She said that my voice, "once heard, could never be forgotten... People marveled when he opened his mouth to sing, and such a strong and beautiful voice emerged."

Kinneret tried to summarize my travels, saying I went to sing in places like "Buenos Aires, Rio de Janeiro, Caracas, Mexico, Lima, Costa Rica, Chicago, Los Angeles, Strasbourg, London, Paris, and not once or twice or even five times." There were many, many more places. I like to summarize my travels this way: I've sung all over Europe, in cities all over North, Central, and South America, in cities in the Middle East, and in several countries in Africa. Kinneret continued: "Remarkably he was also invited to two places where Jews were scarce: Teheran under the Shah, and Istanbul." I wasn't exactly invited to Teheran, but I did visit that place on my way to Israel. She asked me what the best part of my career was, and this is what I told her, and it is still true fifteen years later: "My highlight was every *tefilla*. Every *davening*, I gave my best. I always knew I was standing before God. I didn't *daven* to entertain people. I *davened* for God."

Journalist Diane Koven, who covered the actual three-cantor event for the *Ottawa Jewish Bulletin,* called the concert "a tribute to a man who is, himself, respected and admired around the world." The emcee phrased it like this: "This evening would have been amazing even had Cantor Kraus merely been an invited guest from out of town – to have had the privilege of having such an internationally recognized *ḥazan* in our midst would have been a tremendous coup for Ottawa. However, Cantor Kraus is not an invited guest from out of town – he is one of us, a resident of Ottawa, and that adds an element of enormous pride to the occasion for us all."

Each of the three cantors also spoke about me in accolades. I think my head grew three sizes that night.

Five years later, in 2011, I was honored by a first-rate Jewish day school called the Torah Academy of Ottawa, which merged with Ottawa's second Orthodox school. Perhaps the most remarkable part of this event was the colorful, glossy, fundraising booklet. It comprised interesting articles about me and Rivka and the school, as well as beautifully written congratulatory letters from the mayor of Ottawa, the premier of the Province of Ontario, the prime minister of Canada himself, and finally, from Rabbi Meir Lau, the former chief rabbi of Israel.

With respect to all of these events, I am overwhelmed and humbled by the thoughts and outpouring of love that came with them. I can never forget them.

These days, I am often asked what message I would give the younger generations of Jewish children, who will never visit or experience the idyllic hasidic towns of 1920s Eastern Europe because they were eradicated by Hitler; who will, *barukh Hashem*, thank God, never experience the increasingly restrictive decrees put on Jews in Europe in the 1930s; and who will, *barukh Hashem* again, never see the inside of an operational Nazi death camp. This is my message: I am an older man, and I do not know how much longer I will live. But I love people, and you should, too. There are no bad Americans in general, there are no bad Canadians in general, there are even no bad Germans in general, and no bad Jews in general. There are good and bad in every legitimate group. Don't put a negative stamp on a whole body of people, saying they are bad. Do you know how many Germans put their lives in jeopardy and died to save Jews? Go to Yad Vashem in Israel and you'll see the German names. Many Germans were killed doing these selfless acts. I had the honor to meet Oskar Schindler. But he was only one of so many.

Conclusion

About fifteen years ago, I found myself sitting beside a US senator on a plane. I wish I could remember his name. Somehow, we got to talking about antisemitism. I told him it does not really exist, and by this I mean there are only good and bad people. Only bad people are antisemitic, and of course, not all bad people have that evil characteristic. Good people are never antisemitic. So antisemitism is an evil part of some bad people, not a reasonable idea or a rational subject to discuss. It does not exist in the normal and moral world.

But, we must never forget what the evil Nazis did. Never. It must never happen again.

In our den, Rivka and I have a ten-gallon glass bowl full of a collection of matchboxes from all over the world, from most of the cities we visited. Just looking at how full that bowl is, I can see we had a rich and wonderful life. That bowl of matches represents my vast experiences, not all good by any stretch of the imagination, as I've shown in this book. But I think you now have an idea of my many gifts from God. Which brings me to the other message I want to give: Whatever problems you have in your life, no matter how bad they are, God is available to help you overcome them. Let Him in through prayer and meditation. Through Him, you – and you don't have to be Jewish to find God – will find a meaningful life, full of joy and love.

Thank you profoundly for taking the time to read this book and I pray to God it will help to fill you with understanding, acceptance, compassion, and gratitude.

Tales My Father Told Me

We, Hasidim, learn *ḥesed*, lovingkindness, from anyone. My dear father, of blessed memory, told me and my siblings many hasidic tales when we were children. It was his way of teaching us to have a life of *ḥesed*. Here are some of the tales he told us that have never been published – until now.

Two fathers, a rich one and a poor one, decided to make a *shiddukh*, a marriage match, for their children. The rich man was very kind, and he offered to pay all the expenses for the wedding. But before the ink was dry on the catering contract, the rich man went bankrupt. The poor man went to their mutual rabbi and told him he wanted to break off the *shiddukh*. "I am glad you came to me first," the rabbi said, "before you did something rash. Listen, your future potential *maḥutin*, in-law, could have gone to you and called off the wedding. Or it could have been you who had been rich and gone bankrupt. Many different scenarios could have happened. Let your children get married. Calling it off now is too big a deal.

Money does not mean that much." The wedding went ahead and the couple had a long and prosperous marriage.

This is the tale of Shloime. He was a hasidic Jew who used to visit the Chortkover Rebbe Nochum Mordechai Friedman quite regularly. Reb Shloime was always dressed in his hasidic clothes, his long capote, his black hat, and showing his tzitzit. One day, he arrived at the Chortkover Rebbe's place, wearing a completely different outfit. He had on a short jacket, a tie, a modern hat, and his tzitzit tucked inside his pants so no one would see them. The *rebbe* asked what was happening. Shloime reluctantly answered: "You know, *rebbe*, I just moved from a small village to the big city. I was told the gentiles here don't like Jews. Therefore, it is preferable not to stand out wearing hasidic clothes. After a moment of silence, the *rebbe* turned to Shloime and said, "Tell me, Shloime, now that you are dressed in modern clothes, do the gentiles like you?"

A rabbi's wife was quarrelling with her servant – who happened to be an orphan – because she believed the servant had broken a dish. The *rebbetzen* was telling the orphan servant that she had to pay for the broken dish out of her wages. The servant denied breaking the object, and refused to accept that she had to pay for it. The *rebbetzen* said, "We will have to get a *din Torah* from the *rav*," a legal judgement from the rabbi. So, the *rebbetzen* went to get dressed to go out to see the *rav* at the *beit din*. Her husband, the rabbi, saw her changing into her best clothes, and asked her, "Where are you going?" She explained everything to him. When she was finished, he started to get dressed up as well. "Where are you going, husband?" the *rebbetzen* asked. "I certainly do not need you to help argue my case to the *beit din*. I can argue the case myself." Her husband responded: "I know you can. You are perfectly capable, but who will argue the case for the orphan servant?"

After traveling for three days and three nights, Yoel the innkeeper finally arrived at the town of Kotz. He ran quickly to the *rebbe*'s house, in order to beg him for a blessing for the complete recovery of his very sick wife, whom he had left at home with their little children. He had to do this, as there was no one around to help his wife. Arriving at the *rebbe*'s, he saw that there were already a dozen or so people waiting to go in to see him. He stood in line, too, and waited, and waited, and waited. He finally got to the door at the front of the line; he was next to go in. Suddenly the door opened, and out came the *rebbe*'s *gabbai*, whose name was Reb Lipman. Reb Lipman announced: "That's it for today. The *rebbe* isn't seeing anybody else." When Yoel heard this, he went crazy. He ran up to Reb Lipman and stood face to face with him, tears running down his cheeks. "Reb Lipman!" he cried. "I have just left my sick wife and my small children at home. Have pity and let me in to see the *rebbe*. I must travel back home again tonight." Reb Lipman answered gruffly: "No, I cannot and I must not let you in. When the *rebbe* says that this is it for the day, then that is it for the day." Deep dread fell over Yoel. He panicked and slugged Reb Lipman in the head with his closed fist.

Tumult and chaos followed. "Wow!" the witnesses gasped all at once. One said, "A Jew has slugged the *rebbe*'s *gabbai*." Hearing the commotion from inside, the *rebbe* came out of his study. "What is going on?" he asked. "Someone slugged the *gabbai*," a witness answered, pointing to Yoel. Yoel threw himself at the feet of the *rebbe*, begging and crying. "*Rebbe*, have pity and give me a blessing for the complete recovery of my sick wife. The *rebbe* ordered Yoel to stand up. "If Reb Lipman will forgive you, only then will I give you a blessing," said the *rebbe* before leaving the waiting room and closing the door behind him. Yoel looked around and asked whoever was still there, "Where can I find Reb Lipman?" Someone answered, "In the *beit midrash*," the study hall.

The Life of Moshele Der Zinger

Yoel raced off to the *beit midrash* and found him studying Gemara. Crying bitterly, Yoel said, "My dear Reb Lipman, have pity and forgive me!" Reb Lipman replied, "No! I will forgive you on one condition. Let's go to the *rebbe* and I'll tell you the condition there." When they arrived back, the *rebbe* asked, "Well, Reb Lipman, have you forgiven the innkeeper?" Reb Lipman replied, "No, I have not." The *rebbe* now looked sad. "How can that be?" he asked. "Surely you know that the Creator is like a shadow. Whatever a human being does, his shadow does. So, too, whatever a human being does, the Master of the Universe does. If you forgive, then the Master of the Universe forgives you." Reb Lipman responded, "Alright, I will forgive him, but only on one condition." Yoel started to turn red with frustration. "I have already told you that I will do anything if only you will forgive me. Reb Lipman, what is your condition?"

Reb Lipman replied: "The condition is not set on you, Yoel. It is set on the *rebbe*. I want the *rebbe* to give a blessing for the complete and rapid recovery of Yoel's wife, Bracha bas Golda, Bracha the daughter of Golda. This is because it was not Yoel the innkeeper who hit me. It was his bitterness over the illness of his wife that hit me. If his wife were healthy, he would not have hit me."

The *rebbe* stood up and raised both of his hands to heaven and said: "Oh, Master of the Universe! Oh, Holy Father in Heaven. Send a complete recovery to Bracha bas Golda, in the merit of such people that You have created, like Reb Lipman. At the same time, I would like to beg of you to bless all of humanity with success along with all that is good, so that nobody should sin. Because after all, why do people sin? Out of bitterness that they lack health, and that they lack a livelihood, and other things they need. If You were to see to it that they lack nothing, then You would see that nobody would sin, and it would happen that all that You have fashioned will know that You are their Designer, and all that You have created will know that You are their Creator, and all who have a soul

Tales My Father Told Me

in their breath will proclaim: 'Hashem, the God of Israel, is King and His Kingdom is everywhere.' Amen."

This hasidic tale is called Zalmen Hasid. In the village of Kozhnitz, there was a man called Zalmen Hasid. Everyone wondered why "Hasid" was added to his name. There must be a special reason, they thought, to be called Zalmen Hasid. The reason why the Kozhnitzer Rebbe Yisroel Hopsztajn added the word Hasid to the name Zalmen is as follows. It is historically well known what a bitter life the Jews suffered in Russia under the antisemitic laws and cruel rules of the czars. One of the worst decrees was called in Yiddish *huppers*, which meant catchers or kidnappers. The *huppers* used to raid Jewish homes in the early hours of the morning, arriving well-armed and with official documents. This was done to "recruit" boys from the age of ten and older for the army, where they had to serve for twenty-five years. No words can describe the pain this situation caused for the Jewish families. When the *huppers* came, the mothers would cry and scream and beg to avoid the kidnapping of their children, but to no avail. Now, about Zalmen Hasid. There was a widow who lived with her only son, Zalmen, who was fourteen. He was her whole world, understandably. She watched over him day and night. One early morning around 2 am the *huppers* came to her home and grabbed Zalmen. The mother's yelling and screaming did not help. The men threw Zalmen into a covered wagon and drove away.

The hysterical mother ran to the famous Kozhnitzer Rebbe who slept every night from midnight to 3 a.m. At that time, his *rebbetzen* brought him a hot cup of coffee, which he enjoyed very much. This night, just as he was about to sip from the steaming cup, the door flew open and the distraught widow rushed in and screamed: "They kidnapped my Zalmen! Please, *rebbe*, you are the only one who can save him." The *rebbe* closed his eyes and gave her a blessing: "With God's help, Zalmen will be saved." With

The Life of Moshele Der Zinger

that, he reached for his hot coffee. The widow ran to the table and pushed the drink away. "Sorry, *rebbe*," she said through her sobs. "No coffee until Zalmen is back." The *rebbe* was moved beyond words with the love this woman had. He took his Book of *Tehillim*, Psalms, and he began to pray, including some special prayers. All of a sudden, the door opened and Zalmen walked in with another boy, and both were panting hard. The mother and son embraced, and she asked him how he got away, who saved him. "The *rebbe* saved me," he said, pointing at Kozhnitzer Rebbe Yisroel Hopsztajn. "What do you mean?" said the mother, starting to calm down. "Tell me what happened." Zalmen answered: "When they threw me into the wagon, I found there another boy who had also just been kidnapped. We fell into each other's arms crying over our bad luck. Then I heard someone shouting, 'Zalmen, Zalmen!' I looked out the back and saw the *rebbe* running behind the wagon. He was shouting, 'Zalmen, jump, Zalmen, jump!' I shouted back, 'Not without my friend.' The *rebbe* repeated, 'Zalmen, jump, Zalmen, jump!' And I repeated, 'Not without my friend.' This went on for several minutes. Finally, the *rebbe* said, once again: 'Zalmen, jump!' And I said, 'Only with my friend.' And the *rebbe* agreed."

A Hasid called Shloime came one day to the town of Kotzk and went to visit the *rebbe* there. The *rebbe* asked him, in Yiddish, "Shloime, *vos machst do?*" which means, what are you doing? "Thank God," he replied. "My family and I are healthy." The *rebbe* asked him the same question again. "Thank God," he answered again, a little confused. "I have *parnasa*, I make a good living." The *rebbe* repeated, "*Vos machst do?*" Shloime did not know what to answer. "I don't understand," he replied, befuddled. "*Rebbe*, why do you repeat that question so many times?" The *rebbe* said, "I am asking what you are doing, and you answer me that you are well, that you have *parnasa*, *nahat* from your family and good health. But all that is the doing of the *Ribbono Shel Olam*. What are you doing?"

A man in Europe was walking to a city. He came to a fork in the road, not knowing which way to go. He saw the name sign lying on its side, but he had no idea where the sign was supposed to be placed when it was standing up properly. He had an idea. He knew where he'd come from, so if he stood the sign up and held it so the right word pointed to the place he came from, he'd also know the names of the forks and where they led. He did this and found his way. The moral of the tale is: If you know where you came from, you will know where to go.

This is the story of the Ger Rebbe Yitzchak Meir Alter. When the Ger Rebbe was only nine years old in 1807, he was already known as a genius. A learned Hasid with a sense of humor said to him, teasingly, "Yitzchak Meir, I will give you a gold ruble if you can show where the *Ribono Shel Olam* is." Yitzchak Meir answered back, "I'll give you two golden rubles if you can show me where He is not!"

The great Koritzer Rebbe came to the *beit midrash*, and found his pupils engaged in a heated discussion. *"Kinderlach,"* he asked, "Children, what are you conversing about?" One pupil answered, "We are discussing how to stop the *yeitzer hara*, the evil inclination inside all of us, from chasing us." The *rebbe* said back, "Oh, don't worry, *kinderlach*. You are not at the stage in life where the *yeitzer hara* is chasing you. So far, you are chasing him."

***

Mr. Rothschild is very rich. A young man selling lottery tickets comes to his home, and says, "I have come to sell you a lottery ticket." Mr. Rothschild asks, "How much can I win?" The man answers: "One million dollars." Mr. Rothschild says, "I have enough, so I do not need to buy a ticket." The young man replies, "You don't need it, but I need it. If you don't buy a ticket I will not have *parnasa* for my wife and my children." Mr. Rothschild takes out a hundred dollars and, without buying a ticket, hands the money to the man. The young man thanks him: "I really appreciate what you just did. Have a really good day." Mr. Rothschild likes the reply, and calls him back. "I will buy a ticket after all," he says. Well, as we all know, money goes to money, so Mr. Rothschild wins a million dollars. The young man comes to tell him he won. Mr. Rothschild checks his ticket, agrees, and is happy. "Since you sold me the ticket, you get something too," he says. "I have two propositions for you. One, I will give you fifty thousand dollars all at once. Or two, I will give you a thousand dollars every month for life." The young man thinks for a few minutes and then says, "I will take the cash up front." Rothschild gives him a check, and then says, "You are not a ḥakham, a smart person. This money I give you will disappear soon and then you'll have nothing left. But if you had taken the thousand dollars a month, you'd have had money for your whole life." "Yes," the young man replies, "but the way your luck seems to go, I would probably die tomorrow."

In *shul,* one Tuesday when I was twelve, I heard my father, of blessed memory, finish the *shmoneh esrei,* the most fundamental prayer of the liturgy, then look around, and sigh heavily. Standing next to him, I heard him say, "Oy!" I lifted my head and asked, "Tatty, what is the matter?" He said, "I will tell you in a while, son." Later we sat down to eat dinner, and I noticed my father was still not his usual relaxed self. After we finished eating and praying Maariv, he said to me, "Let's go."

We went to see our neighbor, Israel Klein. We went into his home, which was dark. "Please Myer, forgive me," he said to my father. "I know I was supposed to bring you one hundred kronen today. I do not have it because yesterday my wife was sick and I had to take her to the doctor. I had to use the money I had for you for the doctor and the medication. I thought, "Praise God, I will give

Myer the hundred kronen next week. I hope you..." My father was finally able to interrupt Israel Klein. "That is not why I am here," my tatty said. "I came to give you something." My tatty took an envelope out of his pocket, put it on the table and said, "Have a good week." We left. On the way home Tatty explained to me: "When I *davened shmoneh esrei*, today I saw that Israel Klein was also there. I remembered he was supposed to pay me the money and when he didn't, I knew he did not have it. So, I worried that maybe he did not have money for Shabbat. It has happened before that he has needed money and he has come to me. But this time, I think he was too ashamed to ask me for money again. Therefore, I sighed and said, 'Oy!' That is why I was anxious and uncomfortable. I knew he did not have the money and would not ask me. I wanted to go and give him more money right away, another hundred kronen. Moshele, let's go home." Postscript: We had a custom on Shabbat of asking around the table if someone had something positive to say. Sometimes my father asked who could say something about ḥesed. That week, I talked about my tatty's ḥesed.

This is a hasidic tale about the mitzva of honoring one's parents, *kibbud av ve'em*. Someone whose name I never knew was simply called the holy Jew. He loved to attend a *shiur* every afternoon. He would race home after his morning obligations, eat a quick lunch that his mother prepared, and then race out to the rabbi's place to be on time to listen to the *shiur*. The rabbi always had one special question at the end, and the holy Jew always tried to answer the special question. One day after eating, the holy Jew's mother asked him to get something from the attic for her and bring it down. The holy Jew answered, "I can't because I am going to be late for the rabbi's class. I am sorry I cannot fulfill your request." As he walked along to the rabbi's, the holy Jew had a sudden consideration. "What is the use," he thought, "of learning about the mitzva of *kibbud av ve'em* if you don't put it into practice, if you don't do what you were taught?" He turned around and went home to perform the task his mother had asked him to do. She was overjoyed to see him and have the job done.

The holy Jew arrived a little late to the rabbi's lecture. When he came in the rabbi lifted his eyes to look at him. Then he got up very excitedly, knowing from the look in the holy Jew's eyes that he had done something good, an important mitzva. "What mitzva did you do?" he asked the holy Jew. The holy Jew told the whole story. Right away the rabbi said, "I got the answer to my question today." The rabbi explained that he had been bothered by something at the beginning of the class, but he was unsure what it was. When the holy Jew arrived and told about the mitzva, the rabbi was satisfied, and he told the story of his own parents: "I was born after my father died, and not long after that my mother died. Therefore, I was given the name Asher ben Yerucham Yasom." Yasom means orphan. He also explained that he had been raised with the custom of accompanying anyone home who did the mitzva of honoring parents in a special way. Rabbi Yasom went home with the holy Jew and met his parents and ate a meal with his family.

This is a hasidic tale about the *yahrzeit* of Rabbi Elimelech of Lizensk. Lizensk is in Poland, and the rabbi lived from 1717 to 1787. When I was in Israel, I often davened in the *beit midrash* of Rabbi Gutman. One day, I saw lot of candles burning. I realized it was the *yahrzeit* of Rabbi Elimelech of Lizensk. So, I lit a candle, too. After davening, I drank a *Leḥaim*, toast, with the people who were there, as was custom. One of the Jews there was actually from Lizensk. We talked and said another *Leḥaim*. Then he said, "I want to tell you a story about the gravesite of Rabbi Elimelech of Lizensk. The Nazis came to our town. As if that was not bad enough, we heard a rumor that they found out the gravesite of Rabbi Elimelech was a holy place for Jews. We heard the Nazis decided to go there and destroy the protective house around the grave and do whatever other damage they could. The Nazis opened the grave, but when they saw the *tzaddik*, he was perfect, not rotting at all. He was not a skeleton, but a flesh-and-blood human. The Nazis became so frightened they ran away. Two Jews, Rabbi Yosef Fovel and Israel Zeiner, went in after to close the grave."

The man who told this story had been in a bunker hiding from the Nazis. He continued the story, "When my food and water were gone, I decided to go out and find more, new reserves. When I left the bunker, I had to pass the cemetery. I decided to go to the grave of Rabbi Elimelech. I was tired so I lay down on it and I cried and my tears ran like water. I was there for a long time praying and making requests. When I got up I was full of sand. The idea came to me take some of the holy sand and keep it. It would not be missed, and it might bring me miracles. I put some holy sand in my handkerchief, which I put in my pocket. I went through many horrors of the Holocaust, including labor camps, and death camps. I even survived Auschwitz. Through it all, I managed to keep the handkerchief. After the war, I had a dream. In front of me was the nicest dressed man, who spoke in a pleasant voice. He said, 'Please give me back the sand wherefrom you took it.' In the morning, I took the train and went to the cemetery and put back the sand with a lot of prayers of gratitude. I thanked Rabbi Elimelech of Lizensk from the bottom of my heart.'"

You could translate the mitzva of *kibbud av ve'em*, honoring parents, to mean that you are paying them back for bringing you up, for all the worry and love they gave you, for the food, drink, spiritual support, and education, for teaching you Torah and Torah values, for helping you learn to love and fear God, for everything. But what about the case of neglected children? What if your parents refused to love and protect you, to educate and look after you? Should such children honor their parents? Are they expected to perform *kibbud av ve'em*? When you borrow, you give back. If you do not borrow from your parents, when they lend you nothing, what do you have to give back?

Rabbi Meir Simcha HaKohen of Dvinsk, who died in 1926, commented on this issue. A unique Torah scholar of the twentieth century, he was famous for two works: *Or Sameaḥ,* a highly intelligent commentary on the Rambam's Mishne Torah, and *Meshekh Hakhma,* an outstanding explanation of Ḥumash. Rabbi Meir Simcha HaKohen discussed the subject *kibbud av ve'em* this way. Even if you have a terrible father, you must honor him. The commandment to honor your parents was given while the Jews were wandering in the desert. There, there was no need to feed your children because there was manna, food from heaven given by God to the wandering Israelites after they came out of Egypt. It was given by Him when their supplies ran out. They didn't even have to give their children water, as this came from wells. Everyone's clothes were ironed by the clouds. In other words, they had everything they needed, yet they still had the commandment to honor their parents. The mitzvot were given on Mount Sinai, and it is your duty to carry them out and to pass them on from generation to generation, even if your father and mother did not care for you and did a bad job looking after you.

A Hasid from Bulgaria – Europe's sixteenth largest country bordered by Romania, Serbia, Macedonia, Greece, Turkey, and the Black Sea – left his hometown of Vizitsa to visit a *rebbe* to ask for his help. The Hasid announced he was prepared to pay the *rebbe* a large sum of money to have his request fulfilled. The *rebbe* replied, "This is not the way of the world. The world does not behave this way." The Hasid was adamant: "I will pay!" The *rebbe* still refused to help. The Hasid from Vizitsa then asked how it was that he, the holy righteous rabbi, used to take money in exchange for helping people. The rabbi said, "If you can bring me one example of how I did this, I will help you." So, the Hasid gave an example. "A rich woman came to a rabbi. She did not have children, and she asked the rabbi to assure her she'd have a boy. This rich woman was intelligent. She knew how *tzaddikim* behaved, so she knew it might not happen the way she wanted. She urged him to accept the money for the promise of a boy. She believed her wish would then be real. She begged him to take some money, saying it was for her son's *pidyon haben*, a ceremony of redemption for a firstborn son involving five silver coins. The coins are given to a Kohen – a priest who is descended from Moses' brother Aaron – in exchange for the baby's redemption. The rabbi refused the money.

"As she started to leave, the rabbi also started to leave to go *daven* Minḥa. The woman, however, knew the custom of this rabbi, and how he would leave the room carefully so as not to go out and come in from the same door. The woman ran and stood in front of the door from which he planned to leave. She refused to move until he accepted the money for the *pidyon haben*. Seeing he had no choice, the rabbi said, 'You'll have a son and you will call him Shlomo. But in exchange, you must give 375 coins.'" In *gematria*, a numerical system whereby numbers are assigned to each letter of the alphabet, the name Shlomo works out to 375. The Hasid continued, "The rich woman said, 'Rabbi, you are right, but let's call him God, then there are only seven coins.' The rabbi knew she was right, but he added: 'What if God commands differently?'" The Hasid finished his story. He had concluded that what God commands, you will give, and you will understand how much *pidyon* you have to give. According to his name, this is how much you give.

This is a story of charity. A poor man came before Rabbi Nochum Partzovitz, a rav who was born in Trakai, Lithuania, and who was known internationally for his intellectual clarifications of Talmudic subjects. Rav Nochum, who died in 1986, was said to have run off barefoot to his morning ḥeder lessons when he was a child, since his shoes took too much time to put on. Rav Nochum was happy to receive the poor man into his study. The man explained to the *rav* his sad situation. "I have an eighteen-year-old daughter," he said. "And I have no money to give to any man to marry her." Rav Nochum didn't hesitate. He reached into his pocket and gave fifty coins to the poor man. "This is for silk for a dress and the rest is to give to a *ḥatan*," a groom, said Rav Nochum. The man was so happy he ran out of the rabbi's office and went right to the pub where he got drunk. When some friends of Rav Nochum saw what was happening, they went right up to the poor man and grabbed what money he had left. They brought it back to the *rav* and told him what they had seen. "He was not a decent man," one of them said. Rav Nochum replied by shouting very loud: "I heard a declaration from Heaven saying that Nochum behaves the same as God. God is good to good people and also good to bad people. And you want to take that away from me?" The friends ran back to the poor man and returned the money. Rav Nochum was one of the great *tzaddikim*.

Rebbe Menachem Mendel Morgenstern of the Kotzk hasidic dynasty mused out loud one day about bringing dead people back to life, but he pondered further: "What I really want to do is make living people really live! It is more important than making dead people alive."

Rabbi Moshe Leib of the Sassov hasidic dynasty lived until the early nineteenth century. He was glancing out the window one day, and saw a filthy drunk lying in the street. He thought to himself, "If someone like this is in God's world, is made by God, how can I not let him in my wonderful clean home?" He opened his door and invited the intoxicated man in, and then cleaned and fed him.

Reb Leib used to ask, "What does it mean to love a human being?" He answered his own question. "I was taught what loving a human being means by two drunks, Ivan and Stephan, lying in filth on the street. They were embracing, and I overheard their conversation. Stephan asked, 'Do you know how much I love you?' Ivan called him a liar. 'I swear with my whole heart, with all that is holy to me,' Stephan stated decisively. Ivan replied, 'If this is true, then tell me what hurts me, now.'" Reb Leib said he learned from two drunks that to love someone is to know and care about their problems and pains.

***

Hasidic Rabbi Chaim of Tzantz used to say, "When I was between eighteen and twenty years old, I wanted to control the world. When I was between twenty and thirty years old, I wanted to control the city. When I was between thirty and forty years old, I wanted to control my community. When I was between forty and fifty years old, I wanted to control my street. When I was between fifty and sixty years old, I wanted to control my home. Now that I am seventy years old, I know if I can control myself, I have achieved everything."

Rabbi Zalman Leib Teitelbaum of the Sighet hasidic dynasty was known to favor quiet situations. He used to say, "Problems are caused by too much talking. Often, if you keep your mouth shut, you will solve your problem." He was asked if he ever got tired of so much silence. "Why would I?" he asked; then he went quiet again.

A hasidic Jew went to his local tailor and ordered a new suit. The tailor took his measurements, and helped him choose the material. "When will it be ready?" asked the Jew. "In ten days." The Jew arrived back in ten days but the suit was not ready. "Give me another ten days," said the tailor. The Jew came back in another ten days, but the suit was still not made. "I don't understand," said the Jew. "In six days, God made the Earth, but in twenty days you cannot make a suit?" The tailor agreed. "Yes, but see what the world looks like!"

A woman was having a difficult time giving birth to her baby. Her friend gave her excellent advice: "Say *yizkor*," a special memorial prayer for the departed recited four times a year in synagogue. She explained that since during *yizkor* all the children leave the sanctuary, maybe the baby will feel it is time to leave as well.

Mementos

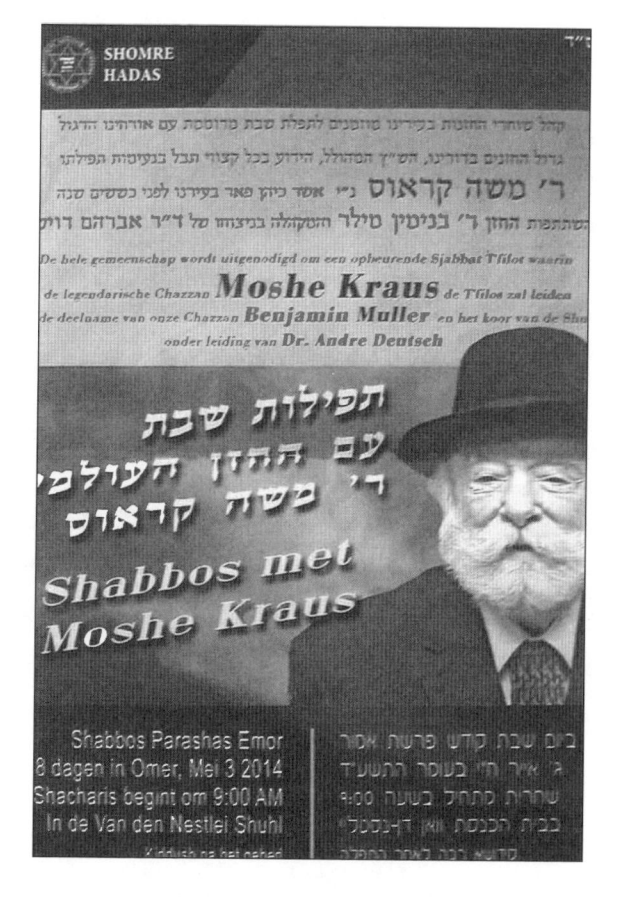

Shabbat with Cantor Kraus in Antwerp

The Life of Moshele Der Zinger

Hanukka lighting service in Budapest

Mementos

My dear Moishele,

Were it not for the fact that I had to go to Petra and chair an extraordinary conference of Nobel Laureates, sponsored by King Abdullah and myself, I would certainly be with you and your friends tonight and celebrate your life and its remarkable achievements.

We have known one another for six-seven decades. I remember your visit to Sighet when we were both younger. You conquered the entire community with your warm and inspiring davening. After the Tragedy, your voice became even more melodious and evocative, and your Nussa'h even more meaningful.

May you continue, Moishele, in the many years ahead, to bring joy and pride to all those who are close to you.

Your friend,

Elie Wiesel

Letter from Elie Wiesel

Concert in Manchester

Mementos

Caricature of Moshe Kraus, Istanbul 1963

The Life of Moshele Der Zinger

Concert in Johannesburg

Concert in Paris

Cantor Kraus with Israeli Ambassador Simcha Pratt

The Life of Moshele Der Zinger

Der Präsident
der
Bundesrepublik Deutschland

Berlin, im August 2022

Herrn
Kantor Moshe Kraus

Ottawa

Verehrter Kantor Moshe Kraus,

zu Ihrem 100. Geburtstag gratuliere ich Ihnen von ganzem Herzen. Ich wünsche Ihnen einen erfüllten und glücklichen Tag und hoffe, dass Sie die Vollendung Ihres persönlichen Jahrhunderts mit den Menschen feiern, die Ihrem Herzen nah sind.

Verbinden möchte ich meinen Gruß mit dem Ausdruck großer und aufrichtiger Wertschätzung: In einem jungen Alter haben Sie als Sohn einer jüdischen Familie in Deutschland unsägliches Leid erfahren müssen. Die Erfahrungen, die Sie und viele andere Menschen gemacht haben, waren entsetzlich. In all den grausamen Zeiten haben Sie durch Ihre Lieder und Ihren Gesang anderen Menschen Trost gespendet und für Hoffnung gesorgt. Viele Menschen sind Ihnen zutiefst dankbar hierfür. Ihnen gebührt auch meine tiefe Anerkennung.

...

- 2 -

Besonders dankbar bin ich Ihnen, dass Sie als Zeitzeuge von Ihrem Lebensweg berichteten, unter anderem in Schulen, und sich der Holocaust Erinnerung und Education besonders stark gewidmet haben. Sie haben sich leidenschaftlich und unermüdlich eingesetzt für das Gedenken an den Holocaust und für das Aufklären über die universellen Lehren aus der Shoah. Ich bin sicher, dass Sie viele junge Leute inspirieren konnten, Antisemitismus und Rassismus zu erkennen und sich dagegen zur Wehr zu setzen.

Auch ich werde weiterhin dafür eintreten, Antisemitismus und Rassismus weltweit zu bekämpfen und dafür zu sorgen, dass jüdische Menschen Deutschland als ihre Heimat betrachten. Denn in einem Land, in dem Juden nicht leben können, können und wollen wir alle nicht leben. Nur wenn Juden sich in Deutschland vollkommen sicher und zuhause fühlen, ist auch diese Bundesrepublik vollkommen bei sich.

Ich wünsche Ihnen Gesundheit und Wohlergehen sowie Gottes Segen.

Mit herzlichen Grüßen,
Ihr
Frank-Walter Steinmeier

The Life of Moshele Der Zinger

RIDEAU HALL

August 15, 2022

Dear Mr. Kraus,

Congratulations on your 100th birthday!

During your lifetime, the country has undergone some amazing shifts: a transition from one century to the next. Evolution of technology, society, community. Times of great challenges and of great joy. No matter what role you played in the last one hundred years, you have been an essential part of our country and we are grateful for all your contributions.

Your experience is valuable and respected, and we can all learn from the wisdom you have to share.

In the language of Inuktitut, from the South Qikiqtaaluk, *nalliuniqsiutsiarit!* In English, happy birthday!

I wish you a wonderful day filled with happy moments and memories.

Yours sincerely,

Mary Simon
Governor General of Canada

Mr. Moshe Kraus

Mementos

BUCKINGHAM PALACE

PALAIS DE BUCKINGHAM

Mr. Moshe Kraus

I am delighted to hear that you are celebrating your one hundredth birthday. I send you my warmest congratulations on this happy occasion and good wishes for an enjoyable day.

Elizabeth R.

Congratulatory Messages from Her Majesty The Queen

Her Majesty The Queen personally approved this message, which was specially designed for the transmission of Her Majesty's best wishes to Canadians. The photograph was taken during The Queen's Royal Tour, from June 28 to July 6, 2010; Her Majesty visited Halifax, Ottawa, Winnipeg, Toronto and Waterloo.

Message de félicitations de Sa Majesté la Reine

Sa Majesté la Reine a personnellement approuvé l'utilisation de ce message pour transmettre ses meilleurs vœux aux Canadiens. La photo a été prise durant la Tournée royale de la Reine qui s'est déroulée du 28 juin au 6 juillet 2010; Sa Majesté avait alors visité Halifax, Ottawa, Winnipeg, Toronto et Waterloo.

© Her Majesty The Queen in Right of Canada represented by the Office of the Secretary to the Governor General (2011).
© Sa Majesté la Reine du chef du Canada représentée par le Bureau du secrétaire du gouverneur général (2011).

The Life of Moshele Der Zinger

From the desk of
RIVKA REICHBERG
1348-41st Street, Brooklyn, NY 11218 | 718.810.2323 | baishayotzer5653@gmail.com

ב"ה

May 27, 2002 / 26 Iyar 5782

At this momentous occasion, at the marking of your 100th birthday (ad me'ah v'esrim), I remember the tumultuous times that have passed over us.

The childhood years we spent growing up together with our siblings in the home of our holy parents (may their blood be avenged);

The agonizing war years we spent in the concentration camps under the claws of the evil Nazi beast;

And with G-d's grace we have survived, flourished and are now approaching our 100th birthday.

My dear brother, I find the pen and paper not eloquent enough to express my feelings to you, my older brother, whom I always looked up to – and who always thought about me and my welfare.

So many years have passed, yet your dedication to me and my great love to you has never diminished, it has actually grown and deepened.

May the Holy One blessed be He, to whom you have cleaved to and believed in during the most difficult times, bless you and your dear, devoted wife Rivkah, who is always faithfully at your side. May you be blessed with many more long years, enjoying continued good health, to be happy and content, and able to carry on with your daily lives, until we merit the coming of Moshiach, speedily in our day, amen.

Your devoted sister,
Rivka Reichberg (Kraus)

Mementos

Cantor Moshe Kraus

It is a great pleasure to send you best wishes and warmest congratulations on the occasion of your one hundredth birthday

Prime Minister of Canada
Ottawa 2022

*The Toby Press publishes fine writing
on subjects of Israel and Jewish interest.
For more information, please visit www.tobypress.com*